RESEARCH in EDUCATION

Doing
RESEARCH in EDUCATION
Theory and Practice

Edited by
IOANNA PALAIOLOGOU
DAVID NEEDHAM
TREVOR MALE

Los Angeles | London | New Delhi
Singapore | Washington DC

Los Angeles | London | New Delhi
Singapore | Washington DC

SAGE Publications Ltd
1 Oliver's Yard
55 City Road
London EC1Y 1SP

SAGE Publications Inc.
2455 Teller Road
Thousand Oaks, California 91320

SAGE Publications India Pvt Ltd
B 1/I 1 Mohan Cooperative Industrial Area
Mathura Road
New Delhi 110 044

SAGE Publications Asia-Pacific Pte Ltd
3 Church Street
#10-04 Samsung Hub
Singapore 049483

Editor: Jai Seaman
Assistant editor: James Piper
Production editor: Victoria Nicholas
Copyeditor: Mary Dalton
Proofreader: Kate Campbell
Indexer: David Rudeforth
Marketing manager: Dilhara Attygalle
Cover design: Shaun Mercier
Typeset by: C&M Digitals (P) Ltd, Chennai, India
Printed and bound in Great Britain by Ashford
Colour Press Ltd

© Ioanna Palaiologou, David Needham, Trevor Male and
contributors 2016

First published 2016

Chapter 1 © David Needham
Chapter 2 © James Ma
Chapter 3 © Ioanna Palaiologou
Chapter 4 © David Needham
Chapter 5 © Lynda Pinnington-Wilson and David Needham
Chapter 6 © Krishan Sood
Chapter 7 © Tina Byrom
Chapter 8 © Mark Connolly
Chapter 9 © Yu-Hao Kate Lin
Chapter 10 © Trevor Male
Chapter 11 © Trevor Male
Chapter 12 © Ken Spencer
Chapter 13 © Glynn Kirkham
Chapter 14 © Gary Beauchamp

Library of Congress Control Number: 2015937797

British Library Cataloguing in Publication data

A catalogue record for this book is available from
the British Library

ISBN 978-1-4462-6674-8
ISBN 978-1-4462-6675-5 (pbk)

At SAGE we take sustainability seriously. Most of our products are printed in the UK using FSC papers and boards.
When we print overseas we ensure sustainable papers are used as measured by the Egmont grading system.
We undertake an annual audit to monitor our sustainability.

CONTENTS

LIST OF CONTRIBUTORS

Professor Gary Beauchamp is Professor of Education and Associate Dean (Research) in the School of Education at Cardiff Metropolitan University. He worked for many years as a primary school teacher, before moving into higher education where he has led undergraduate and postgraduate courses in education. His research interests focus on ICT in education, particularly the use of interactive technologies in learning and teaching. He has published widely in academic journals, books and research reports. He is also Additional Inspector for Estyn, Chair of Governors in a primary school and has served as external examiner for many universities.

Dr Tina Byrom is currently employed as Academic Team Leader for Undergraduate and Post Graduate Education at Nottingham Trent University and contributes to the undergraduate joint honours and doctoral programmes. Tina also has significant experience of teaching in secondary schools and has worked on numerous research projects including: Understanding Teenage Pregnancy in Nottingham; Health Imperatives in Schools; HE Participation Rates in Nottingham North; FE Provision in Nottingham City. Her research interests include issues around social justice and inclusion, pupil voice and the educational experiences of young people who are the first in their family to go to HE. She is currently conducting research in collaboration with the Nottingham Youth Housing Association.

Dr Mark Connolly is an educationalist working in Cardiff University's School of Social Science. Mark's work incorporates many aspects of education including culture and creativity, adult learning, and children, risk and outdoor education. Mark has a particular interest in the rights of children, especially in relation to research ethics within qualitative research.

Glynn Kirkham is based in Prague and an independent consultant in education and educational leadership and management. In this role, he has worked in the UK, Europe and the Middle East. He has been a successful teacher, headteacher, inspector, university lecturer (four UK universities), doctoral supervisor, Director of CPD and external examiner. He has presented many international conference papers, lectured on leadership on four continents and published articles, chapters and books on leadership and competencies. His research interests are in school leaders' standards and competencies, headteacher mentoring and coaching and the selection, recruitment and continuing professional development of headteachers.

Dr Yu-Hao Kate Lin is currently employed as the director of IB Office at Kang Chiao International School East China and oversees the authorisation process towards an IB World School to offer the International Baccalaureate Diploma Programme. Prior to her current role in an international school setting, she was working with the IBO as a research manager for programme development and responsible for prioritising, overseeing and utilising research projects to inform curriculum development decisions and promote better understanding of key values and approaches underlying the IB programmes. Her special areas of research interest include programme evaluation and development; inquiry and concept-based pedagogical and learning approaches; metacognition and thinking skills; knowledge management and continuing professional development.

Dr James Ma is a linguist. He received his PhD from the University of Bristol and undertook subsequent postdoctoral training at the University of Oxford. Prior to this, he studied at the University of Nottingham. Over the past few years, his scholarship has centred on semiotic philosophy and its relevance for learning and education, resonating with his longstanding interests in sociolinguistics, cultural-historical activity theory (CHAT), critical discourse analysis (CDA), corpus linguistics, hermeneutic phenomenology and a priori methods. He holds membership of learned organisations including the International Association for Semiotic Studies (IASS), the International Society for Cultural-historical Activity Research (ISCAR), the British Association for Applied Linguistics (BAAL), and the British Educational Research Association (BERA).

Dr Trevor Male is an education consultant having worked full-time for over 20 years in higher education during which time he held lecturing and managerial posts at Brunel University, the University of Lincoln and the University of Hull. For the first 20 years of his career he was a teacher, an LEA officer and a tutor for the Open University. Trevor has been published widely in books and journals nationally and internationally and is a regular contributor to research conferences. He is now a Research Associate at the UCL Institute of Education where he supervises postgraduate dissertations and theses in education and works as a consultant and trainer on international development programmes.

David Needham is a senior lecturer in the School of Education in Nottingham Trent University with a background embedded in business education and formerly at the University of Stirling. In his current role he supervises a number of research students. David's evolving research interests have focused upon and related to how young people learn within the business classroom as well as enterprise education. Over the years he has brought in many contract research projects for local authorities and quasi-educational bodies. He has analysed the use of case study techniques for developing an understanding of how business studies students learn, and has also looked at a range of classroom pedagogies and techniques for improving learning within the classroom. His recent work has focused upon notions of art or science within education, the influence of reflexivity upon teacher trainees' experiences within the classroom, as well as those of staff new to higher education teaching.

Dr Ioanna Palaiologou has worked as a lecturer and researcher in HE for the last 20 years and is now returning to her career as a child psychologist. She is a Chartered Psychologist with the British Psychological Society with specialisms on child development and learning theories. During her time in HE education she has worked for five universities and among her main responsibilities was the supervision of postgraduate research students and the mentoring of early career researchers. Her research interests are focused on ethics in research, child development and implications for pedagogy and the epistemic nature of pedagogy.

Dr Lynda Pinnington-Wilson is a Deputy Principal with the New South Wales Department of Education and Communities and a part-time lecturer in the Primary, Secondary Education and Indigenous Programs within the University of Western Sydney. Recent research projects included studies into how graduates progress into a profession and service learning within the initial three years of practice. The experiences led to a Consultancy role which assisted practitioners towards Teacher Registration/Accreditation. She is co-architect of the *Classmates* project, a partnership between the University of Western Sydney and the New South Wales Department of Education and Communities to place University of Western Sydney Teacher Education students in secondary classrooms while undertaking their Masters of Teaching level qualifications in-situ. Current interests include the maintaining of Accreditation status with the NSW Institute of Teachers.

Dr Krishan Sood has over 36 years' teaching experience gained through being a Science teacher, Head of department, assistant head and in an advisory teacher role for a Local Authority. He has run a multicultural resource centre, led in-service education for staff, governors and leaders on equality and diversity. He has been a governor in a secondary and a special school and has taught in four UK universities. He is currently actively involved in research and publication locally, nationally and internationally and his research interests currently focus on leadership and management; CPD; teaching and learning, diversity, gender and Early Years.

Dr Ken Spencer has been a lecturer and researcher in Higher Education for over 40 years. He has been a member of the Institute for Learning and Teaching in Higher Education since October, 1999, and has held governorships in Hull schools for the past 20 years. He has extensive experience as a reviewer for international journals, the Czech Science Foundation and the Economic and Social Research Council (ESRC). Throughout his academic career his research has evaluated the effectiveness of technology in education, including the efficiency of orthographic systems. His current research examines the relationship between orthographic metrics and early reading in the development of statistical models for predicting children's reading and spelling difficulties for common English words, reaching the conclusion that English is a dyslexic language.

PREFACE

We have produced this book in order to help and guide students who are required to undertake research projects as part of their degree programme and early career researchers in education seeking publication. Most degree programmes in education now require learners to produce an extended study or some form of thesis, dissertation or project, often based on primary research. Consequently this book has been prepared with students of education in mind and is suitable for those on taught undergraduate and postgraduate programmes as well as those studying for a research degree. In addition we are mindful of early career researchers, normally employed as lecturers in education departments, who are expected to develop their research profile. The overarching aim of the book, therefore, is to provide advice and guidance to successfully engage in a research project in education which may be published as a report, a dissertation or thesis.

The basis of successful research is the production of evidence that supports conclusions and recommendations for action. The researcher investigates a situation, a set of actions or an experience, draws a conclusion and may then offer a recommendation for action. In all instances they have to support these conclusions and recommendations with evidence that stands up to some searching questions. So you will need to think about the rigour of evidence supplied in research studies. How do we know what is true? How can we be sure that what is told to us is representative of what happened? Consequently the effective researcher will have to devise a way of assembling information that will allow a body of evidence to emerge which takes account of potentially different outcomes to the basic questions asked.

Although there are general research issues, we have sought in this book to recognise the complex nature of education systems that impact on the researcher working in this field. Much of the methodology that forms the more traditional approach to research stems from the scientific, or *positivist* approach. In this scientific paradigm, it is often possible to eliminate intervening variables when conducting a research study. You could, for example, undertake an experiment in laboratory conditions which eliminates all normal conditions and establishes a unique environment. In the real world, however, it is impossible to eliminate the effects of the environment which can be manifested in a number of physical or psychological ways. Furthermore in education it is neither practical nor ethical to conduct experiments on human subjects, particularly children and young people, who could be considered vulnerable. Even if we put ethical issues to one side for now, however, the interaction of human beings within society at large or within a particular setting tends to militate against the establishment of scientifically controlled investigations. An alternative view has emerged, referred to as the *non-positivist* paradigm, which suggests that research into social systems can only really be undertaken with a view to understanding the views and experiences of the participants.

Both viewpoints are the polar ends of a continuum, however, that tends to overlook the potential of each approach. It is possible, and recommended on occasion, that education researchers will need to establish an overview of the way things are and will thus make use of a positivist approach. This will almost inevitably involve the collection of data from as large a body of respondents as possible in a *quantitative* study. This type of inquiry is normally based on testing a theory or hypothesis, composed of variables, which is then measured with numbers and analysed with statistical procedures in order to determine whether the predictive generalisations hold true. Alternatively, the study sample or situation may not yield sufficient quantities of data to satisfy any of the key factors of validity, reliability or generalisability expected within quantitative approaches and may instead require the investigation of a particular phenomenon. This is the *qualitative* paradigm which is defined as:

> [...] the process of understanding a social or human problem by building a complex, holistic picture, formed with words, reporting detailed views of informants, and conducted within a natural setting. (Creswell, 2013: 2)[1]

Both quantitative and qualitative approaches are valid, however, and education researchers should be prepared to make use of either approach, even within the same study if necessary, according to circumstance and need. In high quality research the choice of approach should be governed by issues relating to the quality of evidence rather than employing a pre-determined methodology. Our recommendation, therefore, is to choose methodological approaches which address the hypothesis or research question(s) you establish for your enquiry. This may result in your research being quantitative, qualitative or a combination which is referred to as *mixed methods*.

This book is designed, therefore, to guide you through research on a step-by-step basis and is organised accordingly. The early chapters focus on the issues relating to conducting research and highlight some of the key issues required when conducting enquiries in education. **Chapter 1** seeks to help you appreciate the purpose of the research process and understand the nature of educational research. **Chapter 2** then explores key methodological principles in the research process and raises awareness of the fundamental differences between social science research and natural science research. The contents of this chapter will help you identify both the ways in which you can approach research and the relationship of theory and praxis in social inquiry. **Chapter 3** focuses on the nature of ethics and the standard expectations for the conduct of education research. A major feature of this chapter is the discussion and

---

[1]Creswell, J. (2013) *Research Design (International Student Edition): Qualitative, Quantitative and Mixed Methods Approaches* (3/E). Thousand Oaks, CA: SAGE.

recommendations for the way in which relationships between researcher and researched are conducted. By the end of these three chapters you will have been required to consider personal values and your position as a researcher in order to undertake ethical research.

Chapters 4, 5 and 6 are designed to guide you with the design of your research project. In **Chapter 4** firstly you will be given the opportunity to identify a topic and it then provides tools designed to help you to develop and expand your ideas. The chapter then moves you toward considering the key role that hypotheses and research questions play in helping you to plan and deliver your research project. **Chapter 5** is about project management and identifies the skills you require in order to present a report, dissertation or thesis. Simple project planning tools are provided to help you organise, manage and monitor your project. **Chapter 6** will develop your skills in writing a proposal for research, a fundamental requirement for projects which need approval from supervisors, employers or funding agencies.

Chapter 7 focuses on the requirement for all projects to demonstrate the underlying theory base that relates to the planned enquiry. This is the production of what is commonly called a literature review, although here it is suggested you should be thinking of referring to this as a literature section as you are using relevant theory and associated research previously conducted to frame your own ideas and argument and preparing the foundations for your study. This chapter provides the thinking tools that allow you to clarify your understanding of the uses of literature and previous research that legitimise your own planned enquiry.

The next five chapters examine the range of methods that can be used in research, with a particular emphasis in their use in education. **Chapter 8** will give you the means to determine the best approach you can adopt for your planned investigation by making the link between your hypothesis/research question(s) and the methods you intend to use. An excellent feature of this chapter is the way in which it allows you to distinguish between methods which will generate data in the form of numbers and words and identify the methods which are the appropriate tools for *your* research project. **Chapters 9, 10, 11 and 12** then provide practical guidance on the collection and analysis of both qualitative and quantitative data.

The last two chapters of the book provide details of how best to present the outcomes of your research. **Chapter 13** has been designed to help you understand the difference between reporting results, undertaking analysis and presenting your conclusions, whilst **Chapter 14** focuses on how you express lucidly in writing what you have learnt and report those ideas clearly to others.

All chapters in the book provide practical tips, examples and activities that will support you as a researcher. In addition you are directed toward further resources by each of the authors in the form of relevant websites and further reading.

This book is dedicated by us to all aspiring researchers in education who desire to identify and undertake enquiries that provide high quality evidence for their reports.

COMPANION WEBSITE

Doing Research in Education is supported by a wealth of online resources to aid study and support learning, which are available at:

https://study.sagepub.com/needhamandpalaiologou

The resources include:

Examples of annotated questions and projects giving you even more insight into how theory works in the real world.

Exercises to help test your methods knowledge.

Weblinks directing you to relevant resources to broaden your understanding of chapter topics and expand your knowledge by linking to real world organizations and conversations on education research.

Selected SAGE journal articles allowing you to read more widely and reinforcing key chapter concepts. They are also an ideal place to start for literature reviews, dissertations, or assignments.

1

THE PURPOSE OF RESEARCH: WHY DO WE DO IT?

DAVID NEEDHAM

Chapter Aims and Objectives

This chapter aims to help you to:

- understand the nature of educational research;
- appreciate the purpose of the research process;
- classify the different types of educational research;
- understand your role as an educational researcher as you put together your research strategy;
- write a good piece of educational research;
- understand the role of your supervisor.

Introduction

When you go into an educational setting, do you ever ask questions that help you to find something out? Sometimes conversations with professional people enable you to learn from what they do and may prompt you to ask even more questions so that you explore issues and improve your understanding of some of what you observe. It could be argued that as human beings it is instinctive for us to ask questions, often internally to ourselves, and that research is something that we all do most of the time.

Intuitively, and in different ways or at different levels, we want to discover knowledge, often by prefacing our thoughts with words such as 'why, how, might, what if, does, could, do, when, where, suppose or even "surely"!' It was Kagan (1972) who argued that people are motivated to reduce their sense of uncertainty between themselves and their environment. This is simply part of our behaviour. We all have a desire for knowledge which is why we seek explanations. It simply helps us to make sense of the world. The instinct of human beings is to ask questions and then try to answer them by finding the answers. Reading, research and finding things out just makes life so much better!

It is not easy beginning a research project and subsequently writing a report or constructing a dissertation or thesis. This is because in some cases it may take a great deal of time to complete, possibly spanning at least a whole academic year and maybe longer! It is important, therefore, to choose an area that you are genuinely interested in and fascinated by. Perhaps it is clichéd to say that research is something that is very personal, but it is something that you, the researcher, control from the outset. It is your topic and is different to that chosen by anybody else. It is also something that you are going to complete and do differently to the way in which anybody else would carry out their project. It is you, with your very human qualities, who will make your project unique. That makes it very exciting! Through your project you are going to gain an insight into an area of education in a way that enables you to become a specialist within your chosen topic.

Definition – Thesis or dissertation

A detailed document based upon an element of research submitted in full or part fulfilment of an academic degree or professional qualification.

?	?	?	?
Why	How	What if	Does
?	?	?	?
To what extent	Could	Do	When
?	?	?	?
Suppose	Surely	Which	Where

Figure 1.1   Prefacing questions

What is Educational Research?

The starting point for this is to think about the word 'research'. The picture that often comes into our minds when we think about research is that of scientists in white coats experimenting in a laboratory. We may also think about doing research, however, by exploring the Internet or through reading books and browsing journals in a library. Each of these images contains similar characteristics in that research is something scholarly that involves some form of investigation in order to find something out within a particular discipline such as education (Newby, 2014).

The word *research* comes from the French word 'rechercher' (to travel or survey, or establish facts and relationships). This is not like being in a classroom or a lecture hall where you might listen or take notes. In those instances you are at the receiving end of the educational process. Although these sessions are important in providing you with knowledge and understanding it might not be answering all of your questions or allowing you to test your thoughts. Research is something that involves an investment and enables you to develop new knowledge and understanding (HEFCE, 1999). In this sense it helps you to seek answers to questions (Tuckman and Harper, 2012). Involving yourself in research helps to make your learning active and makes it relevant and exciting. Research is, therefore, a practical process for you. However, let us not forget that research also involves a sense of your own personal reflection in which you ponder and make sense of what you have learnt.

We all have experience of an educational environment. Inevitably, your early experiences within school will have had some part to play in developing your views or ideas about education. The problem with forming views, and we all have them, is that they create unsubstantiated reasoning. There is often little basis upon which to make statements or observations other than through our own experience. This is where educational research comes in. Educational research is about the reorientation of ideas on the basis of information obtained through an investigation. It is a process of discovery through which reading and data help to reduce any sources of error within our reasoning to create a better sense of authority. Think of it as a process of putting contact lenses or spectacles on to help you to see the world more clearly. As you do so you come closer to understanding the real answer to all of your questions. It is through this that with authority and confidence you find out a little bit more about all that is happening within the world of education.

Educational research is something that engages with the practice of education. For example, it could include a focus upon schools, classrooms, learning, teaching, management, policies, and legislation and might cover issues related to sociology, psychology, history, politics, child development, teacher education, culture, gender, economics, art and creativity, life sciences, ethnicity, technology, media, mathematics, language, recreation and human physical or social performance. The list is almost endless. There is also logic about educational research which ensures that the procedures for constructing the project and undertaking the research help to make it a valuable tool for understanding the chosen area. For further guidance on this it is worth referring to the SAGE book *Research Methods in Education* (Check and Schutt, 2012).

Educational research thus involves an organised and structured process or approach by the researcher – you – to find the answers to a hypothesis or research question or attempt to solve one or more problems, likely to be related to one or more of the areas above, by reading, collecting data and through searching for explanations (Anderson and Arsenault, 1998).

In other words, by gathering data from one or more sources and by undertaking a thorough examination of relevant literature the researcher is trying to improve their understanding of the issue upon which they are focused in a way that produces unbiased findings. This involves:

- reading literature and gathering data to use;
- developing new knowledge;
- creating a qualified understanding of issues related to learners and education;
- processes of discovery about issues that really matter to the researcher;
- being careful, rigorous, measured, accurate and precise as the process of research is developed;
- developing an unbiased process that attempts to solve a problem;
- satisfying and informing the interests of the researcher;
- enjoying the journey. Research is not a fixed process, but is iterative and creative. Along the journey you may adapt and refine your approaches and direction.

Practical Tip

So, what do you really want to find out? In the early stages of your project this can be difficult. Before you begin your project or, during the early weeks, it can be useful to keep an *Ideas Diary*. Into this put everything that you are thinking about your research. You are not making notes in here about the literature. It is for your eyes only so that you can record and reflect upon your thoughts as your ideas develop.

Researching an educational environment can be unpredictable and messy. It was W.C. Fields, the American comedian, who penned the phrase 'never work with children or animals'. Your research may take place in early years settings, schools, colleges, universities or other educational organisations; it could involve talking with specialists such as teachers or child psychologists. You may meet members of other related occupations such as carers, parents, police officers or employers. It could involve listening, observing, asking questions, recording and meeting individuals of various ages and from different backgrounds. However, in most instances and, at the heart of many areas of educational research, are children or young and perhaps vulnerable people. Things often go wrong. It can sometimes be difficult to arrange meetings with busy people or observations in educational settings. As research involves dealing with people, there are also many ethical issues which should be at the forefront of any project. It is never easy being a researcher and an ethical code of conduct is really important (this will be discussed more fully in Chapter 3). Educational research takes many different forms and may demand many different approaches. As you undertake the role of a researcher you will want to seek answers and improve your understanding of issues related to your chosen area. You may be trying to find out, for example, whether reading differences in children within a Year 2 classroom depend upon their birth date, whether sex education programmes within a secondary school impact upon teenage pregnancy, how speaking English as a second language impacts upon the experiences of an early years child, whether gender influences outdoor learning or whether role play within a nursery might help children to develop life skills. The list is endless and everybody's approach to solving their research problem is different. This is what makes educational research so interesting, not just for the researchers, but also for the tutors and supervisors.

Educational research allows you to pursue your interests and to learn something new. It is an academic exercise that enables you to hone your problem-solving skills and to challenge yourself in new ways as part of your own learning. As you do so you work closely with your supervisor who is likely to be an experienced researcher and with whom you should meet regularly. Then as a researcher you seek answers to questions that you are genuinely interested in. Remember that it is you who chooses your approaches and the tools or your research as you read and articulate your ideas while you gather and analyse your data.

Activity

Either on your own or within a group, think about the potential benefits that could arise for teaching and learning from good educational research. Discuss your thoughts with others.

The Purpose of Educational Research

As part of their daily activities, anybody who works in education is a consumer of research and also a producer of their own research. For example, in working with young and vulnerable people you might be reflecting upon your own practice and also want to strive to improve your practice. In this sense educational research is about raising questions. This might involve experimenting with different techniques in order to test their effectiveness. Similarly, published research into pedagogies that has been substantiated across a range of situations might suggest ways in which practice could be improved.

Research is essentially about acquiring knowledge. Ongoing research might add to what a practitioner might already know about how people learn. From the practitioner's point of view they can then adapt learning processes within their particular setting. As there are many areas about which there are gaps in research, processes of research constantly help to create new knowledge. It is difficult to either understand or be cognisant of the complexity of learner needs and how and why they might change. Research is an inclusive process that engages with complex needs in a way that enables educators to interpret research for their own practice.

Education is not a field that stands still. Similarly the environment in which education takes place is constantly changing. We only have to look at schools 40 years ago, for example, to realise that we have moved forward inexorably. Some of these changes have included different types of schools; more scientific management of performance data; an increased focus upon assessment and league tables; more rigorous inspection systems; changes to qualifications; increasing use of technology within the classroom; policies by successive governments upon curriculum, school improvement and teacher training; changes to leadership; different pedagogies within the classroom; childcare provision; bullying; parental choice and the introduction of a national curriculum. However, and maybe ideally, for these changes to take place informed decisions are needed, requiring some element of educational research which is applied to the challenges facing the changing school environment. This is known as applied research. The users of such research would therefore include:

- the government and policy makers;
- teachers, headteachers and childcare practitioners;
- parents and families;
- academics involved in carrying out their own research.

In this sense applied educational research is something that engages with the world in which it serves so that it can make a difference; in other words make it better. Applied research is about searching for solutions to questions that are focused upon live issues within the world of education. This involves some level of critical enquiry that helps to inform educational decisions.

Educational research can also be basic research. Basic research is about research for knowledge and using educational theory to develop an understanding about aspects of education. For example, basic research might focus upon some element of philosophy or sociology. Although it might not be immediately obvious how such research might help in terms of understanding educational issues, at a later stage elements of applied research might take findings from basic research into the educational world to further build and develop an understanding of issues related to student learning needs. Both applied and basic forms of research have their value in playing a role that helps the researcher to understand a particular set of circumstances.

The nature and purpose of any particular research project will determine the type of research project or study that is undertaken. The problem is that, as there are many different categorisations of research, trying to describe each one would not be helpful and might be obfuscating. So, for the purpose of this text, I have simply been selective in using the main types of student projects I have experienced within my field. The different types of research project could therefore include:

1. *Exploratory research* – As the word 'exploratory' implies, this is conducted into a research problem or issue that has not been clearly defined. There are likely to be very few studies into the area of research focus for this type of study. The starting point for this type of study is for the researcher to become familiar with the area being researched in order to look for patterns, perhaps by using observations, discussions or a case study. Exploratory research provides insights into a chosen area being researched.

2. *Descriptive research* – This type of research provides information that describes phenomena, situations and events as they are observed. In doing so it elicits factual or systematic information about the characteristics or elements of a problem or issue to provide a picture of what is happening. For example, a descriptive research question might be what television programmes do children between the ages of five and seven prefer, or how might the health of students impact upon their academic success? As this research is descriptive, questions usually start with a 'what' or 'how' because the aim of the research is that description of characteristics should provide a picture of a data set.

3. *Analytical or exploratory research* – This research goes beyond the boundaries of descriptive research which merely describes characteristics to analyse and explain why something is happening. This type of research identifies causal relationships between phenomena. It therefore focuses upon the effects of something or the outcomes. For example, it could analyse whether the rights of children influence how parents and carers manage their behaviour or the influence of a home environment upon the holistic development of under 5s.

4. *Predictive research* – Whereas analytical research explains what is happening amongst variables, predictive research goes further by forecasting the likelihood of something happening. In this sense predictive research could forecast the success of children at school within the world of work or the way in which using the outdoor environment with a group of primary school children might impact upon their learning of mathematical concepts. It could be argued that predictive research is more generalisable as it could apply to problems elsewhere.

5. *Historical research* – Research that is historical describes events, situations and activities that have occurred in the past. To find out about such events census figures, historical documents, newspapers and local records could be analysed. Sometimes, to understand the world we live in today, we have to make connections with our past. Historical research is a critical analysis of the past in order to develop a contemporary interpretation of events.

6. *Evaluative research* – Almost every day there are circumstances in which we have to make judgements about something we observe or something that we do. Evaluative research is a form of applied research that involves evaluating the effectiveness of a programme or initiative. This involves making judgements about outcomes (Stern, 1990). At the heart of this type of research is the notion of a judgement and this involves acquiring a critical and informed viewpoint. For example, the extent to which technology within a mainstream school can be used for speech and language therapy would involve making judgements about the effectiveness of technology.

7. *Action research* – This involves a professional enquiry within an educational context. As the name 'action' suggests, the researcher implements a planned change in practice by using the planned action as a tool for the research. This action is then monitored, evaluated and reflected upon as, with any decision or strategy, the outcomes are uncertain. For example, a teacher might introduce materials in a classroom that help children to write more detailed answers to questions. Some aspects of the strategy might work and others might not. So, the teacher would then revise their strategies, perhaps by refining the materials.

Activity

Clearly most small-scale research projects, including for a dissertation or a thesis, would include elements of several of the classifications of research above. Although this might be difficult to say at this stage, when thinking of how you are going to develop your study, which of these classifications might relate to your research project?

There is an uncertainty about many of the processes of educational research. At the start you need to keep an open mind as you seek answers to the issues you explore. As you read about your chosen area you begin to make relationships between theories and discover how you might construct and develop knowledge. There are many different strategies and approaches that can then be used within an educational setting. When you encounter children as an educational researcher, for example, there is a real opportunity to be creative. You have to choose your own approaches. It is then a bit like any investigation. You suddenly become a detective as you need to look for evidence that supports your findings. Some of the evidence might be tenuous or even contradictory. But even if you feel that it is overwhelming it may not be proof that you have answered your question. Knowledge created through a process of educational research is always likely to be tentative. There is often no clear-cut answer. However, having undertaken the process of research you have created knowledge and your approach is then significantly more informed.

Practical Tip

One of the problems with writing an extended piece of work such as a dissertation is that you tend to work on your own. This can be lonely and sometimes you might need somebody to talk to about your work; somebody who can be trusted and might be able to provide some provocative questions and help you to reflect upon your own work. This person would then be your 'critical friend'. Is there anybody that you know who would be able to help you in this way?

So, what would the world be like without educational research? Inevitably without educational research there would still be universities, colleges, schools, lecturers and teachers, and politicians would still be making policies. However, there would be less knowledge about teaching, learning, poverty, technology, unfairness and the multitude of questions that it is possible to ask about the processes of education. Nobody would be challenging the system or finding out how education could benefit both individuals and society. Education would be much more static and much less creative. There could be lots of prejudice and dogma with decisions becoming a matter of convenience. It would be easier to use education for political purposes. Thus there could be a dull acceptance of education as a given product with little emphasis upon an informed process of change and a constant movement forwards in thinking and actions. Changes in education could fail to reflect changes in society and in its external environment. As a result and inevitably, the educational world would also be a lot poorer.

Case Study

Deidrea James

Deidrea James was an international student from Bermuda studying for an educational degree at a university within the UK. She felt that *starting* her dissertation was difficult. Deidrea found that if you approached a project in terms of each of the sections, it was easier to get to grips with. As her dissertation progressed she found that change was inevitable. This is because unlike an essay where you argue points, within a dissertation the researcher learns as they move forward. If she could have done anything differently she would have started sooner and taken more time to understand the aims of her research and the processes that it had to go through.

Putting Together a Research Strategy

Compared to other pieces of work, starting a dissertation or a piece of research may feel daunting. As a new researcher you must ask yourself not just 'where do I start?' but also 'how do I start?' Nobody would ever claim that research is easy. In order to meet your completion deadlines and targets you will need to construct some form of research strategy.

From an early stage you will probably realise that undertaking a piece of research does not follow a linear direction. It is not a case of gathering sources, reading them and then simply writing a report. As thinking is involved in all stages of a research project you constantly need to refer back to information in a way that redefines your approaches, the nature of your project and your research strategy. If anything, research is more of a cyclical process which involves reading and making notes. Having read you need to think about the implications of the reading for your research and this may involve some reflection. Then, when you reflect upon what you have learnt, you may wish to revise some of your approaches or look for different materials. It is all a process of discovery and enlightenment which is why critical thinking is an essential part of the research process. Educational research, therefore, is not a static process. More commonly it is amorphous and, as you go through the processes of discovery, it constantly changes its form. Much as you try to control it through being organised and disciplined, you soon realise that it has a life and personality of its own.

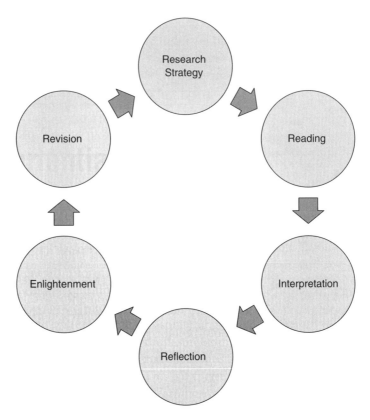

Figure 1.2   The cyclical nature of a research strategy

From the outset it is important to be organised. Even the best and most able of individuals struggle if they do not manage their projects properly. You need to be able to keep and manage materials, have a good filing system, set aside regular times to visit the library and work on your dissertation. You may need to think about how to plan your primary research, when to see your supervisor(s) and all of the physical resources that you require in order to support your project (see Chapter 13).

Choosing an appropriate research question or hypothesis is critical to your research. Although it can be difficult to do so, you need to think about what you as an individual want to get from your research project. For example, how will your dissertation topic support you in your potential choice of career? What experience and expertise will it give you? How will it help and support your curriculum vitae? These are key issues as you think about the outcomes. For probably the first time in your life, you have the opportunity to choose your own curriculum and area for study.

Writing a Good Piece of Research

Some of you will undoubtedly find the prospect of writing up your research to be daunting. If you are studying a postgraduate degree, for example, the research project will have a major impact on your degree grade. It is very easy to talk a good research project, however, without doing the necessary work to get it completed on time and with the quality that you are happy with. Writing is something that involves a considerable amount of self-discipline.

Writing is, and should be, built into the planning process with time allowed for the composition of each part. In fact the writing for a research project should start almost immediately the project begins. As soon as you start reading the literature, you should take notes and then write them up in a way that allows them to be edited and themed into some form of literature section.

Tips when writing up include:

- Begin the writing as soon the project starts, usually by making notes about the project proposal and justifying the choice and then by looking and reading the literature. As each part of the literature is read it should be written up or summarised.
- Writing regularly, sometimes weekly, is a good way of making sure you are on target with deadlines. If this means that you go beyond the word count, the work can be trimmed at a later stage.
- Ensure you have continuous consultation with a tutor, supervisor or critical friend so that work can be seen as and when it is written, thus enabling them to provide constant and ongoing feedback that improves your overall outcome. For students, the evidence is that those who regularly consult their tutors and supervisors perform better. Constructive feedback will help (Silverman, 2013).
- You should keep writing up and contributing to sections. It never stops. As the research evolves, it is perfectly possible to come back and make some revisions, particularly if you come across some new literature.
- You should write at a time of the day when you feel 'inspired'. This may seem like a strange comment, but some people work better in the morning, while others work better in the evening and some burn the midnight oil and work through the night.
- Writing to a routine is important. One method of working is to form study groups. It may be possible for a group of you to meet regularly, perhaps three or four mornings a week, where you can work together in the same resource centre. The aim of the study group is not just to provide a regular way of working; it is also a mechanism that enables you to support and proof-read each other's work.

- It is always useful for you to work in a place where distractions are minimised. This can be difficult.
- Think about your audience. There is no single approach to writing and no set of rules to follow (Denscombe, 1998). Something which may concern many of you is your writing style. Try and get feedback about this. It is really helpful if you produce two or three paragraphs from your literature section, for example, that so you can get some detailed feedback.

Practical Tip

Think carefully about how you might organise yourself for an extended study such as a thesis. Do you use post-its or different forms of notes for reminders? How do you file and keep materials? How are you going to keep and manage any notes that you make? What electronic devices could you use to support this process? Do you foresee any problems or issues associated with the organisation of your project?

As a student, from the start of your project you will have been told the word count or length of your piece of work. It is important to try to keep to this. Longer is not necessarily better. It is the quality that counts. It is best to divide up the word count between various parts of your dissertation or thesis. Everybody always asks about word count, but there is no fixed word count for each part. However, it would be really silly not to allocate a sufficient word count to your literature section, methodology or analysis and discussion.

Your writing style is probably the most important part and for many is the most difficult thing to develop. It involves the use of language, the amount of detail that you go into, the use and discussion of references and the way you use language for analysis. It may also include the quality of analysis, the length of sentences, paragraphs and anything that makes the research report interesting and distinctive to read.

One way for you to think about and try to improve your level of analysis is to look at Bloom's Taxonomy (Bloom et al., 1956). Taxonomy is a form of scientific classification into a hierarchy. In 1956 Benjamin Bloom and some colleagues at the University of Chicago identified what became known as 'Bloom's Taxonomy'. The taxonomy is helpful in creating a lens that provides a more precise focus on the 'cogs' that you need to perform at the highest levels. These 'cogs' appear in examination literature and assessment schemes, in a way that illustrates how they have been adapted from Bloom (Needham and Flint, 2003).

The role of the cues in Table 1.1 is to provide you with tips about how to improve your level of analysis, so that much of it provides evidence of higher level intellectual skills such as those involved with evaluation.

Developing these higher level skills should not simply involve using long sentences and long words! In fact it is not good practice to use lots of long sentences. Mixing and matching sentence length to provide a coherent writing style is instead important. Long and

Table 1.1 The Cogs of Cognition adapted from Bloom's Taxonomy

The 'Cogs'	Forms of Response/Cues
Knowledge • rote memory – e.g., of facts, terms, procedures.	• Making observations, recall, mastery of subject matter, knowledge of major ideas • **Cues**: list, define, describe, identify, collect, show, label, tabulate, name, quote …
Comprehension • an ability to translate, paraphrase, interpolate, extrapolate	• Understanding information, interpretation, translating knowledge into new context, prediction, ordering, grouping, comparing, contrasting • **Cues**: describe, summarise, interpret, predict, distinguish, discuss …
Application • a capacity to transfer and apply knowledge in unfamiliar settings	• Use information, methods, concepts, solve problems using knowledge and skills • **Cues**: apply, demonstrate, calculate, illustrate, examine, discover, solve, modify, complete, calculate …
Analysis • the ability to break down information into its integral parts and to identify the relationship of each part within a *structure*	• Seeing patterns, identification and organisation of parts, recognising hidden meanings • **Cues**: analyse, separate, order, explain, connect, classify, compare, arrange …
Synthesis • the ability to combine existing elements together to create something new	• Using old ideas to create new ones, for example generalising, making connections between knowledge gained from different domains • **Cues**: combine, integrate, rearrange, design, plan, formulate, prepare, generalise …
Evaluation • the ability to make judgements about the value of something by comparison with a standard	• *compare and discriminate between ideas* – similarities/differences and the basis for such discrimination • *assess value of theories and presentations* – desirable, appropriate, good/bad *on the basis of who, what, where, how, why* • *make choices based on reasoned argument* – What is the precise subject – theme, form of thinking, feeling – of your argument? What is the precise object – thing to which actions, feelings are directed? Identify strengths/weaknesses of theoretical positions. Recognise sources of opinion/anecdotes etc • *verify the value of evidence* – sources of triangulation, authority/legitimacy of the sources used • **Cues**: assess, decide, rank, grade, convince, judge, explain, recommend …

convoluted sentences can be difficult to understand, and not make appropriate points. Similarly, long words may be misinterpreted and are not always a good indicator of your academic abilities.

Punctuation and, spelling are important. There is nothing more annoying than reading a project that has clearly not been spell-checked, or simply comprises what seems to be an endless paragraph.

There are likely to be times during the course of a report when you may have to accept feedback that might not always be complimentary. This might be difficult, but whether formally written or informally provided, sometimes you have to take the criticism and use it to improve your own learning outcomes. Feedback is really important during the writing up process, and the more feedback it is possible to get, the better the potential learning outcomes.

Things to avoid in writing up research reports are:

- A report that is not seamless. You should remember that you are answering a question or meeting a hypothesis and so there should be a notion of 'fit' running throughout the report.
- Dialogue that contradicts. Again this relates to the notion of 'fit'. It is all right for you to identify references that contradict, because you can then make fine distinctions about them in relation to the context. However, it is important that the argument you put together should not contradict itself unless you talk about it as a contradiction, particularly in a way that shows a limited understanding of the issues.
- Do not fill your report full of generalisations. It is easy to make broad comments, particularly when setting the context, but these have to be justified on the basis of your reading. The wider the statement you make, particularly in your literature section, the more you will need a multiple reference. It is important to learn to be measured in your dialogue.
- Reaching conclusions without the evidence. Sometimes researchers seem to know what their report is trying to achieve and what the results are even before the research takes place! You have to remember that this process is investigative, and that surprising results might occur. Avoid any pre-conceptions that make your project value ridden.
- Research that is not completely transparent and honest (Roberts-Holmes, 2014). When others look at your project it must be clear exactly what you have done and how you have reached your conclusions.

When presenting diagrams or graphs it is important to express the information in a way that is clear and can be easily understood. If a table is difficult to interpret, then it is important you should refer to in within the dialogue in a way that provides the reader with an understanding of what you are trying to do. Figures and tables or any other diagrammatic form should be given a number and a title.

The purpose of a research project is to bring everything that you have learned together, in a way that enables you to apply learning to something that involves your own idea. It is one of the few occasions within education when you take control of the project yourself for the very first time. It is both exciting and also potentially very challenging.

The research project should have:

- provided you with the opportunity to test concepts and techniques that the you have learned about within other parts of your programme;
- linked your own knowledge and ideas with existing literature;
- provided you with the opportunity to undertake a process of learning of your own choice, possibly focused upon your own career preferences.

Practical Tip

Record everything that you do and back everything up. Save your work regularly and make hard and electronic copies. Use your email, hard drive, pen drive and whatever it takes to make sure that you have multiple copies of everything you observe, undertake and collect. (See Chapter 14 for more guidance on these processes.)

Working with a Supervisor

For degree students it is important that before you start the research project you fully understand the terms of reference. If you have a module handbook or a regulations handbook, this needs to be read carefully. These will vary by each course and within each institution, but are fundamental in ensuring that the project is delivered in an appropriate format. The guidelines for your research project may also have specific requirements about duration, supervisory guidelines, hours and attendance. For example, there may be a number of lecturers or seminars to attend on research methods. There may then be a requirement to submit a work-plan or project proposal by a particular date so that it can be approved. You may also find that elements of the assessment might include a poster presentation or a viva. Sometimes, a course is sorted into small seminar-style groups of critical friends who meet regularly to share ideas and provide each other with formative and supportive feedback. In some courses it is expected that you will provide a presentation of the results of your research to peers in a more formal and traditional setting, and this forms part of the assessment process.

Early in your course you will be allocated a research supervisor. Your course handbook should set out the roles of the supervisor. Usually when you undertake a research project you are allocated a supervisor who will provide support. It is particularly important that you regularly maintain contact with your supervisor(s), and either email or constantly provide copies for their work for supervisor approval.

Although your supervisor may be familiar with the area of your research, their skills and expertise may not exactly match your choice of area. This is because there are so many different projects, areas of research and possibilities that it is impossible for one person to be an expert in every area. In fact as you undertake the research you will become an expert yourself in your own area.

Supervisors contact students in various ways and will develop a routine for meetings and consultations. It is always useful to be prepared for the meeting you attend by taking notes and resources, questions and materials that you can discuss. It is important to make the best use of time with your supervisor. Your supervisor will provide you with:

- formative advice and notes;
- feedback on your ideas, notes, dialogue and thoughts;
- support in developing your research question and aims;
- sources of information;

- advice upon various elements within your project such as the literature section and methodology;
- help to critically interpret and analyse all that you see and find;
- help to plan your project, and;
- most importantly, counsel if things start to go wrong.

Before you visit your supervisor it is often useful to send them some notes so at least they can be prepared for the meeting and provide you with an element of response. A good supervisor will ask you lots of questions and should, from time to time, challenge you. This is really a positive thing. Sometimes, we need to reflect upon criticism and be put into a situation where we have to justify our approaches.

Any form of research is a journey and nobody would describe it as easy. In many ways, and unlike most other modules, it involves and interlinks with your own personal development as you become aware and activate your academic skills. In this way, it is a process of discovery which, no matter what the tensions and pressures you face as you work towards a degree grade that meets your hopes and expectations, is an engaging form of learning.

Key Points to Remember

- Educational research is an area that engages with the practice of education. As the world of education is very large there is almost an unlimited array of potential areas of research in which you might want to engage.
- Educational research is not an area that stands still. It is a constantly evolving area that endeavours in a variety of ways to influence and improve people's lives.
- There are many different types of research approaches and projects that you can construct. It is a testing time and, as you do so, you need to think carefully about how you write. At the same time you need to take advantage of the skills and support of your tutor, supervisor or critical friend.

Further Reading

The books below are helpful sources for beginners in research in the field of education:

Cohen, L., Manion, L. and Morrison, K. (2011) *Research Methods in Education* (7/E). London: Routledge.
Opie, C. (2004) *Doing Educational Research: A Guide to First Time Researchers*. London: SAGE.
Thomas, G. (2013) *How to do your Research Project* (3/E). London: SAGE.
    As guides for beginners both of these books are particularly helpful to all studying in the field of education. They are both particularly good as points of reference and have many illustrative examples that support the reader.

Robert-Holmes, G. (2014) *Doing your Early Years Research Project: A Step by Step Guide* (3/E). London: SAGE.
    This book is very helpful to all studying early childhood studies or childhood studies degrees.

Useful Websites

- Whether an undergraduate, graduate, early career researcher or faculty member, SAGE Research Methods provides a comprehensive guide to research
  http://.srmo.sagepub.com/publicstart;jsessionid=D9DAFB1A07761509155328ED23795BD6?auth
     Rejection=true

- The Open University provides a useful website focused upon developing study skills and this includes a section on post-graduate study
  www2.open.ac.uk/students/skillsforstudy/

- The Scottish Educational Research Association has a series of bulletins on their site that discuss topical research issues
  www.sera.ac.uk/

References

Anderson, G. and Arsenault, N. (1998) *Fundamentals of Educational Research*. London: RoutledgeFalmer.

Bloom, B., Engelhart, M., Furst, E., Hill, W. and Krathwohl, D. (1956). *Taxonomy of Educational Objectives: The Classification of Educational Goals. Handbook I: Cognitive Domain*. New York: David McKay Company.

Check, J. and Schutt, J. (2012) *Research Methods in Education*. Thousand Oaks: SAGE.

Denscombe, M. (1998) *The Good Researcher Guide for Small-scale Social Research Projects*. Buckingham: Open University Press.

(HEFCE) Higher Education Funding Council of England (1999) *Research Assessment Exercise 2001: Consultations on Assessment Panels' Criteria and Working Methods*. Bristol: HEFCE.

Kagan, J. (1972) 'Motives and Development', *Journal of Personality and Social Psychology*, 22: 51–66.

Needham, D. and Flint, K. (2003) 'Uncovering the Truth Behind Vygotsky's Cognitive Apprenticeship: Engaging Reflective Practitioners in the "Master-Apprentice" Relationship', *International Journal of Learning*, Volume 10. Melbourne: Common Ground Publishing.

Newby, P (2014) *Research Methods for Education* (2/E). London: Routledge.

Roberts-Holmes, G. (2014) *Doing Your Early Years Research Project: A Step by Step Guide* (3/E). London: Paul Chapman.

Silverman, D. (2013) *Doing Qualitative Research* (4/E). London: SAGE.

Stern, E. (1990) *The Evaluation of Policy and the Politics of Evaluation*. The Tavistock Institute Annual Review.

Tuckman, B.W. and Harper, B. (2012) *Conducting Educational Research* (6/E). Baltimore, MD: Rowman & Littlefield.

For additional online resources please visit the book's website:
https://study.sagepub.com/needhamandpalaiologou

2

MAKING SENSE OF RESEARCH METHODOLOGY

JAMES MA

Chapter Aims and Objectives

This chapter aims to help you to:

- understand the prime function of research methodology, as well as the universal value of methodological principles, in the research process;
- recognise the importance of making sense of the connection between methodology and methods for how methodological considerations are enacted through the research design;
- conceptualise the discussions relating to the relationship of theory and praxis in social inquiry, in addition to raising awareness of the fundamental differences between social science research and natural science research.

Introduction

The defining of methodology is laden with values, beliefs, desires and expectations that are subliminally brought to such an act. This chapter seeks to accentuate as well as preserve the enduring primacy of methodology in the research process. It brings into focus a collection of theoretical constructs that are used as guiding principles for scholarly research. Mindful of this, it departs from defining methodology within the narrow confines of methods or instruments for investigation, instead highlighting such theoretical constructs as necessary foundations for both practical and academic research. More specifically, it considers methodology on logical grounds to be the basic principle on which research design is premised and shaped. This is the core purpose of this chapter, which argues that methods of data collection and analysis are to be predicated on and underpinned by methodological principles.

Traditional academics, and those who comply with the conventions of scholarly activity, habitually avoid the practice of doing research devoid of or lacking theoretical gravitas. However, there are times when this is less clear and the road begins to fork: one branch heading towards what might be signified as theory-driven academic direction, and the other as vocational direction characterised by the application of theory. Consequently ontological (underlying concepts of reality) and epistemological (knowledge base) positions can be differentiated in terms of 'academic/vocational divisions' (Young, 2008). The former direction maintains that failure to theorise issues and concerns in research can result in the failure to do so in reality. Nevertheless, this is not to say that doing research is for the sake of theory or for merely living in the world of theory. Rather, it is for sustaining academic enquiry in which the pursuit of knowledge and truth takes precedence through an engagement with 'rationality, methodological principles, objectivity and logical argument' (Bloch, 2012: 2). It is important to note, therefore, that the interaction of theory and practice is a dialectical relationship. They are inseparable in that each shapes and is shaped by the other through a cluster of 'situations, institutions and social structures' (Fairclough and Wodak, 1997: 258). Thus, the research process is to be construed as a synthesis of theory and practice to which dialectical thinking and reasoning is of vital importance. With due diligence, the resolution or reconciliation of contradictions and differences can yield new understanding of and insights into the phenomenon under scrutiny.

Taking this as a starting point, this chapter will provide an account of the central planks of research methodology in terms of ontology, epistemology and paradigm, together with other key methodological constructs and their underlying conceptions and assumptions. In order to enact the dialectical relationship between theory and praxis in the research process, this chapter is coupled with a series of case studies, terminology definitions and differentiations, writing exercises, pointers for reflection, and questions for discussion that are specifically tailored to facilitate and consolidate an understanding of the relationship of methodology to the research design.

Terminology differentiation

Methodology and Methods: Methodology is generally concerned with a set of theoretical constructs and concepts deployed as a conceptual framework for solving the research problem. Methods are often referred to as denoting concrete approaches to, or instruments for, collecting and analysing the data. It is thus important to recognise that any scholarly investigation should be galvanised by the researcher's will for and commitment to methodological principles rather than simply methods. In this sense, understanding methodology is a prerequisite of understanding methods during the research process.

Construct and Concept: Construct pertains to a thinking block generally associated with the theoretical domain of a particular discipline. Concept is often related to a particular theoretical idea. It is widely known that the abstract nature of theoretical constructs and concepts requires a high level of intellectual contemplation of theory. Such constructs and concepts often leave the impression that they are abstruse and woolly, as opposed to practical matters and affairs. This calls for commitment and devotion to theoretical thinking and reasoning.

Practical Tip

1. Methodology is the cornerstone of academic research and it is essentially concerned with a system of knowledge with specialised vocabulary and grammar. As such, methodology should be approached in a technical sense rather than in an uninformed, practical manner.
2. Understanding the primacy of methodology in the research process can prevent the researcher from being lulled into an unprincipled, sloppy sense of doing research as a way of solving a problem or issue in the real world.

The Nature of Social Science Research

The domain of social sciences is wide-ranging, with core disciplines including anthropology, sociology, psychology, economics, politics and cultural studies. Although the general conception of how it is defined may be influenced by the notion that social sciences are invariably a science in the same sense that natural sciences are a science, there are examples that suggest the contrary. For example, there is no single, unanimous method of investigation and interpretation that can be employed in both social and natural science research. The aim of social sciences is to understand human society at both individual and collective levels. In this chapter I maintain that it is imperative to recognise ways in which social sciences differ from natural sciences prior to conducting a research project in education.

Natural sciences are sometimes labelled 'hard sciences', e.g. physics, mathematics, chemistry and biology, as opposed to social sciences often being referred to as 'soft sciences'. What is prioritised in natural sciences is that reasoned (*a posteriori*) knowledge is dependent on empirical evidence, with the use of inductive logic. Natural scientists are committed to objective explorations in which the role of consciousness is excluded to the extent that the sum of the parts equals the whole. They are particularly concerned with natural phenomena or events and ways in which they are configured to abstraction or generalised to laws. On the other hand, social scientists are more interested to attain derived logical (*a priori*) knowledge independently of empirical findings, through a deductive approach. It should be recognised, however, that some approaches, such as ethnography, still emphasise the need of 'observing the same relationship in several more cases and finally constructing a general theory to cover all the cases' (Gilbert, 1993: 22–23).

Social scientists, therefore, are inclined to foreground the qualitative aspects of the social world as to what, how and why such aspects are as they are – which cannot be dealt with in natural science terms given that there is an inherent focus on the meaning conferred on such aspects. In social science research, an important, unmitigated factor is that the researcher is a social actor who duly recognises his or her role as an instrument for studying the social aspects of other human beings. This is in contrast with natural science research in which the researcher uses laboratory or other technical equipment. Moreover, hypotheses in social sciences are essentially retrospective and inapt for prediction, with the sum of the parts to be conceived of as greater than the whole. It is widely recognised that the findings of social science research are, for the most part, open, emerging and incapable of abiding conclusions.

This brings to the fore fundamental differences between social science research and natural science research:

1. The object of investigation in social science research is the social, behavioural dimension of the human world, as opposed to the objectivity of investigation in natural science research being the inanimate or consciousness-free dimension of the physical world independently of what is assumed in terms of mental concepts.
2. Subjectivity is ubiquitously inherent in social science research due to the researcher's biases and prejudices. Considering that the fundamental aim of natural science research is to obtain objective knowledge, such biases and prejudices have no role to play in dealing with the data and results.

To sum up, the demarcation between these two domains of research can be seen as tinged with the researcher's values and beliefs, albeit determined by ways of dealing with different subject matters. A natural scientist's approach to data analysis and interpretation is based on scientific methods, whereas a social scientist asserts an orientation towards a contextual understanding of human existence. This is often reflected in their ontological and epistemological positions for understanding the essence of the phenomenon under scrutiny.

Definitions – *A priori* knowledge vs. *a posteriori* knowledge

A priori and *a posteriori* are two rival concepts of philosophy. *A priori* knowledge derives from a top-down approach to investigation, involving a process of 'deduction' that proceeds from the general to the specific, in which the causation principle is applied to denote a conceptual move from 'cause' to 'effect'. In contrast, *a posteriori* knowledge derives from a bottom-up approach to investigation, involving a process of 'induction' which proceeds from the specific to the general, in which the causation principle is applied to denote a conceptual move from 'effect' to 'cause'. The logic of deduction means 'particularisation', whereas the logic of induction is 'generalisation'. These two types of logic are frequently used in social science research, e.g. the construction of theory requires induction, whereas the application of theory requires deduction (see *A priori* theorising on p. 28).

Case Study

'It is important to realise that induction is not foolproof. It is certainly possible to construct erroneous, misleading or over-simple theories. For example, induction has led us straight to the theory that high suicide rates are the product of economic and social change. Unfortunately, this is not the whole theory. Denmark and Finland both have high rates of suicide compared with other industrialised nations, yet neither has experienced great political or economic changes recently.

(Continued)

(Continued)

These counter instances can be put to good use, however. The theory can be extended in scope and deepened in its explanatory power if we look to see what characteristics Denmark and Finland share which might explain their high rates. The answer, as Durkheim discovered from his data, is that economic and social change is only one influence on suicide rates. The degree of integration of the dominant religion is also important and this is the reason, he argues, that Protestant countries, such as Denmark and Finland, tend to have much higher suicide rates than otherwise similar countries.' (Gilbert, 1993: 24)

Activity

Explore the following questions:

1. How do social science and natural science differ in terms of the object of study?
2. Why is social science sometimes labelled 'soft science' or even 'retarded science'?
3. Why is biology classed as natural science despite its object of study being humans and non-humans?
4. Is there a single, unanimous method of interpretation for both social and natural sciences? Why?
5. Can social sciences be value-neutral and to what extent can the researcher's self-function as instrument for research be accomplished?

Ontology and Epistemology

Ontology is a branch of philosophy in association with *metaphysics*, a theoretical domain of philosophy placing the notion of *being* at its very core. As such, ontology is normally referred to as the theory of existence, with specific reference to the nature of being and reality. It asks philosophical questions such as: *What can be said to exist? What is there to be known? What is the nature of social and physical phenomena?* These questions encapsulate a distinction between the conception of reality as detached or independent from human knowledge and the conception of reality as socially constructed and culturally organised. On logical grounds they are intended to forge an ontological proposition and the making of such propositions requires deductive argumentation, i.e., the process of making an argument by the use of deductive logic, proceeding from a general premise to a specific one. It is noteworthy that any ontological arguments are deductive in nature. In social sciences, ontology highlights the nature of what is being examined as a social phenomenon. It can assist in the construction of knowledge by the recognition that there are different ways of viewing the world in terms of what there is to be known. For example, the perception of happiness varies from individual to individual due to different genetic inheritances and environmental influences. It is plausible to say that happiness is biologically cultural and at the same time culturally biological.

There are two ontological positions to be distinguished: *positivist* ontology and *constructionist* ontology. For positivist ontology, the world is *out there*, operating in a systematic and lawful manner, with myriads of discrete and observable events in which reality is separate from human sense-making. For constructionist ontology, on the contrary, the world is semiotically constructed and reconstructed, with different ways of meaning fused together through signs and symbols, amongst which language plays a central role.

Following ontology, *epistemology* is concerned with the theory of knowledge, with specific reference to the nature and forms of knowledge. It asks philosophical questions such as: *What is knowledge? How is it acquired? How should we know what we know?* In a similar vein, these questions encapsulate a distinction between the notion that the observation of reality can be carried out by any individual in the *same* unvitiated, impartial manner and the notion that an individual's interpretation of the world is subjective and this always has an influence on what is being observed by that individual.

In the educational domain, researchers may hold different views about knowledge and truth. Knowledge is, on the one hand, something that can be *objectively* transmitted or acquired in a concrete, palpable way and, on the other hand, something that has to be *personally* experienced. In the former, the researcher would take a detached, observer role with an allegiance to methods used in natural science. In the latter, the researcher will insist on having a psychological involvement with what is being studied and reject the methods of natural science.

Practical Tips

1. For natural scientists, the physical phenomena or events are examined through systematic observations in order to establish a scientific model or routine for prediction. In contrast, for social scientists, the individual action and the collective action are viewed as bi-directional, each shaping and being shaped by the other.
2. In terms of epistemological position (i.e., how reality should be understood), social scientists are more inclined to adopt a synergistic approach to what is under investigation, by weaving together strengths of different methods or instruments.

Epistemological positions provide fundamental aspects of research as they concern the philosophical question of what counts as reality and how beings come into being as well as what constitutes knowledge and how knowledge comes to be established. There are two epistemological positions to be distinguished: *positivist* epistemology and *constructionist* epistemology. For the former, knowledge can only be obtained by gathering facts in a systematic and objective manner, predominantly by experimental methods or by testing of hypotheses. For the latter, knowledge is a representation of the reality carried out by the researcher who construes knowledge as subject to time-space configurations and as a manifestation of social relations of power. Scientists and their institutions shape the production of knowledge by their choices and values. It is important to note that, on logical grounds, ontology leads to epistemology and epistemology subsequently informs the choice of research paradigm. This is the universal value of academic and practical research in terms of its ultimate aim as being capable of making contributions to knowledge.

Definition – Ontology argument

An ontological argument is commonly defined as a manifestation of the individual's worldview in terms of what he or she is looking at for an investigative study and the reason for it. When composing an ontological argument, the logic of deduction is applied in order to demonstrate a process of ascending from the general to the specific. This process requires the construction of three propositions that are sequentially organised into a logical order: an analytical proposition is followed by an evaluative proposition that is then followed by an argumentative proposition.

With regard to the origin of ontological argument, Bertrand Russell writes:

> St Anselm was, like Lanfranc, an Italian, a monk at Bec, and Archbishop of Canterbury (1093–1109), in which capacity he followed the principles of Gregory VII and quarrelled with the king. He is chiefly known to fame as the inventor of the 'ontological argument' for the existence of God. As he put it, the argument is as follows: We define 'God' as the greatest possible object of thought. Now if an object of thought does not exist, another, exactly like it, which does exist, is greater. Therefore the greatest of all objects must exist, since, otherwise, another still greater, would be possible. Therefore God exists. (Russell, 2004: 388)

Activity

Questions for discussion:

1. How do you describe your ontological and epistemological stance for your proposed study, linking this to either positivist ontology/epistemology or constructionist ontology/epistemology?
2. To what extent does your ontological and epistemological stance inform the search for knowledge through your proposed study?
3. What would be the potential limitations of your proposed study, linking this to your ontological and epistemological viewpoint?
4. How do you examine a human condition (e.g. learning disposition or temperament) from your own ontological and epistemological standpoint?
5. What do you think might be the debate to which ontology and epistemology may contribute?

Activity

Ontology and epistemology are infused with *axiology* (your cultural values and norms). Therefore, the construction of one's ontological and epistemological position requires a commitment to deliberate thoughts by tapping into a deeper layer of the consciousness. Write a short account of how your own axiology has come to affect the following aspects of the research process:

a) choosing your research topic;
b) formulating your research questions;
c) explaining the choice of research paradigm within which your research is situated;
d) deciding on the methods for collecting and analysing the data.

Paradigms

Paradigm, as a philosophical term, is conventionally associated with Thomas Kuhn (1922–1996), an American philosopher of science. A *paradigm* pertains to a school of thought or an intellectual tradition within which scientific concepts and practices operate. The term is also related to a set of values and beliefs shared by a scientific society for their research enterprises. In his seminal work, Kuhn (1996) popularised the concept of 'paradigm shift' which denotes the change of paradigmatic constructs resulting from one paradigm being overthrown by intellectual revolution when it has served its term. He advocates a holistic approach to scientific knowledge by which the whole is seen as prior to its parts and the logic of induction as inadequate for generating theory. For Kuhn, sciences are paradigm-orientated and paradigms are established through the collective work of an intellectual group; the notion of paradigm shift is to be conceived of as being enacted at a collective level rather than an individual one.

It would be in some sense preposterous or at least inappropriate for a novice researcher or practitioner to claim to have accomplished a *paradigm shift* prior to the research design. Such claims may be ascribed to a perceptual illusion or conceptual fallacy in which the idea of paradigm shift displaces what is in effect objectified to be a personal ontological and epistemological move from one point of view to another for the sake of the inquiry undertaken. Given that paradigmatic transition involves an array of the vicissitudes of ideas and concepts at micro and macro levels, the researcher needs to be sensitive to the dynamics and complexities of such transitions, rather than seeing this as something that can be irrationally construed or wilfully manipulated. This leads me to conclude that understanding the essence of paradigm shift requires discernment and prudence.

There are different conceptions of the nature of the social world which have different effects on ways in which research is conducted. Two major paradigmatic traditions are defined in Bassey (1999) as positive research paradigm or *positivism* and interpretive research paradigm or *interpretivism*. Both paradigms claim their roots in sociology.

- Positivism has influences from functionalism, a modern successor to early behaviourism, and structuralism, a doctrine considering social phenomena as intelligible and meaningful in the sense that they are interrelated;
- Interpretivism has a bearing on symbolic interactionism, initiated by George Herbert Mead (1863–1931) who argues that human life is symbolic in nature with shared meaning conveyed through social interaction, and ethnomethodology, an approach to ways in which people make sense of the world, e.g., conversation analysis by Harvey Sacks (1935–1975) with an emphasis on language use and social interaction.

For positivism, the connection between the world and the human perception of the world is direct and in social sciences there are the same capacities for understanding reality as there are for natural sciences. For example, any observable events can be examined by excluding the mediating effect of the human mind and its social and cultural environments. It is thus possible to obtain true knowledge of the world, provided human perceptions are impartial and objective. Hence the social world can be understood in terms of general statements about human actions and interactions. As an allied doctrine of positivism, *empiricism* construes human knowledge of the world as a derivation of what is perceived through the generating of hypotheses that can be tested by means of observation. For empiricists, objectivity is achievable in the sense that general causal links can be established between social events and phenomena.

However, interpretivism remains at odds with positivism, rejecting the notion that reality can be understood irrespective of the unique, individual characteristics of the human mind. Interpretivists consider the description of human action as being tied to particular social, historical and cultural contexts. They strive to establish a shared understanding of the world with other social beings by hermeneutics as a way of developing perspectives on, and insights into, the social phenomenon under scrutiny. They emphasise the capacity for reasoning and sense-making as varying from individual to individual, recognising the role of the researcher as a potential variable in interpreting the world, with a personal influence upon the inquiry. This value position is also held by *relativists* who share the same ontological position with interpretivists. Both relativists and interpretivists maintain that reality is not fixed but socially constructed and therefore cannot be examined in an objective manner.

With regard to instrumentation, the methods used by positivists are often termed as '*quantitative*' due to their prioritising of measurable quantities and statistics, e.g. surveys. Positivists claim allegiance to methods employed by natural scientists in their analytical approach, with minimal explanatory interpretations but maximal generalised causations. In contrast, interpretivists employ *qualitative* methods in tune with their ontological and epistemological stance for the inquiry, i.e. human knowledge about the world is socially constructed, pluralistic, relative, provisional and emerging. They often use interviews, field notes, conversations and other qualitative methods that are not open to quantitative analysis. Given that the notion of measuring or testing is not apt in their approach, interpretivists are often confronted by the problems of *reliability* and *generalisability*. Nevertheless, in the debate on social science research in terms of quantitative versus qualitative, there is not such a dilemma that social science researchers have to make a 'stark choice between words and numbers, or even between precise and imprecise data; but rather with a range from more to less precise and imprecise data' (Hammersley, 1992: 163). This may suggest that qualitative and quantitative methods may complement each other in terms of managing 'the tension between reality and representation' (Gubrium and Holstein, 1997: 114). The table below offers an overview of the key differentiation between qualitative methods and quantitative methods (Bryman, 2012: 393):

Table 2.1 Qualitative vs. quantitative methods

Qualitative	Quantitative
Words	Numbers
Points of view of participants	Points of view of the researcher
Researcher close	Researcher distinct
Theory emergent	Theory testing
Process	Static
Unstructured	Structured
Contextual understanding	Generalising
Rich in depth	Hard reliable data
Micro	Macro
Meaning	Behaviour
Natural setting	Artificial setting

In qualitative research, there are four traditions: *naturalism, ethnomethodology, emotionalism* and *postmodernism*.

- *Naturalism* is concerned with exploring the social world in its own right through the interpretation of social phenomena based on observations. The aim of naturalism is to develop a new theory or verify an existing theory by drawing on support from empirical data, e.g. ethnography. The logic of induction is commonly used in naturalism as a bottom-up approach to investigation.
- *Ethnomethodology* is the study of human interaction designed to understand how social order shapes and is shaped by social interactions and power relations, in which the notions of inclusion and exclusion are relevant.
- *Emotionalism* focuses on the role of subjectivity in human relations. For example, knowledge and intelligence vary from person to person. It can be argued that knowledge and intelligence in terms of diversity and hierarchy are a source of exclusion rather than inclusion.
- *Postmodernism* emphasises the constructing of social reality through discourse. Social reality involves social relations and practices. Discourse pertains to something beyond verbal interaction, relating to 'a patchwork of thoughts, words, objects, events, actions, and interactions' (Gee, 2005: 7).

These traditions tend to have a common analytical approach, characteristic of *a priori* theorising with 'well-informed theoretical aims, specified concepts for analysis, reflection on, and specifications of, the processes of pursuing analysis using these concepts' (Gibson, 2010: 57). Such theorisation can be found in many qualitative approaches, such as critical discourse analysis and semiotic analysis.

Definitions – Positivism vs. Interpretivism; and Empiricism vs. Relativism

These are two sets of methodological constructs associated with different philosophical doctrines, each set consisting of two rival conceptions of knowledge about social reality.

Positivism vs. Interpretivism: A fundamental difference between these two doctrines lies in their differing assumptions about knowledge and ways in which knowledge is acquired. Positivism considers knowledge to be obtained objectively and in a value-free manner, whereas interpretivism foregrounds an individual's personal involvement in knowledge acquisition and appropriation.

Empiricism vs. Relativism: The main difference between these two doctrines is a concern about the perception of knowledge. For empiricism, knowledge is rooted in experience, i.e. knowledge is both derived from and justified by experience. In contrast, relativism maintains that statements made within a given area of knowledge can be true for one individual or the members of one social group but false for another individual or those of another social group.

Definition – *A priori* theorising

The usual character of an a priori approach is a pre-existing body of concepts and ideas that are put to work in the course of doing analysis. Many approaches to analysis have this character, such as critical discourse analysis, rhetorical analysis, semiotic analysis and critical narrative analysis, to name but a few. To work within these approaches/paradigms is to orientate to their body of work and assumptions. Of course, 'orientate to' does not mean 'agree with' or even 'stick within the confines of', but it does mean that there is existing theoretical and conceptual work that is used to organize analysis from the outset of a research project. (Gibson, 2010: 57)

Activity

Writing exercise:

Make a list of theoretical ideas and concepts that you intend to apply to your study and then write a short account of how these ideas and concepts are organised into a coherent whole as a method of *a priori* theorising for your analysis and interpretation of the data.

Activity

Questions for discussion:

1. Can our observation and perception of social reality deceive us? Why?
2. On what grounds should human societies value the results of scientific research? Why?

3. Is there ethical neutrality in social inquiry? Why? (See Chapter 3 for guidance on ethical issues.)
4. In what ways and to what extent is one's knowledge about paradigms important to the research undertaken? Why?

Practical Tips

1. On ontological grounds, qualitative research takes a constructionist view, i.e. seeing the social world in terms of process. Such processes are on an individual and collective basis and are context-bound. So, as researcher, your own belief and value position always play a part in how you make sense of the social reality.
2. On epistemological grounds, qualitative research takes an interpretivist view, i.e. believing that people attribute meaning to the social environment. From a postmodernist point of view, such meanings are relative and constantly under construction.

Hermeneutics as an Axiological Stance for Social Inquiry

Hermeneutics is the theory of interpretation associated with the work of Martin Heidegger and Hans-Georg Gadamer (Bullock and Trombley, 1999: 388–389). The question of interpretation is posed in terms of the 'hermeneutic circle', involving basic problems such as the possibility of establishing a determinate meaning in a text, the role of the author's intention, the historical relativity of meanings, and the status of the reader's contribution to a text's meaning. Over time hermeneutics has developed into a general philosophy of understanding and interpreting human actions, utterances, products and institutions. It manifests itself as rooted in *circularity*, and the process of interpretation is accordingly conceived of as two basic, coinciding and complementary hermeneutic circles: the 'part–whole' hermeneutic circle of objectivist perspective, which regards what is presented to consciousness as the nature of an object not determined by one's own feelings or sensations, and the 'pre-understanding–understanding' hermeneutic circle of alethic perspective, which concerns the process of interpreting truth based on the interpreter's value judgements.

- The '*part–whole*' circle foregrounds the notion that any part of the whole cannot be understood until the whole is preliminarily understood, and conversely, as the whole consists of parts, it cannot be understood until its parts are understood. For example, an individual's understanding of an artwork must involve an anticipation of the whole that informs his or her view of the parts while simultaneously being modified by them.
- The '*pre-understanding–understanding*' circle highlights the notion that understanding a new text requires pre-understanding and simultaneously, as pre-understanding is to be formed, it requires the understanding of the new text. By moving round the hermeneutic circle from known to unknown, the researcher is able to enrich his or her knowledge base both qualitatively and quantitatively, as well as enhancing the validity and credibility of the analysis (Miles and Huberman, 1994).

In the light of contemporary hermeneutic philosophy human individuals understand the world through historical processes and they are strongly influenced by their culture and the environment of that culture. That is, human experience is, on the one hand, determined by culture and, on the other, creates and transcends culture. As Robson (2011) comments:

> A central feature is the 'dialogic' nature of hermeneutic enquiry. The text is returned to time and time again. Initial understandings are refined through interpretation; this then raises further questions, calling for a return to the text and revision of the interpretation. Throughout this process, one is trying to understand what it means to those who created it and to integrate that meaning with its meaning to us. Hermeneutics has contributed to qualitative research methodology the notion of an active involvement by the researcher in the research process. (Robson, 2011: 197–198)

Such conceptions may have formed an axiological stance that comes to impinge upon the interpretivist research paradigm. More recently, the relevance of hermeneutics for discourse studies has been given prominence across several social science disciplines in that hermeneutics has affinity with and can bring illumination to theories of discourse analysis (e.g. Ma, 2013). It seems that hermeneutics is becoming a paradigmatic framework for the intertextuality of human actions in a broader social, cultural, economical, political and technological milieu of postmodernity.

Case Study

The work of Ma (2008) on parental involvement in reading proposes a hermeneutic approach to children's learning through 'guided participation' (Rogoff, 1990), i.e. the interpersonal engagement during shared reading. This approach is informed by a socio-cultural understanding of meaning as co-constructed in cultural, historical and institutional contexts through which the interpersonal processes are mediated and transformed into the intrapersonal functioning. The researcher is therefore involved in an active process of insight-driven and hermeneutic organisation and interpretation of empirical data. The analytical feature of this approach is that data from different empirical sites are triangulated, i.e. the data from the interpersonal plane is triangulated with data from the institutional and personal planes. This analysis is governed by an explanatory framework – within which guided participation as a foreground-focus of the analysis is conceptually connected with 'apprenticeship' and 'participatory appropriation' (Rogoff, 1990) as a background-focus of the analysis. Endorsed by the hermeneutic part–whole circle, guided participation is interpreted with reference to apprenticeship and participatory appropriation which illuminate the articulation of guided participation.

⊣ Practical Tips ⊢

1. A key analytic feature of hermeneutic interpretation is that data from different empirical investigations are triangulated in order to enhance the validity of findings. Such triangulation is often concerned with the examination of one object from more than one position in order to develop insights into the hermeneutic whole.

2. Hermeneutics has broadened the scope of discourse studies for examining the social world
    in terms of a wide range of verbal and textual materials in various contexts. This has meth-
    odological implications for educational research, e.g. collaborative learning and intervention
    in different educational settings.

Validity and Reliability in Qualitative Research

In qualitative research, validity and reliability are closely related to the possibility of achieving them in practice, as well as ways in which qualitative research is defined. In view of
different researchers taking different ontological and epistemological positions to conduct
their research (Robson, 2011), validity appears to be a contested methodological concept.
There are different ways of seeing qualitative research as being valid. If validity is taken to
be an observable criterion in qualitative research, then it is possible for qualitative research
to claim to be valid.

Lincoln and Guba (2000) propose two criteria for assessing validity in qualitative study:
credibility, i.e. whether the findings can be trusted; and *transferability*, i.e. whether the findings can apply to other contexts (see Chapter 9 for more guidance in this issue).
Hammersley considers validity to be 'the extent to which an account accurately represents
the social phenomena to which it refers' (1990: 57). Lecompte and Goets (1982) identify
two forms of validity: *internal validity*, i.e. a sound contest between the researcher's observation and the theoretical ideas to be developed; and *external validity*, i.e. the extent to
which the findings can be generalised. Internal validity is also termed *casual* validity in
terms of 'the degree to which findings correctly map the phenomenon in question' (Denzin
and Lincoln, 1994: 100). i.e. measuring what is supposed to be measured.

There is always a concern that social inquiry is a construction and the conclusion about
the findings reflects the social reality under investigation. In the view of Schutt (1996),
researching the social world means conducting research that achieves the goal of validity
in terms of making correct statements about the empirical reality. Thus, the credibility of
such inquiries is prioritised, i.e. data analysis and interpretation are trustworthy in the sense
that they are true descriptions of the phenomenon. Moreover, as Bryman (2012: 36) comments, 'qualitative research is stronger than quantitative investigations in terms of
ecological validity'. For example, ecological validity is viewed as a central theme in qualitative research, premised on the view of the participant on a particular subject matter.

Like validity, reliability is, too, a contested methodological concept in qualitative
research. As such, it is important to take into account the nature of qualitative research
when defining reliability. Lecompte and Goets (1982) use *internal reliability* to refer to a
case in which more than one observer agrees to what has been observed, and *external reliability* to refer to the extent to which the study can be replicated. Hammersley refers to
reliability as 'the degree of consistency with which instances are assigned to the same category by different observers or by the same observers on different occasions' (1992: 67).
Bryman offers a definition of reliability in the sense that the 'measures that are devised for
concepts in the social sciences are consistent' (2012: 31). This may suggest that reliability

addresses the link between a measure and a concept and that the concept of consistency is important should reliability be concerned with generating a measurable concept.

Case Study

A case study undertaken by Ma (2008), based on video observation and interview, aims to understand guided participation as interpersonal engagement and relationship, with a focus not on extracting factors, but gaining a better understanding of video-recorded mother-child shared reading. On the basis of clarifying meaning in the video data, validity is facilitated through interviews and observations. Different data sources (interviews and observations) are incorporated in the approach to analysing the video data. That is, the video data are analysed in terms of how they are corroborated by the data from interviews. To enhance validity, a circular process is prioritised: interpretation → interrogation → interpretation. In this process, superficiality and bias are reduced to a minimum possible level, and the accuracy of video-data transcription and translation is scrutinised. Furthermore, peer examination of the transcription is used as additional validation of the video-data transcripts alongside these processes.

It is often difficult and almost impossible to replicate a qualitative study, in that data are derived from a specific context and understood within that context. Reliability in this study is demonstrated through data triangulation as a method of increasing the credibility of video-recorded data and interpretation. By examining the intersection of different data, the interpretation of video-documented data can be enhanced. It appears to be inappropriate in this research that reliability is addressed in the quantitative sense of replicability, because the value of this study resides in the uniqueness and instrumental significance for understanding human cognition as being sociocultural in nature. Thus, the issue of reliability is concerned with how data are analysed and interpreted as an appropriate way of answering the research question. In addition, over an extended period of time in conducting home observations, the researcher developed a friendship with the child observed. This ensured a better condition for data collection but also called for reflexivity.

Subjectivity and Objectivity

Subjectivism and *objectivism* are often likened to an axis around which the theory of knowledge revolves, i.e. how the knowledge of the subject matter should be obtained by attending to subjectivism and objectivism. Subjectivism versus objectivism has hitherto been one of the main polarities in philosophy.

Philosophical polarities are also termed complementarities, dualities or binaries, e.g. mind and body, yin and yang, Eros and Thanatos. Eros is the life instinct and Thanatos the death instinct, as defined in Freudian theory. Eros is the Greek god of love and hence the principle of life, whereas Thanatos is the death drive. Freud believed that the human psyche, i.e. the soul, is the interplay of these two forces which he described as interpenetrating forces. For example, the Electra complex and the Oedipus complex are two interpenetrating forces of infantile development in his psychosexual theory. Human consciousness exists beyond, rather than being constrained or limited by, time and space. It is therefore not susceptible to empirical experiments, resulting in the subjectivity of our mind as a defining feature of the human race.

Subjectivity refers to the quality of dealing with objects as *internal* to the mind, i.e. *internal experience*. It is an approach to the subject matter based on individual or personal analysis and interpretation. This means that the subjective is of singularity, i.e. only one individual is involved and the meaning is characteristic of being neither directly public nor knowable to another individual. In qualitative research, the subjectivity of the researcher intimately manifests itself in the research process, e.g. from the choice of the topic to the review of the literature, from the formation of research questions to the design of the inquiry. In social sciences, the recognition of subjectivity encapsulates the notion of how subjectivity comes to affect objectivity. Subjectivism makes the assumption that all perspectives are different ways of making sense of the world. It denies the possibility of examining social and physical environments objectively.

In contrast, objectivity refers to the quality of dealing with objects as *external* to the mind, i.e. *external experience*. It is an approach to the subject matter characterised by *freedom* from individual biases or prejudices. This may be understood as there being a 'pure' kind of knowledge that is not vitiated by subjective experiences. Objectivism often renders the researcher a passive recipient of stimuli encountered in social and physical environments. It is important to note that qualitative research in social sciences has an objectivist strand. This means that the subjectivity of the researcher allows him or her to accurately comprehend the social world, although such subjectivity can give a bias to the researcher due to his or her own psychological reality. Objectivity was hitherto an important concept in social sciences. Being objective requires an immediate awareness of the subjectivity of our own minds. It would be simplistic to think that social science research can be conducted without recognising that social sciences are by nature subjective and self-evident. Why are social sciences subjective and self-evident? Because they use humans to study humans – and every human is unique and has particular brain physiology and a particular perspective deriving from his or her particular experiences in life, e.g. upbringing and culture. So what is evident to one person is not necessarily so to another person. The subjectivity of the human mind never fails to cast a shadow over objectivity and the way of being objective.

Activity

Pointers for reflection:

1. It is important to understand that subjectivity is a condition of the human consciousness. The use of analytical reasoning, synthetic reasoning and logical deduction can be a way of achieving objectivity since it compensates for the subjectivity of mind. Think of how your own subjectivity is intimately involved in the process of your research.

(Continued)

(Continued)

2. To recognise subjectivity is to reflect on whether it increases or decreases objective understanding. What kind of knowledge can be said to be objective? It is the kind of knowledge which requires subjective processes. These subjective processes are active and sophisticated, involving analytical reasoning, synthetic reasoning, logical deduction and the differentiation of essence from appearance. Remember that subjectivity casts a shadow over objectivity.

3. In social sciences, the researcher's self-function as instrument for research must be recognised first and foremost. Natural sciences, such as physics, chemistry and biology, study natural phenomena. In social sciences, however, the very concept of ethics has two distinctive aspects: universal and local. The universal aspect refers to knowledge and people – here the concept of people does not simply mean the people you are studying but rather has more to do with the people who are conducting the research. The concept of knowledge means that by doing research the researcher makes a claim to knowledge, to epistemology, to the very notion of how we see what we see and why. The local aspects of ethics refers to things like informed consent, privacy, anonymity – they should never override the universal aspect of ethics – around which social sciences can evolve.

Reflexivity

Reflexivity is more than a mere retrospective examination of how a research problem is identified and solved. It is beyond a 'personal tale of what went on in the backstage of doing research' (Ellis and Bochner, 2000: 741). It encapsulates the researcher's immediate critical conscious awareness of what he or she is thinking and doing when designing the research as well as collecting and interpreting the data. For example, as described earlier, researchers working in the ethnomethodology tradition are more inclined to see reflexivity as taking different aspects of the social reality and ways in which it is interpreted and analysed into one consideration. In social science research, reflexivity is generally enacted on the following grounds:

1. The nature of social research is self-evident. Differences in perception and conception give rise to differences in data analysis and interpretation.
2. The researcher's self-function is seen as instrumental for research. Social sciences and natural sciences can be differentiated in terms of how social scientists use themselves as instrument for the research whereas natural scientists take a detached view of, and use laboratory equipment or technologies to master, the external world.
3. The analytical approach used in social science research is often hermeneutic and contextualist. The researcher's positionality in terms of knowledge, background, experience and relationships comes to affect his or her understanding of the phenomenon under scrutiny.
4. Knowledge about the social world varies from individual to individual and there is an intimate relationship between knowledge and knower.
5. From an ethical point of view, it is important to establish transparency and trust in the reader. Within the education domain, the researcher has less rigid adherence to the use of the passive voice in writing a research report.

| **Practical Tip** |

Pointers for reflection

1. Reflexivity can be understood as a 'personal tale of what went on in the backstage of doing research', considering this idea as a mediator between the researcher and the research process.
2. How to act out reflexivity? Some psychologists and sociologists suggested a metaphor. It's like you looking at yourself in the mirror. For example, Carl Jung said that you turn around yourself and confront what it produces. George Herbert Mead said that reflexivity is a self-analysis in which you can interact with yourself either verbally or non-verbally.
3. In qualitative research, what is 'true' is often in the sense that research findings accurately reflect the situation, and what is 'certain' is in the sense that research findings are supported by the evidence. This is self-evident and therefore there is no absolute sense of truthfulness and certainty. In Greek philosophy, after the three giants, there was a school of thought called the Sceptics. According to Sceptics, knowledge is ever relative and any proof has itself to be proved – this is called ad infinitum.

Key Points to Remember

- When you start a research project it is important to position yourself in terms of what ontological and epistemological perspective you will use.
- You need to ask yourself the following questions:
  - Will you take a constructive perspective?
  - Will you take a positivist perspective?
- You will choose your paradigm in educational research and then decide on your methods of investigation and address the ethical issues that will be raised in your project (see Chapter 3).

Further Reading

Collin, F. (1997) *Social Reality*. London: Routledge.
Lincoln, Y. and Guba, E. (2000) 'Paradigmatic controversies, contradictions and emerging influences', in N.K. Denzin and Y.S. Lincoln (Eds.), *Handbook of Qualitative Research* (2/E). London: SAGE, pp. 163–188.
Plowright, D. (2011) *Using Mixed Methods: Frameworks for an Integrated Methodology*. London: SAGE.

References

Bassey, M. (1999) *Case Study Research in Educational Settings*. Buckingham: Open University Press.
Bloch, C. (2012) *Passion and Paranoia: Emotions and the Culture of Emotion in Academia*. Farnham: Ashgate.

Bryman, A. (2012) *Social Research Methods* (4/E). Oxford: Oxford University Press.

Bullock, A. and Trombley, S. (Eds) (1999) *The New Fontana Dictionary of Modern Thought*. London: Harper Collins Publishers.

Denzin, N K and Lincoln, Y S (Eds.) (1994) *Handbook of Qualitative Research*. London: Sage Publications.

Ellis, C. and Bochner, A P (2000) 'Autoethnography, personal narrative, reflexivity: Researcher as subject'. In N.K. Denzin and Y.S. Lincoln (Eds.), *Handbook of Qualitative Research* (2/E), London: SAGE, pp. 733–768.

Fairclough, N. and Wodak, R. (1997) 'Critical discourse analysis', in T. van Dijk (Ed.), *Discourse as Social Interaction*. London: SAGE, pp. 258–285.

Gee, J. (2005) *An Introduction to Discourse Analysis: Theory and Method* (2/E). London: Routledge.

Gibson, W. (2010) 'Qualitative research as a method of inquiry in education', in D. Hartas (Ed.), *Educational Research and Inquiry: Qualitative and Quantitative Approaches*. London: Continuum, pp. 54–64.

Gilbert, N. (1993) 'Research, theory and method' in N. Gilbert (Ed.), *Researching Social Life*. London: SAGE, pp. 18–31.

Lincoln, Y. and Guba, E. (2000) 'Paradigmatic controversies, contradictions and emerging influences', in N.K. Denzin and Y.S. Lincoln (Eds.), *Handbook of Qualitative Research* (2/E). London: SAGE, pp. 163–188.

Gubrium, JF. and Hosltein, J.A. (1997) *The New Language of Qualitative Method*. Oxford: Oxford University Press.

Hammersley, M. (1990) *Reading Ethnographic Research: A Critical Guide*. London: Longmans.

Hammersley, M. (1992) *What is Wrong with Ethnography: Methodological Explanations*. London: Routledge.

Kuhn, T. (1996) *The Structure of Scientific Revolutions* (3rd edn). Chicago: University of Chicago Press.

Lecompte, M.D. and Goets, J.P. (1982) 'Problems of reliability and validity in ethnographic research', *Review of Educational Research*, 53: 31–6.

Ma, J. (2008) 'Reading the word and the world: How mind and culture are mediated through the use of dual-language storybooks', *Education 3–13*, 36(3): 237–251.

Ma, J. (2013) 'Exploring the complementary effect of post-structuralism on sociocultural theory of mind and activity', *Social Semiotics*, 23(3): 444–456.

Miles, M.B. and Huberman, A.M. (1994) *Qualitative Data Analysis*. London: SAGE.

Robson, C. (2011) *Real World Research* (3/E). Chichester: Wiley.

Rogoff, B. (1990) *Apprenticeship in Thinking: Cognitive Development in Social Context*. London: Oxford University Press.

Russell, B. (2004) *History of Western Philosophy*. London: Routledge.

Schutt, R. (1996) *Investigating the Social World: The Process and Practice of Research*. Thousand Oaks: Pine Forge Press.

Young, M.F.D. (2008) *Bringing Knowledge Back In*. London: Routledge.

For additional online resources please visit the book's website:
https://study.sagepub.com/needhamandpalaiologou

3

ETHICAL ISSUES ASSOCIATED WITH EDUCATIONAL RESEARCH

IOANNA PALAIOLOGOU

Chapter Aims and Objectives

This chapter will help you to:

- understand the nature of ethics in education research;
- review perspectives on ethics in education research;
- explore the relationship between the researcher and those being researched;
- understand standard expectations for the conduct of education research;
- consider personal values and your position as a researcher in order to undertake ethical research.

Introduction

There is much advice to be found in books and articles on education research and professional educational associations and universities have published codes of ethics (see below and Further Reading at the end of this chapter). Roth and Middleton (2004) point out, however, that the complexity of ethics in education lies in the asymmetry of knowledge between researcher and researched. Howe and Moses (1999: 21) identified this complexity as being due to the 'imperative turn and the ever increasing use of qualitative research methods that have accompanied it'. This, they claim, has created a division between traditional approaches to research (where participants were seen as objects) and contemporary approaches (where research participants are considered as subjects). In this chapter, therefore, we will be dealing with how we move from a stage where the researcher is the 'knower' to a dialectical situation where researchers and researched are acting collaboratively. As a consequence participatory and collaborative research has generated new ground rules where participants are 'subjects and architects of research' (Torre and Fine, 2006: 456). Thus in the field of education research a debate has opened up about how we apply ethical practices and how we create possibilities for researching with the participants (Simons, 1995; Clark and Moss 2001; Dalhlberg and Moss, 2005; Cahill, 2007; Christensen and James, 2008; Lindsay, 2008; BERA, 2011). Most contributors to this debate are in agreement that participants should and must be asked for their participation in research, that respect is demonstrated for them and they will be allowed to make choices, withdraw and be able to access the research (Simons, 1995; May, 2001; Creswell, 2003; Evans, 2004; Pring, 2004; Ellis, 2007; Alderson, 2008).

Consequently in this chapter I will argue that ethics in research should be approached from an axiological position which involves the researched in all stages of the research process. Furthermore I will suggest that although prior consent is important in research ethics, this is not the only consideration and that the ethics at stake are inherent at all stages of the research process. When human relationships are involved ethical issues are continuously interwoven and thus are not an isolated act of the researcher. Instead the research process requires collective activities between researcher and participants whether these are adults, young people or children, all of whom could be vulnerable without sensitive attention to ethics. In Chapter 2 the discussion on axiology revealed that the positioning of the research reflects on the analysis and presentation of the findings. In that sense an ethical commitment to participatory, inclusive and collaborative research from the researcher requires practices and power to be shared within the research process. Ethical considerations should thus go beyond ensuring consent and access as such considerations are embedded in research axiologically. In that sense, the role of the researcher becomes a 'collective praxis approach' (Cahill, 2007: 298) where the research process is no longer owned solely by the 'expert' researcher, but is a shared process between researcher and participants.

To aid this examination of ethical considerations in education research, the chapter will explore concepts of ethical praxis (as opposed to practice) in the search for axiologically defined approaches to conducting research that value the role of the participant equally with the ambitions of the researcher.

Ethical Codes of Practice

In order to understand the significance of ethics in educational research it is important to examine the history of research and ethics. The ethics codes evident in most educational settings are normally associated with a wider set of international and national instruments that cover the whole field of human rights. The process of establishing international human rights in the last half of the previous century was mostly a consequence of the atrocities in World War II which drew attention to the lack of international standards on research with human subjects. This led to the formulation of the Nuremberg Code in 1946 and, subsequently, to the Declaration of Human Rights in 1948 (see Table 3.1 for background developments of ethical codes).

Table 3.1 Historical development of ethical codes

Date	Influential Acts	Description	Contribution
1906	Pure Food and Drug Act	First act to raise standards for food and drugs.	Federal rules are established for the first time.
1946	Nuremberg Code	The code was developed after World War II as a number of medical experiments on humans had taken place in concentration camps without participant permission resulting in serious consequences for their physical and mental health. The code was introduced to ensure human safety during research.	First international document to suggest voluntary consent of human participants was considered essential, but it was not reinforced by law.
1948	United Nations Declaration of Human rights	All human beings have the same rights and these are necessary for survival, dignified living, freedom and security.	For the first time in human history all UN state parties agreed to respect human rights.
1959	UN Declaration on the rights of the Child	It set out ten principles which provided the framework for children's rights.	It opened the public debate that rights have to be promoted actively and prepared the ground for the United Nations Convention on Children's Right (UNCRC) in 1989.
1962	Kefauver Harris Amendments to Food Drug and Cosmetic Act	Due to the thalidomide medication about 12,000 babies were born with severe deformities. The Kefauver Harris Amendment or 'Drug Efficacy Amendment' that followed introduced a requirement for drug manufacturers to provide proof of the effectiveness and safety of their drugs before approval; required drug advertising to disclose accurate information about side effects; and stopped cheap generic drugs being marketed as expensive drugs.	The first law to ensure drug efficacy and protect humans' safety.
1964	Declaration of Helsinki	Guided medical research.	Issues addressed in the Declaration of Helsinki include: • Research with humans should be based on the results from laboratory and animal experimentation. • Research protocols should be reviewed by an independent committee prior to initiation. • Informed consent from research participants is necessary. • Research should be conducted by medically/ scientifically qualified individuals. • Risks should not exceed benefits.

(Continued)

Table 3.1 (Continued)

Date	Influential Acts	Description	Contribution
1965	Convention on the Elimination of all forms of Racial Discrimination	All human beings have the same rights no matter their race.	Impact on government was to require them to have policies to protect people from discrimination.
1974	National Research Act	It was enacted by 93 United states and aimed to protect human beings from research experimentations especially medical ones.	It contributed in developing guidelines in research with human participants based on the Human rights.
1976	International Covenant on Civil and Political Rights; International Covenant on Economic, Social and Cultural Rights	Both of these aimed to protect human rights for all people.	For the first time in human history, individuals' beliefs, values, views are acknowledged as important for being a citizen.
1979	The Belmont Report	The report states the basic ethical guidelines of research based on a principled approach focusing on respect for persons, informed consent, assessment of risk–benefits, justice.	Influenced how research is conducted with human beings. A number of international professional bodies introduced a code of practice based on this report.
	Convention on the Elimination of Discrimination against Women (CEDAW)	CEDAW defined what constitutes discrimination against women and set up an agenda to end such discrimination. By accepting the Convention, States commit themselves to undertake a series of measures to end discrimination against women in all forms, including:	Established the basis for realising equality between women and men through ensuring women's equal access to, and equal opportunities in, political and public life – including the right to vote and to stand for election – as well as education, health and employment.

Date	Influential Acts	Description	Contribution
		• to incorporate the principle of equality of men and women in their legal system, abolish all discriminatory laws and adopt appropriate ones prohibiting discrimination against women; • to establish tribunals and other public institutions to ensure the effective protection of women against discrimination; and • to ensure elimination of all acts of discrimination against women by persons, organisations or enterprises.	The Convention is the only human rights treaty which affirms the reproductive rights of women and targets culture and tradition as influential forces shaping gender roles and family relations. It affirms women's rights to acquire, change or retain their nationality and the nationality of their children. States parties also agree to take appropriate measures against all forms of traffic in women and exploitation of women.
1984	United Nations Convention against torture	Protection of survival rights.	Governments had to make commitments for fair and free of harm imprisonment.
1985	Declaration on the Right to Development	Development is defined as not only biological and cognitive but mental, emotional, social and cultural.	Led to the Convention on the Rights of Children.
1989	United Nations Convention on the Rights of the Child	It lays out rights according to the special needs and situation of children. It is special in that it covers the whole range of economic, civil, political, social and cultural rights stressing the indivisibility and inter–relatedness.	It recognised that rights have to be actively promoted and places an obligation on governments to do so. It changed the way children are seen and moved away from old stereotypes of children as innocent and powerless. Children were seen as becoming politically active.
1991	Code of Federal Regulations for the Protection of Human Subjects	Discusses the obligations when humans are involved in research.	Provides protection to any human participants in any research. Special protection is provided for 'vulnerable people' (e.g. children, prisoners, the mentally ill).
1994	United Nations Convention on the Status of Refugees	Protected rights for refugees.	Governments have to act upon these issues.

The acceptance of the human rights conventions is important and has led to the development of regional Human Rights Charters where these rights are enshrined in international legal agreements and are not just promises, but entitlements (see link to Department for International Development (DfID) paper in the Activity below). Such charters set out the duties and responsibilities of states to protect, promote and ensure the achievement of rights. This is not just a top-down approach, but also one where people have a right to demand that governments fulfil these duties and responsibilities and can be held accountable if these rights are not implemented.

Activity

There are a set of regional Human Rights Charters. A general summary of the human rights which are enshrined in these and other instruments can be seen at: www.odi.org/publications/1537-dfids-human-rights-policy-scoping-study

The key issues that they cover are:

- rights necessary for survival and dignified living;
- rights and freedoms necessary for human dignity, creativity and intellectual and spiritual development;
- rights necessary for liberty and physical security.

Now explore these two questions:

1. The UK government, for example, has committed itself (at least in terms of policy) to achieving the rights for each individual. If you work in the UK to what extent do you consider that these policies have been effective?
2. Why do all these issues become relevant to the issue of educational research?

In the light of the policy changes, and changes in thinking that were brought about by all these international conventions, a number of professional bodies such as the British Psychological Society (BPS) and the British Educational Research Association (BERA) have introduced codes of ethical practice when research is conducted with human participants (for more such guidance see Further Reading at the end of this chapter). Although in this chapter I will refer to the ones that are prominent in the UK, it may be that as a researcher you may need to refer to the codes that are in use in your country or region (please see an indicative list in the Practical Tip box opposite). The main issues are the protection of human rights and conducting research in a way that should comply with institutional and professional association codes of practice, emphasising the importance of informed consent. More and more it has become a requirement for researchers to apply for ethical clearance of their own institutions and/or sponsoring body, often with the establishment of mechanisms to examine research proposals, review the research designs and keep records of the research (see example in Chapter 6).

This debate has led a number of universities to examine their research practices and it is now common practice for all to have a localised code of ethics based on guidance on how to carry out research. Most universities have ethics committees and all researchers need to comply with the ethical practices of their academic departments. In all of these codes the basis on which contemporary assertions of the rights in research are demonstrated includes moral attitudes such as respect for human life, belief in the dignity of the individual human being, a concern for the preservation of threatened species and for the long-term future of the planet as the heritage of future generations.

Practical Tip

Influential UK ethical codes:

British Educational Studies Association (BERA) Ethical Code
The Scottish Educational Research Association (SERA)
British Psychological Society (BPS) Ethical Code
National Children's Bureau (NCB)

Influential international ethical codes:

The European Early Childhood Education Research Association (EECERA) Ethical Code
European Educational Research Association (EERA)
American Educational Research Association (AERA)
American Psychological Association (APA)

Links to these codes can be found at the end of this chapter.

Why Ethics?

In all ethics codes the notion of the 'good' is central and the language of the codes stands in between, covering the obligations of researchers in relation to the strategies they adopt in their research. A moral vocabulary, which includes the notion of ethics, is a valued part of the fabric of human activity and goals. Central to Western moral political thought were the issues of values, morality and the problematisation on what are the 'best' ways of living human life (developed from Greek philosophy with thinkers such as Plato and Aristotle, and in more modern schools of thought such as Hume, Kant, Mill, Nietzsche). The branch of philosophy concerned with all these issues is called *Philosophical Ethics* which are relevant to education research in providing rules and codes for following moral ways of doing research. Philosophical ethics are thus concerned with concepts of morality and seek to understand human actions in terms of:

Evil vs Good

Right vs Wrong

Virtue vs Vice

Justice vs Crime

In that sense philosophical ethics aim to understand the moral principles and values that humans use to conduct themselves in dealing with other people in all aspects of life. Although the answers to these questions seem simple and obvious (in what we mean by 'good' or 'wrong'), these are based on a number of factors and there is a plurality of interpretations and explanations which make the questions above complex. The standards of wrong and right, good and evil can be questioned, for example, in terms of values that are influenced by our cultural contexts. This is important in educational research as the researcher has to consider a number of questions such as:

- How are ethics negotiated with participants?
- What power relations and hierarchies become considerations in doing research?
- How can we create an interactive and responsible process for developing ethical codes and agreements with our partners in a way that reflects and honours negotiated process?
- Do responders have different ethical priorities to those researchers may take for granted as 'good practice' and what issues does this raise for practice? (Cahill, 2007: 309)

Take, for example, the sensitive issue of abortion. In some countries it is allowed up to a certain number of months whereas in other countries such as Mexico and Ireland it is illegal. Equally the issue of homosexuality becomes 'moral' or 'sin' depending on religion. All such socio-cultural issues consequently require a responsive approach from the researcher and a critical examination of the researcher's positionality, axiology and power as 'knower/ expert'. Research ethics should aim for a 'mutual respect, dignity and connectedness between research and researched' (Ellis, 2007: 4). With that in mind, and considering the interpretations of what is morally good and true is socio-culturally dependent, still there might be tensions and clashes between institutional expectations, researchers and researched.

It is evident from philosophical ethics that where morality is concerned, there are no truths or facts and no one can judge whose right, or value is the 'best' (Palaiologou, 2012a). This has become the basis of *Ethical Subjectivism* that promotes the idea that our moral opinions are based on our feelings (Peters, 1966, 1967; Rechels, 1993). Our feelings, however, are shaped by our culture which contains language, habits, customs, ideas and religion that lead us to our moral judgements (Palaiologou, 2012b). Such a discourse is complex. The key question that emerges in an era where most communities, especially Eurocentric communities, have become multicultural and diverse is how can one keep his/her identity (thus morality) but at the same time work collaboratively with another's identity and morality to ensure a collective praxis approach in terms of ethics in research?

In conclusion of this section, therefore, central to all the ethical codes is conducting research by the value of an 'ethic of care' which exhibits deep respect for relationships and humanity (Halse and Honey, 2005; Ellis, 2007; Lawson, 2007). This leads us to the question, however, that if ethics are understood to be socio-culturally and contextual specific, how can we co-create an ethical practice with our co-collaborators? (Cahill, 2007: 309).

Activity

Study the ethical guidelines of your institution (or funding body for sponsored research). Try to examine your organisation's ethics code for doing things, its own system values and beliefs, and compare this with the Education Association's ethics code such as the British Education Research Association (BERA).

How do you rate the plurality and diversity of your organisation's ethics code? Do you see any tensions over what is deemed to be good and the power to impose ideas, theories, policies and practices?

Participants as Partners and the Move Towards Participatory Ethics

To guide you in how to conduct education research ethically I intend to build upon notions of participatory research with particular attention to the notion of the collective praxis approach. Praxis (and praxeology, which is the study of human actions) differs from practice, which is a term that refers to human actions in society. Praxis, refers to the process by which a theory, an idea or skill is enacted, practised, embodied or realised. In that sense praxis corresponds to the production of knowledge, the construction of knowledge and the manner in which human actions (i.e. practice) are implemented. In this sense, therefore, when working with human participants the research is made meaningful and relevant to them through constant dialogue.

This recommendation arises in response to the discourse from educational research theorists concerned with what they perceive as an asymmetrical relationship of power between researcher and researched (Howe and Moses, 1999; Torre and Fine, 2006; Cahill, 2007; Ellis, 2007; Pain et al., 2007). The ongoing discussions on this relationship have investigated ways that 'participants must take a more active role than they have traditionally in shaping the research process and in challenging its methods and findings as it unfolds' (Howe and Moses, 1999: 35). The participatory paradigm in research ethics is thus often used in a variety of research practices and methods (e.g. Hart, 1992;

Cahill and Hart, 2006). Such approaches aim to reduce the potential for asymmetrical relationships in research and move away from being merely concerned with techniques or methods towards a commitment to collaboration and to dialectically challenging the power relationships in research. In that sense the researched being considered as 'subjects' and 'participants' in the process is *positionality* (i.e. taking a position as a researcher – see Chapter 2). Conversely (and perhaps ideally) methods which consider the researched at all stages of the process provide evidence of how the researcher is treating the relationship of power and the degree of involvement of the participants in the research process.

In the field of education the publication of the United Nations Convention on the Rights of the Child (United Nations, 1989) brought about an axiological shift in how children are perceived in life at all levels and also opened up the discourse of constructions of childhood, bringing emerging paradigms of childhood that are now impacting on research in schools and other educational settings (Alderson and Morrow, 2011; Harcourt et al., 2011). In contemporary literature on research with young children there are studies that try to move this debate beyond being solely concerned with methods and seek additionally to link participatory research with young children at an axiological level (see, for example, Christensen and Prout, 2002; Christensen, 2004; Abbott and Langston, 2005; Alderson, 2005, 2008; Clark, 2010). There is a danger, however, that although such approaches are valid in the sense that they moved on the debate on how we research young children, they may also have reached a point of fragmentation where certain methods, mainly quantitative methods with young children, have been eliminated when researching young children. Such an approach can be counter-productive and hazardous in educational research, however, it also has the potential to bring back the view of young children as being vulnerable, needy and not able to act as social actors in research. The term 'participation' of children in the field of early childhood has seemingly been misunderstood and has been 'deemed to be akin to a social epidemic with the spread of the idea of children as participants and social actors having agency becoming seemingly irresistible' (Palaiologou, 2014: 690). Thus participation becomes a fallacy unless there is continued dialogue with children; rather than researchers adopting a shallow, simplistic interpretation of 'participation' they have dispensed with a whole range of methods.

The consequences of this debate are that not only do you have to consider the starting points of research, but you will also have to continually explore ethical approaches and principles for research while maintaining commitments to rigour. In that sense ethics goes beyond the legalities of consent and is embedded in the positionality of the research. Thus the idea that ethics can function independently must be rejected. First, in relation to legal requirements that are necessary in research, the concept of consent is not redundant as it allows individuals to make claims not covered by the concept of the duty of care. As discussed above these duties are embedded in human rights and should not appear as two notions but as one. Bradley summarises this precisely:

No right without a duty: no duty without a right and rights. [...] right and duty are sides of a single whole. This whole is the good [...] each is the single side of one and the same relation, fixed apart from the other side. In the good the sides come together, and in the whole first cease to be abstractions and gain real existence. (Bradley, 1970: 208–209)

For example, the entitlements of anonymity and privacy that are part of many consent forms used by educational organisations are difficult to construe in terms of the audience of the research as they often do not even know the existence of the participants. I am anxious at this point not to suggest that the consent form is not a valid and integral part of the ethics of research, but I do argue it should not become merely a mechanical function of a researcher's activity and goals as ethics have an axiological aspect that should be active throughout the research process. Secondly, however (and probably most importantly), the claim that a research participant should be required to sign a consent form seemingly contains the assertion that the participant is engaging in the process of moral evaluation of the research. Instead the ethical discourse should ensure that all participants can be actively engaged in the research and not be seen as dependents or property of the researcher. It is important, therefore, that the process of informed consent recognises the need for researchers' moral language and framework not to be separate from those of the participants. Thus I have argued elsewhere that when we are discussing ethics in educational research we should move away from the terminology of ethical practice and we should discuss ethical praxis in research (Palaiologou 2012b, 2014).

Consequently ethical praxis should be central in research, underpinning and guiding all stages of the process when determining the methodology, design, analysis, conclusions and dissemination of the research. Consideration should thus be given to the following six layers that are interlinked and interwoven to become questions at each stage in the research process (also see Figure 3.1):

- **Intersubjectivity**: the procedures for reaching agreement among all involved in the research project;
- **Indivisibility**: the legitimation and value of the research inquiry in terms of the nature of the knowledge that is about to be acquired and the actual beneficiary of this knowledge;
- **Phronesis**: the necessity of the research, the exercise of judgement and the respect of the participants within the subject of the inquiry;
- **Parsimony**: searching for simple methods, understandable by all (especially where it facilitates the participation of young children);
- **Equilibrium**: consideration of the nature of the research in relation to the extent in which participants are able to be self-conscious and recognise and articulate their own requirements so as to offer emotional agreement to the process;
- **The power of relationships and interaction between researcher and participant**: the quest to avoid false assumptions being made about participant well-being and enable a supportive praxis to ensure their concerns are addressed. (Palaiologou 2012c, 2014)

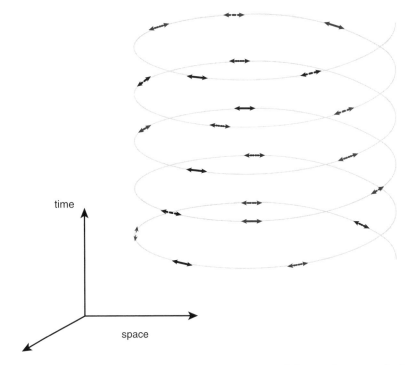

Figure 3.1   Layers of research as an 'ethical helix': Interaction of the six elements of ethical praxis

© Dr. Ioanna Palaiologou

To conclude, therefore, although ethical codes are now seemingly agreed on key issues, it appears evident that participatory ethics and ethics as an axiological approach have profound implications on how one plans and structures the process and how research evolves. Whilst in subsequent chapters of this book support is provided to you in designing your research in an effective way, it is suggested that in order to produce an ethical research process where participants and researchers are bound by a collaborative dialogical process you need to be prepared for the unexpected, be prepared for changes, be prepared for messy situations that will be determined by the subjectivities of the researched and be conscious that the construction of knowledge is more mind dependent than mind independent. Nevertheless this becomes a strength in educational research because your role is not just to facilitate participation, but to collaborate so that researcher and researched both have equal responsibility as a collective praxis approach. In seeking consensus between researchers and researched there is a continuum of negotiation of the ways we explain it to each other and in reaching agreement collaboratively the concepts that the research aims to grasp are revealed and in-depth understanding developed.

Thus I return to the original argument that ethics should be axiologically approached. It is important to recognise that in enabling the researched to become participants in the research process the research becomes inclusive, collaborative and is an approach that recognises the researched as 'knowers', thus creating space for influence on knowledge production. With such an approach to research ethics the researcher and researched are equal partners and complement each other at all levels – methodological strategies, practices and rituals of research – seeking to advance knowledge with dialogue. This will allow the achievement of a 'praxeology of ethically valuable learning approach from a dialectic perspective' argue Hwang and Roth (2005: 4) which becomes the locus of research ethics and achieves inclusion and collaboration as Paolo Freire suggested:

> The silenced are not just incidental to the curiosity of the researcher, but are the masters of inquiry into the underlying causes of the events in their world. In this context research becomes a means of moving beyond silence into a quest to proclaim the world. (Freire, 1982: 30–31)

As Freire (1970) and Gramsci (1971) emphasise, the real value of such an approach is that it will lead to social transformation.

What Are the Ethical Obligations For a Researcher?

So what I am suggesting here is that when the researcher is embarking on a research process they should first formulate the research question(s) (see Chapter 1) before seeking to position the research and offer a paradigmatic perspective on how they plan to undertake it (Chapter 2). Key questions in that process are 'what ontological and epistemological perspectives will be applied in the research?' Consequently it is proposed here that a major part of the ethics process is how the researcher is going to position the project which, as was discussed earlier, should also be approached axiologically.

When doing a research project all researchers are faced with the inevitable challenge to how they can justify the claims the research is making (see Chapter 9 on Collecting Qualitative Data and Chapter 12 on Analysing Quantitative Data). In the process it is equally important to position the research in terms of ethics. One way to overcome some of these complexities is explore the role of the researcher in ethics who, I suggest, should be able to reflect on the research process and develop 'self-efficacy', a term coined by Bandura who defines it as the belief in an individual's capabilities to organise and perform a set of actions required to manage potential situations (Bandura, 1994a, 1994b, 1994c). In other words, self-efficacy is a person's belief in his or her ability to succeed in a particular situation which Bandura described as determinants of how people think, behave, and feel.

In that sense, as researchers the major role and responsibility in terms of ethics is to reflect on the research to demonstrate how the process is perceived and what responses are likely to be made to the situations that will be faced in the process. This echoes Earnshaw's (2014) view of methodological humility when approaching the research design. The researcher should uphold a code of engagement with the participants and the methods should be participatory tools not only in terms of participants' consent, but also in meeting their understanding. Ethics in research are achieved only when we 'listen' to our partici- pants at the deepest level if we are to access, develop and empower their inner philosophical and spiritual worlds. In this way the relationship between researcher and participant can be changed from an asymmetrical one and it becomes the duty of the researcher to create and sustain a symmetrical relationship.

The researcher thus has a duty to sustain a synchronised relationship between the research and the researcher in terms of its constructive reciprocity, but this can only be achieved if the research is not limited by any bureaucratic approach. It should go beyond this level and apply self-efficacy and comprise what is known and what is to be known. To that extent the researched requires a form of language (written, oral or body language) that allows him or her to give an insight into what the researcher asks them. Equally the researcher should accept that the participants might have an opinion separate from theirs and in such a situation to apply self-efficacy in order to be able to respond to the difference of attitudes. Without a 'voice' the participants can merely 'speak' about their own experi- ences and the ways they view the world. In this situation the researcher has the responsibility to work in a collaborative way with the researched and to open a dialogue about the meaning they are trying to make. The relationship between researcher and par- ticipant thus goes both ways in that the participant is 'speaking' for the research and potentially offers the researcher richer data, and views. In turn this empowers the researcher to apply appropriate research questions and to see the world from the perspective of the researched and so gain an insight that would be valuable to the nature of the research.

Ethical Components of the Research Process

All the above discussion has hopefully led you to consider your approach to research design to move beyond just seeking permission at the outset from your institution or employing body to proceed. You will need to take account of several factors when planning your research so that the contribution of the research participants can be maximised. The key elements (each of which will be discussed in turn) are:

- consent, assent and dissent;
- privacy;
- confidentiality and anonymity;
- trust;
- the right to withdraw and the right not to participate.

Consent, assent and dissent

Almost universally among ethical codes is the issue of volunteer permission from the participants. This permission is at two levels, an institutional level where fully informed volunteer consent is required prior to research and, secondly, where researchers are obliged to present information effectively to the participants to support them throughout the research.

These are important elements of ethical approval in any research project and process. Basic elements are to inform the participants fully (adults, young people, children) of the purpose of the research, the methods employed, the time frame, the measures taken to protect participants, and how the data will be protected and shared among the participants.

Privacy

The most recently proclaimed right to privacy sets the individual in the family context against the individual as an atomised subject in an anonymous and indifferent context. This can be considered as privacy that defines us as individuals. It is necessary for this right to be protected and guarded in research against the invasion of the researcher. This will also have implications for the extent to which the research is interpreting findings in relation to how this interpretation may intervene in the privacy of the participants.

Confidentiality and anonymity

Researchers are obliged to prioritise and guard the participants' identity. In contemporary literature, however, there are tensions between the issue of confidentiality and anonymity and the issue of participants as co-researchers. Evans argues that although anonymity and confidentiality may comply with institutional ethical codes in order to achieve the status of participants as subjects, research should be underpinned by 'ethics in content and structure, rather than structure alone' (Evans, 2004: 75). He also argues that the researcher has a moral responsibility to communicate with the participants and recognise the researched as sources of information. It has been pointed out, however, that these issues are in direct conflict with the idea and concept of researchers as participants and they raise the issue under the terms of confidentiality and anonymity, whether 'this means that the stories (and aspects of their lives they choose or feel compelled to share) no longer belong to them' (Fine et al., 2000: 115).

Consequently researchers can be lost in the abstract argumentation of confidentiality and anonymity. It is essential to create spaces for all involved in the research process, however, in order to be able to be part of the interpretations and the creation of critical and reflexive dialogues as to how data might be interpreted, shared and used (Fine et al., 2000; Kelley, 1998). Despite the debate around these issues, it is commonly accepted in ethical codes at international, national and local level that the researcher should safeguard the anonymity and confidentiality of the participants.

Trust

Trust requires actions to maintain commitments the researcher makes to the participants. It needs to be accepted by both parties, the researcher and the researched, that the researcher has the advantages of expertise and experience in the subject and this carries with it hidden forms of power. Conversely for the participant there is not only potential for fresh eyes, but also an ability to bring experience the researcher does not have as well as a problem-solving ability that may provide novel solutions to old problems.

In order to achieve a trustworthy relationship the two parties should command not only unconditional mutual respect, but also a language in which they can both communicate. If trust is to be achieved the relationship will not only benefit both parties, but will also be a step towards developing an ethical commitment from both parties. Consequently a necessary condition to building a trusting relationship is both the ability to speak and the provision of a conversational context in which the relationship is permeable between the researcher and the researched in terms of influence. Such a conversational context acknowledges the need for a symmetrical relationship between researcher and participant, leaving both parties the opportunity to create a dynamic setting which allows greater expression of freedom and access to the methods by which the data can be collected. Thus trust achieved through versatile conversation becomes a reality for both, but it is necessary to acknowledge that this takes time in order to achieve what Cahill (2007: 298) describes as a 'collective praxis approach'.

The right to withdraw, the right not to participate

In the desired context that provides the expectation that the researched are to become research participants it is important to respect the individuality of each participant and allow the right to withdraw at any stage of the process and equally provide the right *not* to participate (Palaiologou, 2012a, 2012b). As devastating as that may be to the researcher's ambition this is a critical aspect of ethical research.

Practical Tip

Avoid research misconduct

In all ethical codes apart from the above key elements, it is important to consider the issues of:

- **Plagiarism**: This can take different forms, for example copying another research, using intellectual property, citing substantial sections of another's work without permission or acknowledgement.
- **Data misrepresentation:** When data is reported in a way that serves the purpose of the researcher rather than as agreed by all participants.
- **Control** of what participants have contributed in the research process.

Activity

Before you embark on a research project, alongside studying your department's ethical code, study the BERA (2011) Ethical Code and try to reflect on how they deal with these ethical issues. Can you identify any tensions between these two?

Case Study

Human Rights vs. Research

The Stanford Prison Experiment

In 1971 Philip Zimbardo wanted to investigate whether certain situations can influence people's behaviours. He conducted an experiment by creating two groups of students, one in the role of prison officers and the other as prisoners. The experiment had to stop as what was observed was that the group of students who had the role of prison officers were abusing the group of students who had the role of prisoners. Critics of the experiment claimed that the situation was manipulated by Zimbardo and that although the participants were aware that research was being conducted, they were not aware of the real aims of the research.

For more information on this please see:

Zimbardo, P.G. (1972) 'Comment: Pathology of Imprisonment', *Society*, 9(6): 4–8.
Haney, C., Banks, W.C. and Zimbardo, P.G. (1973) 'Study of Prisoners and Guards in a Simulated Prison', *Naval Research Reviews*, 9(1–17).

Activity

Reflect on the above research experiment and consider the DifD (Department for International Development) paper's key principles that all human rights are for all people and that they are:

indivisible: because the violation of one right often affects the respect for other rights;

universal: because all people have rights to claim agreed entitlements and all people have equal opportunities. A major problem in most societies is exclusion or discrimination on the basis of social status such as class, gender, age, disability, ethnicity.

- What are the implications for ethics? Are there any rights been violated?
- What ethical considerations apply to your research in terms of human rights?

Conclusion: Moving Beyond Consent – Ethical Praxis vs. Ethical Practice

I conclude by suggesting that ethics are not part of the process in the research, but unfolds at all levels in research. In that sense it becomes *ethical praxis* which is concerned with how people conduct research and how different points of view are considered. Thus educational research is concerned with relationships that are the products of human social and psychological experiences, the causality between actions and people and the effect of the phenomena being studied. In that sense it is proposed that ethical praxis in the field of research should be permissive only – restricted to individuals and their groups – rather than universal. Research ethics is a complex process that unfolds at all stages of research, as will be elaborated throughout the book. At the centre of a research project is a commitment to break away from a bureaucratic approach to ethics by complying with a research application form and it is essential to involve the participants in all stages of the research process.

This idea has implications in educational research. In a field of study where there is a plurality and diversity of research methods the difficulty comes when we start to make judgements of value, truth and morality. A major theme in recent years within the field of education has been to question the way dominant visions of what is 'good' and how to get there; these questions have been strongly debated. This approach has led in some instances to seeing educational research in dichotomous terms such as qualitative versus quantitative research, sometimes seeing one as being better than the other with claims for greater 'truth', whilst also having more efficient/effective 'morality' which leads to 'better' findings. The important question in regard to ethics in research, however, is the determination of an axiological position which can move the researcher away from rivalry debates. In that sense ethics in research combines a set of questions such as 'is this the right action?' or 'is this a good state of affairs?'. These can motivate us to respect the participant as a partner in the research process and develop appropriate knowledge of the research. It will also move us beyond contemporary codes of practice (e.g. BERA and BPS) which can be considered to be little more than statements of aspiration.

Thus before embarking on a research project it is necessary to assess contemporary assertions of 'good' and 'right' as these include fundamental moral attitudes such as respect for the human being. Consequently ethics are essential parts of any axiological, ontological and epistemological discussions making ethics not just a practice in research, but praxis. It is suggested, therefore, that the researcher needs to make sense of their socio-cultural researched context and apply ethics at all stages of the research. Ethical praxis becomes interwoven in the research process and helps to provide factual data at the same time as respecting [participant] actions, emotions, dignity, privacy, autonomy and freedom to have opinions on all matters affecting them and for these to be given due weight (Palaiologou, 2012b and 2014)

Key Points to Remember

- This chapter aimed to discuss research ethics and offers an overview of the context of the ethics. It is important to remember that research ethics cannot be studied in isolation. They are part of a wider set of international instruments that cover the whole field of human rights. The process of human rights started with the Declaration of Human rights in 1948 and this was followed by a number of other instruments which have been summarised in Table 3.1.

- An important point to note is that because these rights are enshrined in international legal agreements they are not just promises but entitlements. These instruments set out the duties and responsibilities of states to protect, promote and ensure the achievement of rights.
- The introduction of Children's Rights (United Nations, 1989) recognised that rights have to be actively campaigned for and challenged traditional views of childhood, promoting the view of children as active members of their societies.
- In the light of the international instruments protecting human rights, research ethics involving human participants are an interwoven part of the research design and process. There are a number of ethics codes that have been published by professional bodies. Universities also now have their own ethics codes that researchers have to comply with.
- Key elements in all ethics codes are: the role of participants in research, consent, assent, dissent, privacy, anonymity, confidentiality, trust, the right to withdraw, the issue of plagiarism and data misinterpretation.
- However, this chapter argued that research ethics should be approached axiologically and it is not just a part of the research process but should be embedded in the research throughout. As researchers in education we should move away from a simplistic, operationalised, mechanical approach to ethics and we should debate whether research ethics should be integrated in the whole research process: research design, methods, collection of data, analysis and dissemination of the findings.
- A researcher can be lost in the abstract, complex argumentation that accompanies research ethics, thus it is proposed that we should deal with ethics as praxis. This is solely concerned with doing research with a collective praxis approach and requires researchers to act from an axiological stance in designing and delivering a research project.

Further Reading

Lindsay, G. (2010) 'Ethical Considerations and Legal Issues in Educational Research', in D. Hartas (ed.), *Educational Research and Inquiry: Qualitative and Quantitative Approaches*. London: Continuum, pp. 110–127.

Punch, S. (2002) 'Research with children: The same or different from research with adults?', *Childhood*, 9(3): 321–341.

If you are doing research with young children here are some key readings:

National Children's Bureau (NCB) (2002) *Including Children in Social Research. Highlight No: 193*. London: National Children's Bureau.

National Children's Bureau (NCB) (2003). *Guidelines for Research*. London: National Children's Bureau.

Pascal, C. and Bertram, T. (2014) 'Transformative dialogues: The impact of participatory research on practice', in A. Clark, R. Flewitt, M. Hammersley and M. Robb (eds), *Understanding Research with Children and Young People*. London: SAGE, pp. 269–284.

Useful Websites

UK ethics codes:

- British Educational Studies Association (BERA) Ethical Code
  www.bera.ac.uk/researchers-resources/resources-for-researchers

- The Scottish Educational Research Association (SERA) Ethical Code
  www.sera.ac.uk/documents/Publications/SERA%20Ethical%20GuidelinesWeb.PDF

- British Psychological Association (BPS) Code of Ethics and Conduct
  www.bps.org.uk/what-we-do/ethics-standards/ethics-standards

International ethics codes:

- European Educational Research Association (EERA) Ethics Code
  www.eera-ecer.de/about/ethical-guidelines

- American Educational Research Association (AERA) Ethics Code
  www.aera.net/AboutAERA/AERARulesPolicies/ProfessionalEthics/tabid/10200/Default.aspx

- American Psychological Association (APA) Ethics Code
  www.apa.org/ethics/code

- The European Early Childhood Education Research Association (EECERA) Ethical Code
  www.eecera.org/ethical-code

References

Abbott, L. and Langston, A. (2005) 'Ethical research with very young children', in A. Farrell (ed.), *Ethical Research with Children*. New York: Open University Press, pp. 37–48.

Alderson, P. (2005) 'Designing ethical research with children', in A. Farrell (ed.), *Ethical Research with Children*. New York: Open University Press, pp. 27–36.

Alderson, P. (2008) *Young Children's Rights Exploring Beliefs, Principles and Practice*. London: Jessica Kingsley Publications.

Alderson, P. and Morrow, V. (2011) *The Ethics of Research with Children and Young People*. London: SAGE.

Bandura, A. (1994a) 'Regulative function of perceived self-efficacy', in M.G. Rumsey, B. Walker and J.H. Harris (eds), *Personal Selection and Classification*. Hillsdale, NJ: Erlbaum, pp. 261–271.

Bandura, A. (1994b) 'Self-efficacy', in R. J. Corsini (ed.), *Encyclopedia of Psychology* (2/E), Vol. 3. New York: Wiley, pp. 368–369.

Bandura, A. (1994c) 'Self-efficacy', in V.S. Ramachandran (ed.), *Encyclopedia of Human Behavior*, Vol. 4. New York: Academic Press. (Reprinted in H. Friedman (ed.), *Encyclopedia of Mental Health*. San Diego, CA: Academic Press, 1998), pp. 71–81.

BERA (2011) *Revised Ethical Guidelines for Educational Research*. Southwell: Author.

Bradley, F.H. (1970) *Ethical Studies*, London: Oxford University Press.

Cahill, C. (2007) 'Doing research with young people: Participatory research and the rituals of collective work', *Children's Geographies*, 5(3): 297–312.

Cahill, C. and Hart, R. (2006) 'Translating global participatory practices with youth'. In C.Cahill and R. Hart (eds): *Pushing the Boundaries: Critical Perspectives on Child and Youth Participation, Children, Youth & Environments*, pp. 16–17.

Christensen, P.H. (2004) 'Children's participation in ethnographic research: Issues of power and representation', *Children & Society*, 18: 165–176.

Christensen, P. and James, A. (2008) *Research with Children: Perspectives and Practices* (2nd edn). London: Routledge.

Christensen, P. and Prout, A. (2002) 'Working with ethical symmetry in social research with children', *Childhood*, 9(4): 477–497.

Clark, A. (2010) 'Young children as protagonists and the role of participatory, visual methods in engaging multiple perspectives', *American Journal of Community Psychology*, 46(1–2): 115–123.

Clark, A. and Moss, P. (2001) *Listening to Young Children: The Mosaic Approach*. London: National Children's Bureau.

Creswell, J.W. (2003) *Research Design: Qualitative, Quantitative, and Mixed Methods Approaches* (2/E). Thousand Oaks: SAGE.

Dahlberg, G. and Moss, P. (2005) *Ethics and Politics in Early Childhood Education*. London: Routledge Falmer.

Earnshaw, O. (2014) 'Learning to be a child: A conceptual analysis of youth empowerment', *Educational and Child Psychology*, 31(1): 13–21.

Ellis, C. (2007) 'Telling secrets, revealing lies: Relational ethics in research with intimate others', *Qualitative Inquiry*, 13(1): 3–29.

Evans, M. (2004) 'Ethics, anonymity and censorship in community centred research of the Island Cache', *Pimarisiwin: A Journal of Aboriginal and Indigenous Community Health*, 2(1): 59–76.

Fine, M., Weis, L., Weseen, S. and Wong, L. (2000) 'For whom? Qualitative research, representations and social responsibilities', in, N. Denzin and Y. Lincoln (eds), *The Handbook of Qualitative Research*. Thousand Oaks, CA: SAGE, pp. 107–132.

Freire, P. (1997 [1970]) *Pedagogy of the Oppressed*. Harmondsworth, Middlesex: Penguin Books.

Freire, P. (1982) 'Creating alternative research methods. Learning to do it by doing it', in B. Hall, A. Gillette and R. Tandon (eds), *Creating Knowledge: A Monopoly*. New Delhi: Society for Participatory Research in Asia, pp. 29–37.

Gramsci, A. (1971) *Selections from the Prison Notebooks of Antonio Gramsci*. New York: International Publishers.

Halse, C. and Honey, A. (2005) 'Unravelling ethics: Illuminating the moral dilemmas of research ethics', *Sings: Journal of Women in Culture and Society*, 30(4): 2141–2162.

Harcourt, D., Perry, B. and Waller, T. (eds.) (2011) *Researching Young Children's Perspectives: Debating the Ethics and Dilemmas of Educational Research with Children*. London and New York: Routledge.

Hart, R. (1992) *Children's Participation: From Tokenism to Citizenship*, Vol. 4, UNICEF Innocenti Essays. Florence, Italy: UNICEF/International Child Development Centre.

Howe, K. and Moses, M. (1999) 'Ethics in educational research', *Review of Research in Education*, 24: 21–60.

Hwang, S. and Roth, W.M. (2005) 'Ethics in research on learning: Dialectics of praxis and praxeology', *Forum of Qualitative Social Research*, 6(1): Art. 19.

Kelley, R.D.G. (1998) 'Check the technique: Black urban culture and the predicament of social science'. In N. B. Dirk (ed.), *In Near Ruins: Cultural Theory at the End of the Century*. Minneapolis, MN: University of Minnesota Press, pp. 39–66.

Lawson, V. (2007) 'Geographies of care and responsibility', *Annals of the Association of American Geographers*, 97(1): 1–11.

Lindsay, G. (2008) 'Ethic and value systems', in B. Kelly, L. Wolfson and J. Boyle (eds) *Frameworks for Practice in Educational Psychology*. London: Jessica Kingsley, pp. 52–66.

May, T. (2001) *Social Research: Issues, Methods, and Process* (3/E). Maidenhead: Open University.

Pain, R., Kindon, S. and Kesby, M. (2007) 'Participatory action research: Making a difference to theory, practice and action', in S. Kindon, R. Pain and M. Kesby (eds), *Connecting People, Participation and Place: Participatory Action Research Approaches and Methods*. London: Routledge, pp. 26–32.

Palaiologou, I. (2012a) 'Introduction: Towards an understanding of ethical practice in early childhood', in I. Palaiologou (ed.), *Ethical Practice in Early Childhood*. London: SAGE, pp. 1–12.

Palaiologou, I. (2012b) 'Ethical praxis when choosing research tools for use with children under five', in I. Palaiologou (ed.), *Ethical Practice in Early Childhood*. London: SAGE, pp. 32–46.

Palaiologou, I. (2014) '*Do we hear what children want to say?* Ethical Praxis when choosing research tools with children under five', *Early Child Development and Care*, 184(5): 689–705 (DOI: 10.1080/03004430.2013.809341).

Peters, R.S. (ed.) (1966) *The Concept of Education*. London: Routledge and Kegan Paul.

Peters, R.S. (1967) *Ethics in Education*. London: HMSO.

Pring, R. (2004) *Philosophy of Educational Research* (2/E), London: Continuum.

Rechels , J. (1993) *The Elements of Moral Philosophy* (2/E), USA: McGraw-Hill, Inc.

Roth, W-M. and Middleton, D. (2004) *Knowing what you tell, telling what you know: Uncertainty and asymmetries of meaning in interpreting graphical data*. Paper presented at the annual meeting of the American Educational Research Association, San Diego, April 12–16.

Simons, H. (1995) 'The politics and ethics of educational research in England: Contemporary issues', *British Educational Research Journal*, 21: 435–450.

Torre, M.E. and Fine, M. (2006) 'Participatory Action Research (PAR) by youth', in L. Sherrod (ed.), *Youth Activism: An International Encyclopedia*. Westport, CT: Greenwood Publishing Group, pp. 456–462.

United Nations (1989) *The Convention on the Rights of the Child*. Geneva: Defense International and the United Nations Children's Fund.

For additional online resources please visit the book's website:
https://study.sagepub.com/needhamandpalaiologou

4

CONSTRUCTING THE HYPOTHESES/CREATING THE RESEARCH QUESTION(S)

DAVID NEEDHAM

Chapter Aims and Objectives

This chapter aims to help you to:

- identify a topic that not only interests you, but is something that you really want to research;
- think about how to develop focus for your investigation as well as use tools that may help you to develop and expand your topic;
- consider the key role that hypotheses and research questions play in helping you to plan your research project;
- understand what are good or bad hypotheses or research questions;
- appreciate how to create hypotheses or construct research questions that deal with the research problem;
- break down the hypothesis or main research question in order to structure your response.

Introduction

Nearly all degree courses require the production of an extended study. This can appear under a variety of guises such as 'thesis', 'dissertation' or 'extended project report' and is something that provides you with the opportunity to take ownership of an important element of learning as part of your course. In fact, it is something that breaks away from formal learning and, using the analogy of driving a car, hands you the keys and allows you to drive on your own down the road for as long as you wish providing, of course, that you are very careful. The great benefit of undertaking such a project is that you have a genuine opportunity to become engrossed in an area that extends your own interests. With a research project, dissertation or thesis, you have ownership and a large element of autonomy. You are able to take control of your learning, as well as the direction that it takes.

When undertaking such a research project you are bridging the gap between being a student and a graduate in order to explore avenues that you may wish to pursue professionally. For example, you may want to undertake a piece of small-scale research that relates to your placement, a part-time job that you have or even to prepare for further academic and professional qualifications that you might want to take. The great thing is that by undertaking a dissertation, thesis or extended project, you are on the way to becoming an expert, or at the very least an enthusiast, in your own field. The title of your final submission is, therefore, something that you can put in your curriculum vitae and be prepared to discuss in a job interview. It is something that helps to make your research distinctive and, in many ways, different from all of the students in your course pathway. In that way it is a real point of differentiation between yourself and all of your peers. Alternatively and, less seriously, writing the dissertation or thesis may allow you to do something that you are genuinely interested in, that would simply be fun. It might allow you to find something out because of a hobby or interest you have in the area and perhaps because the enquiry might help you to gather some answers to questions that you have posed in the past.

Unlike an essay in which you simply write about something as part of a process of directed study, writing up a project, dissertation or thesis involves constructing an investigation. For example, at the beginning of the academic year when students come and visit me to share their ideas they often excitedly tell me about their areas of interest and rationale for their projects. In response, and all too often repeatedly, I seem to be saying 'So, what are you trying to find out?' A research project requires a direction. It needs a focus and clear avenue to pursue. This is why a key element for every project has to be the research question(s) or hypotheses. Questions or hypotheses do not instantly materialise magically, in fact they make take some time to develop. For example, there is little point in constructing questions without doing any reading first. That would be like putting the cart before the horse. There may also be lots of discussions with friends, tutors and colleagues. It is important to get them right and feel comfortable with them as they are the key starting point for your research project (Andrews, 2003).

Identifying a Topic

Conducting a research project for a degree is something that usually takes a considerable amount of time. For full-time students this usually takes a period of about eight months, with more time often needed for part-time and postgraduate students. The time frame for early career researchers will be more variable, however, and dependent on any research contract or publication schedule. The research, therefore, has to be something that you are prepared to live with and be genuinely interested in. You do not want to start a project, get halfway through, and then want to scrap it because you just do not like what you are doing or fail to see its relevance. For this reason, it is really important to choose the right topic and then both clarify and justify why you have chosen it.

Getting started is sometimes the most difficult part of a research project as identifying a topic is not easy. At the two extremes, sometimes individuals have a clear idea about what they want to do, have done some preliminary reading to check out their ideas and are confident about their direction while others may have no specific idea, have read and searched for a suitable avenue, but feel hopelessly lost. Nobody said that writing a research report, dissertation or thesis would ever be easy! You need to think about how to generate your ideas, where they come from – and not just from the top of your head – and, more importantly, whether your thoughts and ideas are going to be meaningful as a piece of educational research (Conrad and Serlin, 2011).

On some degree courses, topics for research are simply allocated to individual students, or they choose from a list of areas. This is arguably prescriptive, but does have the advantage of taking away the creative and sometimes painstaking process of generating ideas. It also ensures that there is some level of continuity and rigour across the projects that students undertake. This tends to happen in more scientific subjects, however, and tends to be rare in education.

So, where are your ideas going to come from? In your new role as an educational researcher there are a number of ways in which you can generate ideas. As well as choosing something that is interesting, you want to choose something that you are going to enjoy researching. There may have been modules within your degree, for example, that you really got involved with and want to learn more about. The list of areas that you will have learnt about may be endless. For example, you may have learnt about Forest Schools, behaviour management, socio-emotional well-being, the impact of family and literacy and so on. All of these are potential areas for further research and the list is endless. Perhaps there is some area within the auspices of education that you have always wanted to learn more about. Undertake some basic research on the Internet and look for any research projects that have already been undertaken. As you do so, think about the unique approaches that you are going to undertake within your research project that will help you to make your work distinctive. Sometimes, simply reading through a textbook or looking through journals, whether online or not, can help you to identify some ideas. You may find that there is a distinct gap in the literature, which you feel could be met through your approaches to your research.

Practical Tip

Your course tutor may allow you to see some dissertations or theses from previous years. These can help as they enable you to understand the nature and type of research projects that have been undertaken as well as some of the parameters that may have limited the research. You may find that your university library stores past extended studies and that, by looking through them, you can generate some ideas. As you look at these projects, try to think about what makes a good project and what makes a bad project. Look at how the projects are structured. Try to think about the strengths and weaknesses associated with the work that you observe.

Another avenue to explore that may lead to a research topic might be any work experience or placement(s) that you have undertaken. You may want to go into the placement to discuss your ideas or send a letter to somebody who may have acted as your mentor. This is always an interesting avenue for research and, if you carry out research in an environment in which you are working, you are a participant observer. Participant observation is particularly good for observing the phenomena within a setting and for eliciting a rich and deep understanding within a social world in a way that helps you to understand the participants well as emphasised in Chapter 9 (DeWalt and DeWalt, 2011). As you work there you understand individuals, the culture and the world that exists within that setting. This type of study is usually linked with ethnography, an area often linked with anthropology, as it involves an understanding of a distinct community and its customs through which interpretations may be made of beliefs and values (Atkinson and Hammersley, 2007).

Definition – Ethnography

Research strategy, often associated with anthropology and participant observation that focuses upon the behaviour of a group of participants within a closely defined context.

But, as a student, what can you do if you are struggling to find anything that might be of interest to you? Diagrams are a really useful way of quickly and easily making links between concepts so that hypotheses, theories or ideas can be simply represented (Crilly et al., 2006). For example when many students are in doubt, they simply construct a mind map. *Mind maps* are a very creative way of constructing a diagram which enables you to visualise your thoughts (see Figures 4.1 and 4.2). At a very simple level they can show just a range of ideas but they can also show how elements depend upon each other as well as relationships between variables. In this way a mind map is a tool that can be used in the early stages for planning a project.

Activity

Consider the following research question:

How might the pedagogies that teachers use in supporting the emotional development of children aged 4–5 result in furthering their resilience skills?

From the question, create a mind map identifying the areas that require investigation, possible topics for a literature review and potential research methods. Consider how and whether the mind map has helped you to represent your ideas for this type of project.

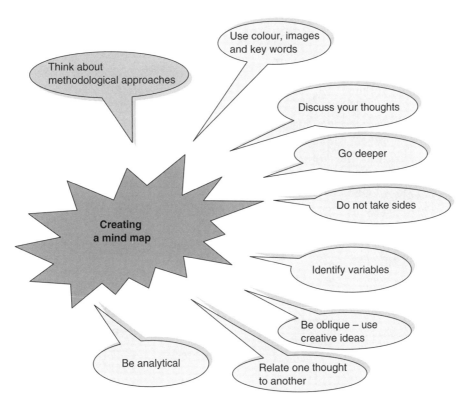

Figure 4.1   Mind maps 1

One similar idea to mind mapping is that of *relevance trees* (see Figure 4.3). This technique was developed by Buzan (2007). Basically, the research starts with a broad concept, which is then broken down into a series of branches from which topics are then further developed and ideas are refined. As you move down and through the branches more potential ideas and topics are examined.

De Bono (1992) identified that random words or images could be used as a lateral-thinking technique in order to stimulate associations that could be used as a thinking tool for a project. By identifying more than one word, the different associations create connections that might help with the development of ideas that would otherwise not have been linked through logical thought. For example, one group of words might refer to methodology such as case study, feminism and gender, ethnography, grounded theory, action research and so on. If you were interested in play, another group of words might include words related to play such as epistemic, heuristic, therapy, undirected, play deprivation, play space, playful learning or play fights. Then a third list of words might relate to a list of completely random words such as religion, reflective practitioner, physiology, exclusion, inclusion, siblings, apprenticeship, self-esteem etc.

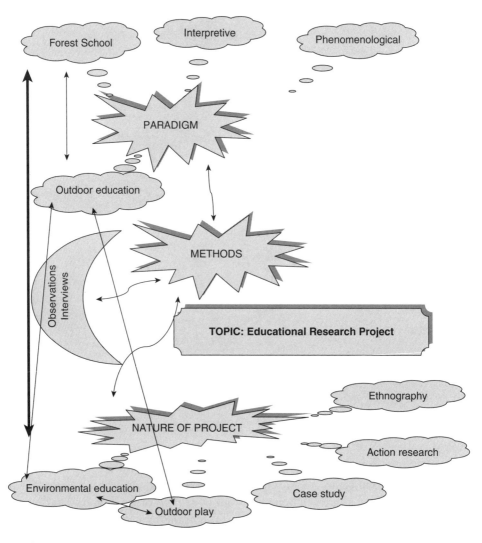

Figure 4.2   Mind maps 2

The trick would then be to take a word from each list and then to try to make linkages between them in order to form some kind of research question, i.e. gender, play deprivation and self-esteem might lead to you focusing upon the extent to which play deprivation might affect the self-esteem of boys within a particular age group. The investigation would then analyse the linkages between such deprivation and its potential to influence self-esteem. Similarly, case study, epistemic play and physiology might create a focus upon health and the development of cognitive and intellectual skills. This might involve creating a case study based upon the influence of exploratory play with objects and materials and how this influences psychological factors as children grow and develop.

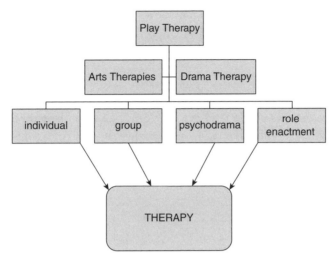

Figure 4.3 Example of relevance tree

A similar way of making linkages across a range of potential variables is through the use of *morphological analysis*. This was first developed by Zwicky and Wilson (1967) in order to analysis potential solutions for multi-dimensional non-quantified problems or relationships.

Definition – Morphological analysis

Associated with form and structure, this is a method of identifying pathways and solutions using classifications for multi-dimensional non-quantifiable problems and issues.

Morphology originates from classical Greek (morphe) which is all about the study of form or shape. The starting point for this is to break down a problem into a range of parameters or dimensions that can then, at its simplest level, be put into a basic matrix. Each of these dimensions could be set out as a column heading as shown in the following example (Table 4.1)

Table 4.1 Using morphological analysis to develop a research topic

Nature of issue	Potential methodologies	Potential methods
School improvement	Longitudinal study	Recording of data over time
Behaviour management	Ethnography/action research	Observer/participation
Mixed age learning	Case study	Interviews/use of secondary data
Outdoor environment	Experimentation	Identifying relationships between variables
Music therapy	Survey	Sampling from key groups
Gender and play	Grounded theory	An appropriate setting

This mix-and-match approach to research allows research interests or topics to form random combinations to constructively relate ways of developing the research question or problem. In effect, what it does is to create combinations which provide the potential for ideas to be developed further.

Undertaking any form of research is an iterative activity as it is ongoing and, although you may have your ideas in place, as you talk to people and undertake your reading, it may change. Talking to experts in the field can be really useful, as their thoughts and feedback may help you to refine and further develop your ideas. If your research is related to a placement, it is always useful to have conversations with any potential users of the research findings. They may have distinct ideas about the implications of your project.

Practical Tips

Once you have identified an area of interest, you need to firm it up by starting to ask yourself questions about it. This will help you to clarify the value of your study. For example:

a) Is your project feasible? Is it possible to research literature and use your research methods to collect data that will provide a strong answer to your question?

b) What are the main elements of literature related to your study? In this early stage when constructing your project you need to familiarise yourself with the main areas of literature. As you read the literature, you may feel the need to refine your question.

c) What are you trying to achieve through your study? Is there sufficient justification for you to carry out this sort of investigation? There should be ample grounds to support your investigation.

d) Are there any words related to your ideas that need further clarification? How well do you really understand the direction that you will be pursuing through your research?

e) How are you going to undertake the project? Think about issues of planning such as timings and deadlines.

f) Is this project going to be of value to you? Consider the benefits, both personal and professional that you will gain from your dissertation.

g) Finally, are you going to enjoy undertaking a research project focused upon this avenue of interest?

You think about the area of research to focus your investigation. This means that you either need to put together a series of *hypotheses* or *research questions*. The purpose of hypotheses and research questions are to orientate the research.

Constructing Hypotheses

Theories or models are variables that have over time provided a series of definitions that classify relationships and these come from the literature. Where there is theory, these theories can be tested by constructing a hypothesis. A hypothesis is therefore a proposition or a statement that can be challenged for causality against variables using empirical evidence, but this approach to research usually tends to make use of statistics. It is for this reason that hypotheses are therefore more often associated with the positivist paradigm in which quantitative methods of analysis are used. Positivism is often considered to be more objective because it is based upon logic rather than values or 'intuitive interpretation' (Collis and Hussey, 2009: 56).

Definition – Hypothesis

Tentative explanations, statements or answers about a research issue that need to be tested, usually against evidence, in order to be verified or proved.

As human beings we naturally look for answers or reasons why things happen as part of our everyday observations. For example, on a winter's day, if your train is late, you might make the statement that it could be that 'the points are frozen at Clapham Junction'. If snow falls, you could hypothesise that you are going to be at least half an hour late for work. Although these may be guesses, they are also hypotheses. You are simply going through rational processes in which you make statements about the probable cause of a situation, based upon your knowledge and experience. You are making a tentative supposition or intelligent guess. Sometimes, we get things wrong. So, if the train is late because of a fault in the rolling stock and not because of the points, the hypothesis is not true and could be rejected. Similarly if you get to work on time, even though it has snowed, again the hypothesis would be rejected. So, we can see that a hypothesis is therefore a good starting point for a process of investigation. Sometimes it can be proved and sometimes it can be rejected.

Case Study

Joseph recently undertook an extended placement within a secondary school. As part of his placement he was asked to work with a 14-year-old boy who had a mild form of autism. Joseph really enjoyed the one-to-one support he was providing for the boy and undertook a considerable amount of background reading about autism so that he knew that he was providing the right form of support for him. For example, he was conscious that autistic children sometimes think in pictures and not in language. So, he became more expressive and used his hands to support any explanations he gave to the boy as well as used visual cues to show him how much work should be done. Joseph also built a daily schedule of activities and started using objects and pictures to help them within the classroom. As he did so, Joseph started to wonder how a more interactive and colourful environment could be used to help children with different levels of autism. For his research project, he came up with the following hypothesis:

(Continued)

(Continued)

> *Multi-interactive learning environments support the educational development of teenage boys with autism.*

Joseph decided to use a hypothesis to underpin his approaches to his research as he wanted to link the outcomes of his research and reading about the creation of colourful multi-interactive resources with the role that he was undertaking with him within the classroom. He wanted to identify all of the advantages and limitations of using the resources and then be able to test whether the resources were actually helping his subject. He believes that if his predictions are borne out and his hypothesis verified, his approaches to helping children with autism will be valid.

Unlike research questions, hypotheses are therefore statements that researchers make which are then tested. In this sense the hypothesis is a prediction about the potential outcomes of the study (Maretella et al., 2013) and is a statement that looks forward, just like an expectation. The hypothesis then guides the researcher into developing tests and experiments that help to test the variables within the hypothesis they have made. For example, we could make the hypothesis that 'low paid teaching assistants are not motivated when their role is enlarged'. Low paid staff would be one variable, motivation is another and the other would be job enlargement. It would be up to the researcher to use research tools to test the hypothesis that they had made.

According to Verma and Beard (1981: 55) a statement of hypothesis is:

> A tentative proposition which is subject to verification through subsequent investigation. It may also be seen as the guide to the researcher in that it depicts and describes the method to be followed in studying the problem. In many cases hypotheses are hunches that the researcher has about the existence of relationship between variables.

So, in this sense, a hypothesis is a hunch that the researcher has about the relationship between variables. Having had this hunch it is then up to the researcher to test the variables. For this reason, hypotheses are more typical in scientific or experimental research, more so because this sort of research can be structured to test the hypotheses. Just stating a hypothesis focuses the research process upon any potential outcomes that a study might have, so that there is a clear link between the statement and the need for a proof.

By using a hypothesis the researcher is able to create a statement that identifies the key variables within the research project. Depending upon the variables the researcher will then collect, analyse and interpret data, more usually using scientific methods in order to verify the hypothesis (Singh and Nath, 2010). From analysing this data they will then be able to confirm and support the hypothesis or reject it.

In the same way that a research question might be broken down into a series of aims, a main hypothesis could be de-constructed into a series of sub-hypotheses (Walliman, 2004).

Again, each of these should contribute to parts of the hypothesis so that when added together they respond to all of it. There may be a distinct relationship between the main hypothesis and the sub-hypotheses based upon the form of testing that may have taken place. For example, the hypothesis below could be broken down into two sub-hypotheses:

Multi-interactive learning environments support the educational development of teenage boys with autism. These are:

- autistic children find multi-interactive learning environments more stimulating;
- when autistic teenage boys operate in a stimulating environment, they learn more and this contributes to their educational development.

Practical Tips

You may want to use the following tips to help to evaluate the quality of your hypothesis:

1. What knowledge do you have of the background to the issue that you wish to study?
2. Does the hypothesis extend thinking in the area of research being undertaken?
3. Do the methods being used to test the hypothesis enable the hypothesis to be verified? If your hypothesis is based upon concepts, you may not be able to test it. You may need to change your hypothesis in order to 'operationalise' it.
4. Having made a hypothetical statement, are you able to undertake the research in a way that does not create bias? One of the problems with a hypothesis is that researchers might undertake procedures in a very fixed way that meets all of the desired outcomes.
5. Is there a danger that by focusing upon a hypothesis, you fail to take into account other phenomena outside the realms of your statement that might influence the broader outcomes of the research?
6. Does the hypothesis use value-ridden terms like 'ought' or 'should' which may make the hypothesis difficult to verify?

Hypotheses or Research Questions?

In contrast to the positivist paradigm, there are researchers who believe that the reality of the research environment in which the research takes place cannot be objective as the experience of the research depends upon their perceptions. This type of research is less objective because it involves an investigation into social phenomena to gain a deep and richer understanding of what is being observed. Instead of proving something based upon quantitative methods, this research is about trying to find out more about the meaning of what is being observed. This type of research does not involve testing statements or proving whether or not hypotheses have been met. In these situations, rather than have hypotheses, it is more usual to frame the investigation around a research question.

Definition – Positivist Paradigm

This is the philosophical framework that guides how scientific research is undertaken where facts are distinguished from values so that knowledge is derived from positive information that is capable of mathematical proof. (See also Chapter 2 for more information about paradigms.)

In my view educational research normally lends itself more towards interpretive approaches. This is because most of you are likely to be trying to make sense of the environment within which you are undertaking your research. For this reason, most of you are probably likely to want to construct research questions rather than create hypotheses.

Definition – Interpretive

Providing an explanation or interpretation of the complex social phenomena within the subject or environment at the centre of the process of research in order to make sense of reality. (See also Chapter 2 for more information about paradigms.)

Whereas research questions are a good way to provide focus in order to answer questions, it is difficult to state them in a way that enables issues to be analysed statistically. Hypotheses, on the other hand, are declarations that can be tested statistically as long as it is possible to identify data to do so. In other words, if you are undertaking qualitative research with interpretive approaches, 'empirical research [refers to] where the data are not numbers but words' (Punch, 2009: 12), then you will construct a research question. On the other hand, if you are dealing with data that are numbers, then really you should be thinking about hypotheses. My experience shows that in most educational contexts, but not all, people tend to undertake qualitative rather than quantitative research.

Creating the Research Question(s)

It could be said that research is about using one's mind creatively to ask questions to which you can then find out the answers. In this way questions help to turn a topic into an investigation. This notion of creating a question is at the very heart of the research process. As an active researcher I constantly go back and back again to the research questions I have asked wherever and whenever I am writing articles for publication. At the back of my mind, is the notion of 'how well I am answering the research question(s)?' The research question and the aims that come from this question influence how I think, write and undertake my analysis. They seldom remain static, however, as new information often leads me to reconceptualise what I am doing. Consequently every part of my research projects is concerned with the efficacy of the research questions and the degree to which my enquiry answers them.

The importance of asking the right research questions

Practical example

Imagine two scenes with stick figures:

1st scene. Police stick figure and male stick figure. Police

stick figure says 'Were you in Boston yesterday evening?'

Second stick figure, 'Yes.'

2nd scene. Police stick figure, 'Well, I am arresting you for theft.

Anything you say etc!!'

Second stick figure. 'But, I was in Boston Massachusetts not Boston

Lincolnshire!!'

WAS THE RIGHT QUESTION ASKED?

Lewis and Munn (1991) showed the crucial part that questions play in the decisions that researchers undertake and how that relates to the sorts of claims that researchers make about the research process by emphasising that the function of a research question is to:

- clarify the area of concern, help to organise the project and give it coherence;
- identify the sort of information that needs to be collected and provide a framework for writing up the project;
- guide the researcher on how to collect information and keep them focused and re-focused;
- provide a framework for developing and writing up the project;
- enable the reader to make judgements about the project.

In other words research questions add focus to the project and provide you with a direction. They help you as a researcher to think more deeply about what you intend to investigate and explore.

Activity

Working with a critical friend or a in a group, identify some hypothetical research questions. They could be about anything. The purpose of this exercise is to create a forum for discussing what might be a good or a bad research question.

Trying to identify research questions is not always easy. You need to think about your area of research interest and of the information that is available to use. Frequently, students on degree courses come up with research questions without having done any preparatory reading beforehand, and then keep going back to their tutor saying 'but, nobody has written about this before. I cannot find anything!' If they had done some reading beforehand, identified an issue, and then used their evolving understanding to identify the main and subsidiary research questions, this would not have happened.

There is another issue here. Your research question is unique because you have developed it. It should be something very special and be an area that you personally want to get involved with. Do not expect that you are going to pick up a book or find a journal that has answered that question before in exactly the way that you have posed the question. It is just not likely to happen. In this way research is a bit like a jigsaw puzzle and you need to read widely. Then you might also want to undertake some primary research to test and further develop what you have read. Later, after organising everything that you have read and coding it, you put all of the pieces out and bring it together (see Chapter 10 for further information on coding and Chapter 14 for advice and guidance on organising your work). Then you can begin to answer the question and think about the implications and findings of all that you have done.

Practical Tips

The research question should not only identify the issue or area of interest, but could also suggest the approach that is being taken to a project. For example, 'how can the Forest School environment be used to motivate children to learn about mathematics within an early years setting?' Finding out about Forest Schools is not too difficult. Much has been written about their approaches and pedagogies in recent years. At the same time you would need to think about how children within their early years learn by referring to aspects of elementary psychology that you have probably covered within your course. As you did so you might look for clues that might, within the later stages of a project, need more focus. You would also need to have a good knowledge of how children within the early years learn mathematics. For example, through observation and interviews with practitioners you may find that developing numeric and mathematical skills may be used by children as a way of solving problems so that they make clear connections between what they are learning and how they can use that information to reason, make decisions, or solve problems in everyday life (Cooke, 2007). By carefully structuring your approaches, undertaking an extensive literature review and through working closely with staff from a chosen organisation to undertake some element of primary research you would create a deeper understanding of the Forest School environment that would help you to answer the question.

It is important to ensure that a research question is neither too broad nor too narrow. For example, you could ask the following questions:

1. What is a Forest School?
2. To what extent can the burden of behaviour management be reduced within a primary school?
3. How might family background, culture and sociological context influence the likelihood of certain types of youth crime?
4. How could pedagogies used by a pupil referral unit (PRU) to promote good behaviour provide the support for young people that helps facilitate their re-entry into mainstream education?

Question One is clearly too narrow, and would simply involve providing a definition of a Forest School. Any answer to this question would be descriptive and not really enable you to develop the depth of analysis required for academic research. This is because there is really only one area of focus. There is no mention of any issues related to Forest Schools, age groups, relationship to child development, notions of types of activities and so on.

Question Two is a better question, but a very difficult one to answer, and is very broad. Behaviour management is a huge area, particularly in terms of its implications for a whole school. There also might be an ethical issue associated with the question. Trying to find out how the burden of behaviour management can be reduced implies that the current approaches may not be good. It would be better to look at some aspect related to this area such as reward systems, a focus upon positive behaviour, seating arrangements within a classroom, co-operative working, low-level disruption or a whole range of other potential issues.

Although the third question is clearly focused there are many ways of answering it and so it is potentially theoretical. There are some distinct areas of possible reading and research and, in fact, perhaps there are too many. It might be better to simply focus upon socio-logical context. Caution will also be needed as there could be ethical issues associated with this question, more particularly in terms of the approaches to answering the question (see Chapter 3 for more guidance on this).

Question Four would be a really interesting question for anybody who has access to a pupil referral unit to answer. There are many different variables within the question as well such as methods of teaching, understanding the purposes of a PRU, behaviour management and the process of transition back into a mainstream school. It would certainly not be an easy question to answer. However, trying to find the answer to this question would be a real adventure. Potentially, this could be a good preliminary research question and a really useful starting point for a research project.

Developing research questions is an iterative process as it is something that takes place all of the time as you undertake your project. As you think about the question and undertake more reading you may want to amend it or revise it in order to give it more focus. Within the early stages, and before you start the research process, you need to think about how your research question relates to the theories required for the study. No enquiry can take place unless it is based upon some element of theory as, at the level you are studying, it is theory that will underpin your approaches. Theory is anything that has been written about your area of research, the body of research that exists in relation to your topic. It is for this reason that a good research question has to be relevant and relatable to a chosen field in a way that underpins the purposes for the research.

Case Study

Alex

Alex volunteers as a teaching assistant in a reception classroom within a local primary school. She is undertaking a degree in Childhood Studies at the local university and wants to develop some experience that complements her course. For the final year of her degree she had to carry out a research project. Alex has two brothers and has always been interested in gender issues both at home and now at work. While at work, Alex wondered why so many boys played with Pop-up Pirates while the girls tended to play at the other side of the nursery in the home corner. Alex is interested in gender issues and is fascinated with the nature/nurture debate. For example, she wonders what it is that prompts children to role play at such a young age. At playtimes Alex would observe how boys and girls would rarely play together. In fact she has noticed that they often opt to play in single gender groups. Within the classroom she has noticed how the girls seemed to be more interested in reading books and felt that perhaps this was a reason why the girls could be doing better in tests.

The following three questions are too big:

1. Why are girls more interested in reading than boys?
2. Does this mean that girls will do much better than boys at school?
3. What sort of things do boys do at school that help them with their reading?

What makes these questions too big? Consider the level of focus and the way that this defines the boundaries of the study.

The following three questions are too small:

1. Every member of James's family has gone to university. Does this mean that he is likely to be a good reader?
2. What impact upon James's reading was there after reading a football magazine with him?
3. Is the fact that James is left-handed significant in his literary development?

Try to write some suitable questions for the study.

As you develop your research questions you need to think about:

- all of the other research that has taken place in your area of interest. It is really important at an early stage to find out about the significant authors and contributors who
might have influenced the different elements of the field that you are about to research.
Talk to your supervisor or critical friend about this. As you start reading articles, look at
the references section. Do some names appear more often than others?
- how realistic your intentions are for the project. For example, are you able to fully
address the issue and all of the concepts that underpin the research question(s)? Your
reading should help you to refine and fine-tune your research question(s) so that you
can become more authoritative.
- the resources, including time, available for the research. It might be the case that in
the early days the research question appears feasible. However, as you undertake your
investigation you may fail to find many appropriate resources and realise that for one
reason or another it is not possible to collect appropriate data. Sometimes it is worth
thinking about one or two avenues of investigation, just in case you have to change your
research strategy.
- the strategies that you intend to use to answer the research question(s). Although this
is sometimes like doing things back to front, it can help if you think about any contacts
that you may have as well as some of the methods that you might utilise as you collect
data. Try to be creative about your ideas for collecting data. This will help you answer
your research question(s) in a rich and meaningful way.

Practical Tips

You may want to use the following tips to help to evaluate the quality of your research question:

1. Is the question focused upon a topic or area that is interesting and helps to extend your
knowledge and understanding of an issue? You need to develop a question that is going to
keep you interested throughout the study.
2. Is the question clear? You do not want to create a question that is too elaborate and
confused. The worst thing is to have an ambiguous research question that is just not clear
(Punch, 2009).
3. How well is it possible to answer the question? If a question is too vague you might struggle to
understand what it really means and this could mean that your whole approach may be muddled.
4. What sort of reading is required to answer the question? At a very early stage, it is useful to
run a simple literature search in order to identify topics relevant to the question.
5. Is the question too broad or too narrow? Either of these could be problematic.
6. What resources might be needed to answer the question? If your research involves primary
research, at a very early stage, think of contacts that you might have as well as contexts
where the research could take place.
7. Do you have a question that can really be answered by undertaking some research? You may
want to talk to others about this, or set up a study group with friends where you can each
test your research question(s).

Good research questions should be:

- easy to understand and clear;
- specific and relate to potential ways for collecting data;
- interesting and worthwhile, worthy of researching;
- constructed in a way that enables data collection and methodology processes to be constructed.

Activity

Work with friends to construct a series of preliminary research questions and then attempt to test them using the format in the matrix below:

Research question	Potential data sources	Strengths	Weaknesses	Justification of question	Ethical issues

---

Constructing Research Aims and Objectives

Having created a research question you then need to begin to form your ideas and plan your research. As you do so there is no instant blueprint for constructing the project (Cohen et al., 2011). It all depends upon you as the researcher to think about how you wish to plan your project. One way of doing this is to construct your research aims and objectives. It is also possible to construct smaller research questions, each of which helps to answer the bigger question. At this stage it is difficult to be prescriptive as different researchers have different approaches to this, and all these ways of constructing a plan to answer the research question could be construed as being useful. To some extent, therefore, it is up to you.

As you construct one or more aims, you should be thinking about the purposes of your research. Effectively aims, like the research question(s), will help to provide an overall direction for your research. Constructing aims helps you to come to terms with the project in your mind as well as helping you to answer the research question(s). For example, research aims can be used to help you think about how you intend to structure your response to the research question(s) with each research aim answering part of the question(s) and all of the research aims together answering all such questions.

Aims are statements that help to emphasise all of the potential outcomes and intentions of the research (Bryman and Bell, 2007). Thus they can be constructed in a logical way to show what is being achieved as the research question is being broached. You may want to provide a single aim in order to help you answer the research question, just a couple of aims or perhaps a number of aims.

For example, the question:

To what extent does a child's vocabulary help to nurture literacy development as children start school?

Might have the aims:

- to develop an awareness of parallel skills that help children prepare for school;
- to understand appropriate activities that enhance a child's vocabulary;
- to appreciate how children develop vocabulary skills;
- to link vocabulary development with reading and language progression;
- to evaluate links between vocabulary acquisition and the preparedness of children for reading.

If you feel that it helps to turn these aims into questions, then this is fine as well. For example, they could become:

a) What parallel skills help children prepare for school?
b) What type of activities help to advance a child's vocabulary?
c) How do children develop vocabulary skills?
d) Is it possible to link vocabulary development with reading and language progression?
e) How do the links between vocabulary acquisition and language progression help to prepare children for reading?

Once you have formed your research aims, you may then want to develop your research objectives. Objectives are generally considered to be a bit more practical as they identify the steps you take in order to answer your research question. In other words, objectives help the research develop a pathway that enables them to answer the aims. In this way the objectives are much more focused and precise in order to relate closely to how the researcher intends to undertake and meet the project outcomes. Remember, the aims identify the potential outcomes for the project and the objectives then describe how you intend to achieve them. It is for this reason that they need to be much more precise and also a bit more practical.

So, for the research question above, we could create the following objectives:

- To find out about the processes and practices used within the classroom to help children to learn to read;
- To undertake a relevant literature review and build an appropriate methodology that underpins the direction of the project;
- To classify the different levels of vocabulary development that early years children have as and when they start school;

- To create meaningful tools that enable the researcher to undertake primary research that links a child's vocabulary to literacy development in order to capture rich interpretive data;
- To critically analyse data so that the meanings, patterns and inferences deduced contribute towards findings.

Clearly, to some extent some of these objectives would be unique to this project, while others could be applied to other projects.

Activity

For the following research question, construct a series of project aims and objectives:

> How might school trips as a form of learning outside the school environment be used to create social interaction that scaffolds the educational development of primary-aged children?

Key Points to Remember

- Getting started upon any research project involves a considerable amount of thought as well as measured judgement. Do not simply leap into an area without doing some reading or without testing your ideas against the range of considerations outlined within this chapter.
- You have to make a decision about whether to construct a research question or a hypothesis. Your choice will depend upon whether your project is interpretive or positivist.
- To support your approaches to answering your research question you may want to construct a series of aims, or for a hypothesis, a series of sub-hypotheses.

Further Reading

Basit, T.N. (2010) *Constructing Research in Educational Contexts*. London: Continuum.
Cohen, L., Manion, L. and Morrison, K. (2011) *Research Methods in Education* (7/E). Abingdon: Routledge.

Useful Websites

- The Education Research Global Observatory comprises a directory of peer-reviewed journals in education. Links lead to the websites of each of the journals
www.ergobservatory.info/ejdirectory.html

- The National Foundation for Educational Research is a leading forum for issues on education
www.nfer.ac.uk/publications/educational-research/

References

Andrews, R. (2003) *Research Questions*. London: Continuum Books.

Atkinson, P. and Hammersley, M. (2007) *Ethnography: Principles in Practice* (3/E). Abingdon: Routledge.

Bryman, A. and Bell, E. (2007) *Business Research Methods* (2/E). Oxford: Oxford University Press.

Buzan, T. (2007) *The Buzan Study Skills Handbook*. Harlow: BBC Active.

Cohen, L., Manion, L. and Morrison, K. (2011) *Research Methods in Education* (7/E). Abingdon: Routledge.

Collis, J. and Hussey, R. (2009) *Business Research: A Practical Guide for Undergraduate and Postgraduate Students*. Basingstoke: Palgrave Macmillan.

Conrad, C.F. and Serlin, R.C. (2011) *The Sage Handbook for Research in Education* (2/E). Los Angeles: Sage Publications Inc.

Cooke, H. (2007) *Mathematics for Primary and Early Years: Developing Subject Knowledge* (2/E). London: SAGE.

Crilly, N., Clarkson, P.J. and Blackwell, A.F. (2006) 'Using research diagrams for member validation in qualitative research', in *Diagrammatic Representation and Inference 4th International Conference*, Stanford, CA, pp. 258–262.

De Bono, E. (1992) *Teach Your Child How to Think*. London: Penguin Books.

DeWalt, K.M. and DeWalt, B.R. (2011) *Participant Observation: A Guide for Fieldworkers* (2/E). Plymouth: AltaMira Press.

Lewis, I. and Munn, A. (1991) *So, You Want To Do Research? A Guide for Teachers on How to Formulate Research Questions*. Edinburgh: SCRE.

Maretella, R.C., Nelson, J.R., Morgan, R.L. and Marchard-Martella, N.E., (2013) *Understanding and Interpreting Educational Research*. New York: The Guilford Press.

Punch, K.F. (2009) *Introduction to Research Methods in Education*. London: SAGE.

Singh, Y.K. and Nath, R. (2010) *Research Methodology*. New Delhi: A.P.H. Publishing Corporation.

Verma, G. and Beard, R. (1981) *What is Educational Research? Perspectives on Techniques of Research*. Aldershot: Gower.

Walliman, N. (2004) *Your Undergraduate Dissertation*. London: SAGE.

Zwicky, F. and Wilson, A. (eds) (1967) *New Methods of Thought and Procedure: Contributions to the Symposium on Methodologies*. Berlin: Springer.

For additional online resources please visit the book's website:
https://study.sagepub.com/needhamandpalaiologou

5

MANAGING THE PROJECT

LYNDA PINNINGTON-WILSON AND DAVID NEEDHAM

Chapter Aims and Objectives

This chapter aims to help you to:

- appreciate the skills you require in order to present a report, dissertation or thesis;
- understand the need to manage a research project;
- use simple project planning tools to organise your project;
- identify the various stages of a research project;
- support you in managing and monitoring your research project.

Introduction

For many, starting a research project can be like stepping into the unknown. The problem is that so much usually depends upon it. Anything could happen on this journey, particularly for those who are unprepared. For this reason, and from the outset, it is important that you think about how you plan and manage your research project, particularly as an emerging researcher.

It may be clichéd, but in a competitive organisational environment the people who succeed are generally the people who take ownership of something or contribute to something in a way that ensures that the outcome is achieved. In other words they 'make things happen'. They succeed because the event, project, product or tangible outcome has met the expectations of others and has been delivered in a way that has met some pre-planned objectives.

All research projects whether large or small:

1. specify a goal or a series of objectives;
2. are not immediately achievable;
3. require some organised and well thought out processes in order to achieve the goals or objectives.

At the heart of this journey there needs to be some form of project management that enables you, the researcher, to complete your work on time and in a way that provides you with the outcome you desire.

Planning

A project has a starting point as well as a place where the project ends. Between the starting point and the finish, there are sequences of activities that involve some form of planning (Bruce and Langdon, 2000). Planning involves effectively achieving a future state of affairs by setting targets that you can work towards and meet. For a research project this might involve a time scale, identifying the stages that break a project up and also ways of monitoring the plan.

It is sometimes useful to think of managing your project as a cyclical and iterative activity as it takes place continually (Carmona and Sieh, 2004). This is because it involves you in thinking about courses of action to structure your project, identifying a way of working, implementing the plan, monitoring the plan and then making revisions as you manage the plan and work upon your project. You have to remember that a plan is not permanently fixed, but is something that needs to be adjusted and refined in the light of reflection and changes to your thinking.

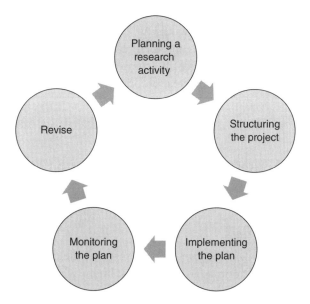

Figure 5.1 Managing the project

The Skills Required to Manage a Research Project

It could be argued that in traditional learning environments learners submissively have to accept what is offered and are simply recipients of what they have to study and how they are expected to learn. Such environments create dependent learners. Undertaking a research project should be very different to this, however, because a large part of conducting research involves elements of self-directed learning. This means that the researcher is the person managing and taking responsibility for the direction of their learning experience as well as for completing the project. Instead of simply reacting to what they are told, researchers, particularly students undertaking degree courses, now have to be proactive in providing their own learning agenda. Although many might think of this as a wonderful opportunity, in some ways it can be much more challenging for the participant. This is because everything is down to the motivation of each person to discipline how they work and manage their own time.

It is your research skills that are going to be required to help you to answer questions, solve problems or investigate issues (O'Leary, 2010). This process fosters the development of abstract thought and the exploration of complex intellectual tasks as part of a major piece of work. One of the reasons for this is that the skills you develop under these conditions can then be applied to other learning situations or even within the workplace. The ways in which you discipline yourself to conduct research will create personal behaviours and practices that may on the one hand challenge you, but on the other could lead to successful and positive outcomes in life.

In this century the workplace increasingly requires employees to be skilled in and capable of ethically conducting research, data analysis and making evaluations as part of their core business of work. Increasingly it is now more common to see job advertisements that list 'project management' alongside skills and other requirements for positions across the professions and beyond. The ideal candidate for a position would have the ability to assess a situation, formulate a problem into a set of essential questions and then plan how to answer questions within a set time, format and resource limitations. Successful completion of a research project should equip you with those skills and we aim to provide appropriate advice and guidance in this chapter.

Practical Tip

To help you manage your project it is useful to keep a diary or a workbook in which you can make notes and map out your priorities. It can also be useful for reflection.

Project Management

Project management has indeed become a rich research field of its own with a set of particular methodologies and approaches to solve problems which are highly dependent on the context of the discipline and the problem to be solved (McKenney and Reeves, 2012). It is easy to think about how projects have influenced our history with the building of bridges, roads, castles and structures. However, at a more manageable level managing your research project simply involves developing skills, tools and techniques that enable you to get your project completed on time in order to meet your personal objectives (Richman, 2012). So, at the heart of managing this process is the notion of getting things completed and delivering results that enable you to succeed with the best possible outcomes.

Activity

Make a list of all of the skills that you think are required in order to successfully complete your dissertation and meet your professional learning objectives.

Remember that a research project is iterative. It lives and will soon have an identity of its own. As it does so, you will have to identify many priorities, monitor the performance of the project, make key decisions and be prepared to make changes to all the things you do. Project management techniques are designed to provide you with more control over your project. Although you may consider some of the techniques time-consuming, they are simply designed to minimise your effort, save you time and reduce any of the risks of failure.

Getting Started

We suggest the starting point for any project is an assessment or reflection of your own personal capabilities and project management skills. How well are you aware of your own strengths and weaknesses and, to what extent do you apply these skills in a focused way within the context of your work? To find out about your own capabilities it is possible to 'audit' and assess your skills. An audit helps you to identify your capabilities within the context of things you have to do and, as you are developing new skills all the time, it is always useful to be reflective in the way you assess them (Burns and Sinfield, 2008).

A simple audit could start by assessing the project management skills you already have. There are a number of approaches to this. For example, you could start by just identifying your existing positive qualities. We have developed a list that might help you to include one or more of the following.

Table 5.1 Identifying positive qualities

Intellectual	Relaxed	Outgoing	Resourceful	Sensible
Cheerful	Organised	Sociable	Sensitive	Energetic
People skills	Aspiration	Motivation	Energetic	Responsive
Patient	Measured	Logical	Practical	Optimistic
Reflective	Idealistic	Warm	Meticulous	Creative
Hard working	Calm	Ambitious	Friendly	Flexible
Mediation	Knowledge	Influence	Empathy	Hopes

Having identified your positive qualities, you may then want to think about how to make the most of these skills as you construct your research project. Many of these positive qualities will influence how you approach your research project and your ability to learn independently. In stark contrast you may be conscious of a range of negative qualities that you may have that could influence the outcomes from your project. For example, these could include some of the following:

Table 5.2 Negative qualities

Lazy	Tense	Disorganised	Childish	Anti-social
Moody	Pedantic	Difficult	Intolerant	Irritable
Unhelpful	Careless	Untidy	Nervous	Disloyal
Subjective	Obstinate	Inflexible	Value-ridden	Singular
Temper	Frustration	Stress	Self-focus	Pity
Addictions	Denial	Withdrawal	Day dream	Irresponsible

As you look through these negative qualities, think about how they could influence the outcomes from your project. Even at an early stage, and particularly as you identify your negative qualities, you have to consider how to overcome some of the problems they might cause you. So, as you maintain, use and make the most of your strengths, consider how you can improve upon your areas of weakness.

Being Creative With Your Project

During your research project you will need to be creative as you design your hypothesis/research question and think about how to conduct your research. There is guidance available to you on Chapter 4 on establishing your hypothesis/research question(s) so we are not going to repeat that here. Instead here we are looking more closely at how you manage that creatively. When we think of how to manage a project we tend to think about 'getting things done' or 'finishing tasks' and 'completing the activity', but we rarely think of the value of creativity. In fact many might view creativity as irrelevant within a research project, but, as Peters (2003) emphasises, 'creativity' is something that generates value to any project. In other words it is what makes writing an extended study very special.

Sometimes it is difficult to develop ideas for a research project and there may be many occasions when you need to think creatively. This involves either working on your own or using a group of people to generate, list, develop and refine ideas. All answers, no matter how extreme, should be recorded and listed in this process. The range of options or ideas is then pared down to those that are most appropriate. A suggested form of activity is 'Mindstorming' which was originally develop by Alex Osborn in the 1930s (Goldenburg and Mazurskey, 2002). Osborn's approach was quite simply based upon two principles:

a) *deferred judgement* – sometimes in a meeting we need to suspend judgement and say what we think in terms of our own ideas;

b) *quantity breeds quality* – the best way to find a good idea is to have lots of ideas, each of which can then be further developed and refined.

Such a process involves suspending the normal rules that you might have in a meeting. Instead different (sometimes outrageous) ideas are explored in order to lead into new avenues and other ideas. Ideas can be short, snappy and visual. Although sometimes considered a bit unscientific in research terms, this technique can be useful if followed by some library and/or Internet research. Sometimes outrageous or extreme ideas, followed by reading, can lead to a rational discussion which might then be used to lead a research project.

Managing, Monitoring and Evaluating Your Project in Action

As the project progresses you have to manage and evaluate it. Organisation, time management and communication are all likely to be important, as are you, in keeping yourself motivated. It will not be easy.

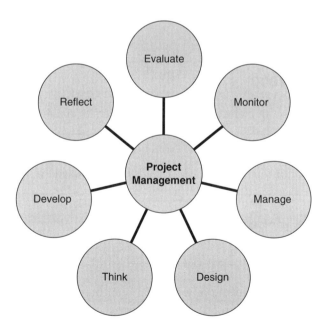

Figure 5.2 Essential project management skills

As writing a project, dissertation or thesis is a learning activity one distinct difficulty for the novice researcher is that the 'body of knowledge' may not be fully known to them

(Maylor, 2001). In fact the researcher may not possess a deep appreciation of the topic until the project has been finalised. So, alongside the process of learning how to research, the learner will also be conducting an investigation into an area about which they may know little. This is why research is a process of discovery.

It is important to note that the theoretical position you may take towards your research and the methodology you choose will dictate to some extent how the research project is to be managed, as set out in Chapters 2 and 4. Your research should, then, be seen as a project to be managed and this will require you to make decisions about knowledge, skills, tools, and techniques. Your research will have both a commencement and due date; however the manner in which you organise yourself within those parameters will be influenced by factors such as time and assessment requirements as well as the quality and scope of your dissertation. Since each research project is unique, as a manager of the process within the project you will need to acquire some generic organisational skills.

The management of a project encompasses the ability to formulate a plan, implement the plan, organise the information or knowledge the research yields then deploy data analysis skills, culminating in a written report on the findings. Some projects, such as a doctoral thesis, involve a Viva Voce (normally just called a 'viva') while others might include presentation to an identified audience. Supporting the researcher are the role of critical friends and, for degree course students, the academic supervisor. Support may take the form, for example, of referring the researcher to an appropriate course for the sorting and storing of data, references of literature and undertaking review of work.

Definition – Viva Voce

Derived from Latin, this is an oral examination for a university qualification.

Regardless of the scale of the research, what needs to be managed is:

- knowledge;
- the transfer of that knowledge;
- the process of gathering and communicating data in various forms; and
- dealing with technology.

Into this mix needs to be added the physical reality of other activities that might happen simultaneously within the research project. The more cerebral demands on your time spent in reflection and to draw conclusions, for example, is often an underestimated aspect of the process. The intrinsic pressure of wanting to achieve highly in view of career aspirations and managing yourself when, in what for some will be a steep learning curve, can all add to the stress of the imposed time limit. For the student researcher these are items to be discussed with your supervisor at regular meetings.

In order to manage yourself and your project, it is vitally important that you build some structural aspects into your plan which ensure success. These must take the form of identifiable benchmarks, milestones, deadlines and you must adhere to those expectations you have set for yourself. For the student researcher benchmarks such as completing and submitting an ethics application to conduct the research (see Chapter 3), seminar meetings and presenting your project will almost certainly be well defined by your university. Other milestones will have to be self-defined, such as data analysis and writing the first draft. While it is advisable to be flexible, a fail-safe and self-imposed deadline should be scheduled in place from the outset.

It is possible to link this listing stage with some of the other project tools that you may use, many of which you may have come across before and some of which we outline below. Sequencing a variety of stages in order to meet project goals and objectives is said to be meeting milestones. A milestone is a key checkpoint in a project. It describes what needs to be completed by a particular stage and before some other activity could be undertaken. Before starting to explore methodological issues for example, the major part of a literature review should be completed. Then, before collecting data, it would be important to complete the methodological discussion and then to write and justify the methods. Milestones serve as short-term goals. As the researcher completes one milestone, they then gear themselves up to reach the next milestone.

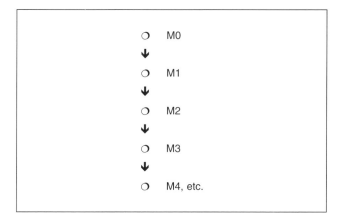

Figure 5.3 Milestones based upon dependencies

Activity

Identify the milestones for your project.

More difficult to plan for are the changes which may occur within the project resulting from literature searches and/or the data collection process. These unexpected results may lead to ambiguity which needs further analysis which will consume time. Data received may also lead to another round of interviews and/or surveys; again this possibility must be considered when planning.

Accepting that there will be some aspects of your planning that you will be able to control and working on those will require self-discipline, but at the same time reduce stress. The fact that some aspects of the research need to be more fluid may increase stress levels. There are unknown aspects of the research such as what participants returned in the data collection phase, the analysis of unexpected data, the discovery of new readings that are difficult to anticipate. In these cases, therefore, research is about putting elements together in order to make some sense of a situation or a set of experiences. In order to answer the research question a less controlling approach to the evolution of knowledge may have to be applied. It will also be important to remember that undertaking new experiences as a researcher and developing new skills to conduct the research will lead to a developing knowledge about yourself.

Using Simple Project Planning Tools to Organise Your Research Project

Perhaps the starting point for any research project is to break the project down into a series of activities that need to be completed. By breaking a project down, it is possible to identify what needs to be completed first and make it easier to see how work overlaps or how some activities influence the timing of others. Effectively, listing is the start of the process of trying to work out a way to meet your research objectives. In other words, 'this is what we want to do and we have set out our objectives'. From this it is possible to work out every activity or event in which you will have to engage in order to make sure that the research project is completed.

Listing helps you to:

1. identify the timings of the activities necessary for the project to be completed;
2. find out the various stages and activities within a project;
3. put the various stages and activities into a logical order;
4. schedule events;
5. discover what tasks are necessary in order to complete the project;
6. group activities together into a sequence of events;
7. think about resource requirements for the project (such as contacting people, finance, equipment, etc.);
8. create a series of events that can then be monitored.

Activity

Create a list of activities that you need to undertake to complete for your research project. As you do so, identify the timings for each of the activities as well as the sequence in which some of them need to be undertaken.

To help you with your planning we will now provide you with information about tools you can use. These are:

- SWOT Analysis
- Spreadsheets
- Force Field Analysis
- Network Analysis
- Critical Path Analysis

One way of examining the relationship between a research project and its environment is to carry out a *SWOT analysis*. A SWOT analysis sets out to focus upon the Strengths, Weaknesses, Opportunities and Threats facing a project at a given moment. It includes both an *internal* and an *external element*. The internal element looks at current strengths and weaknesses of the project. The external element looks at the opportunities and threats present in the environment in which a project takes place. It might be possible to undertake a SWOT analysis for your research ideas and proposals.

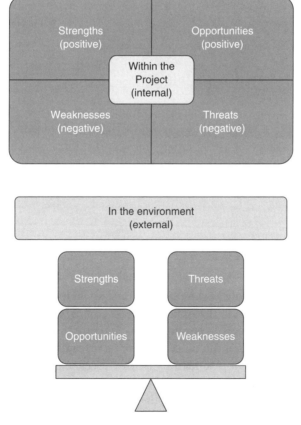

Figure 5.4 SWOT Analysis

Carrying out a SWOT analysis requires research into a project's current and future position. The analysis is used to match a project's strengths and weaknesses with the external forces in the environment. By undertaking a SWOT analysis it is possible to develop approaches that build upon the strengths of the research project, minimise its weaknesses, seize its opportunities and take measures that will cancel out or minimise threats. The SWOT is thus sometimes called 'the planning balance sheet'.

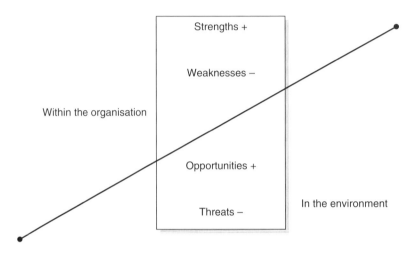

Figure 5.5   SWOT Analysis: The Planning Balance Sheet

A simple Internet search will provide you with much more information on how to use a SWOT analysis and a range of tools that are freely available.

Activity

Create a SWOT analysis for your project proposal.

Force field analysis is a simple technique designed to help project planners with their decisions and presents you with the opportunity to compare the positive features of your proposed project with the possible negative ones. The task thus simply involves identifying the forces that would influence the outcomes from a research project. To carry out a force field analysis the starting point is to identify all the forces that are positive and would help towards supporting the completion of the dissertation and to then identify all the negative forces which are working against achieving the goal. For example, see Table 5.3:

Table 5.3 Identifying forces

Positive forces might be:	Negative forces might be:
Interesting project that relates well to the ambitions and background of the researcher.	There could be ethical issues that could limit the nature and type of primary research undertaken.
There are some unique elements of the project that make it up-to-date as a research project, as well as being capable of generating new knowledge.	The project is unusual and it might be difficult to create an appropriate fit with the literature.
The research is potentially practical and is capable of generating some interesting primary data.	Collecting some of the primary data could be costly.
The project is creative and appropriate for the context of the school environment.	The research project is a little too narrow.

Having identified these positive and negative forces, the next step is to provide a score from 1 to 5 against all of these, allocating 1 as weak and 5 as strong. So, as in Table 5.4, you might get:

Table 5.4 Scoring forces

Positive forces might be:	Negative forces might be:
Interesting project that relates well to the ambitions and background of the researcher. Score = **4**	There could be ethical issues that could limit the nature and type of primary research undertaken. Score = **5**
There are some unique elements of the project that make it up-to-date as a research project, as well as being capable of generating new knowledge. Score = **3**	The project is unusual and it might be difficult to create an appropriate fit with the literature. Score = **4**
The research is potentially practical and is capable of generating some interesting primary data. Score = **3**	Collecting some of the primary data could be costly. Score = **4**
The project is creative and appropriate for the context of the school environment. Score = **2**	The research project is a little too narrow. Score = **1**

So overall, the positive forces for the research project are 12 and the negative forces are 14. The strategy would then be to reduce the strength of the forces against the project and to increase the strength of the forces for the project. So, you could try reducing the costs of collecting the primary data, change the research aims to minimise the ethical issues, spend a long time trying to sort out the fit with the literature and so on until the 14–12 against is reduced and the balance is then swung so that the positive forces for the project outweigh the negative forces against it.

When co-ordinating a project, it is useful to map out the tasks which must be carried out and perform them in a planned sequence. For example, in building a house, the walls are assembled before the roof is put on! These sequences of events can be linked diagrammatically:

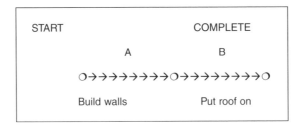

Figure 5.6 Network sequence

However, in many cases activities do not have to take place in sequence; they can be carried out simultaneously. For example, in making a cake, the icing might be prepared at the same time as the cake is baking. *Network analysis* can be used to map the programme of activities in a way that aids project planning.

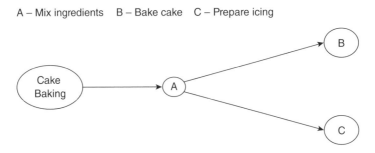

Figure 5.7 Identifying the alternative routes

Critical path analysis is a technique that builds upon network analysis as a tool to help planning. The critical path is the sequence or activities that are crucial because delays to them will delay the project as a whole. Once the critical path has been identified it becomes possible to keep an eye on the sequence of activities to ensure that tasks are completed on time. If problems arise it may be necessary to plough extra resources into maintaining this critical path. The critical path for a research project might start with the literature review, and then be followed by the methodology. As you begin to undertake the methodology you may be in contact with schools or undergoing a preliminary placement at the same time as creating and piloting materials to use for the research.

Case Study

Jessica

The methodological approach that I used within my educational research project was a phenomenological approach, as I used case studies, interviews and focus groups; ethnography research underpinned it as I had worked within the setting and had personal experience of the culture. This was due to the data collected from these methods being more true and beneficial to my overall approach. The purpose of this was to obtain rich and subjective data generated within the participants' natural setting and maintain an open-minded attitude to foresee specific areas within my investigated environment. This mixed methodology therefore allowed me to overcome potential bias and sterility, allowing the research to be generalised from one setting to another.

To conduct the research the main attribute that was necessary for me was perseverance and analysis. Subsequently, motivation and an extensive bank of intellectual skills developed my independence, enabling me to remain organised. Throughout, my commitments were managed alongside my research so that I could ensure that all of my arrangements were met. This was not always easy and at times work suffered due to me needing time off to complete my research and finalise the data collected. Accordingly, I met all deadlines ensuring research was completed to the utmost of my ability. Finally, being open-minded ensured that I followed the flow of my participants ensuring that all research was true which therefore allowed me to manage myself in the development of the study.

I created a critical path analysis to identify the scheme of the project and as a result of this, created a timetable which was agreed between myself and the professional to maintain an academic stance throughout. The timetable allowed me to identify where I held other responsibilities, which identified days and time in which I was able to conduct my research.

Jessica mentions a 'critical path analysis' as well as a negotiated timetable as being tools with which she was able to manage the research project. The advantage of using these tools is that it allows for the practical and realistic eventualities of 'real-life' incidents taking place over the duration of the research project. Her negotiations with her supervisor and the professionals with whom she worked offered her a realistic view of what was required to be achieved in the time frame.

Activity

List all of the activities associated with your project. Attempt to place them within a network diagram. As you do so think about those that are more likely to determine the critical path of the project. Attempt a critical path analysis, albeit a simple one.

Identifiable Stages of the Research Project

There is a generally accepted order in which your research will be completed. Of course the methodological approach used will define the particular steps the researcher must make to complete a project; however, the table below is a simplified version which sets out some of the major stages to use when creating a research plan.

Table 5.5 Potential phases of a research project

Stages of the research	Description of the tasks involved and considerations to be made in the stage
Groundwork	Define a research area and consider the question 'Is this project "do-able" in relation to time, scope and resources?' This stage may include administration of paperwork, an ethics application and/or establishing a research site and possibly defining a target group.
Literature review	This involves wide reading around the knowledge base. The researcher would have to consider what is new and original about the ideas and try to link the literature to the hypothesis or research question (see Chapter 4 for further guidance). It is advisable to consider using a software application to track notes and references. (See Chapter 14 for more guidance.)
Methodology	The researcher has to decide which methodology best suits the hypothesis of the research question and also look at the methods used to collect the data.
Data collection	The researcher will conduct a cycle of data collection as prescribed by the methodology to be used. They would have to consider the needs of the participants with regard to age, ability, time and the impact the research process will have on them. A second cycle of data collection may be required.
Progress seminar or doctoral confirmation/ upgrade	Sometimes there is a progress seminar or formal confirmation/upgrade for doctoral theses. Preparation will include: a firm knowledge of the major strands through the literature on the topic, a justification for the methods used, a summary of the data with some analysis of the returns and a schedule for future work.
Data analysis	Dependent on the nature of the research, a software application may be used to aid with the analysis of data (see Chapters 10 and 12 for more guidance). However, a thorough knowledge of the particulars of the participants and their responses will be required for some methods.
Writing the first draft	Conform to the referencing requirements and assessment guidelines provided in your course handbook. Also review the dissertations and theses contained within the faculty or at the University library in order to observe the layout, style and chapter structure of such a text.
Redrafting	Use comments from a critical friend, supervisors, colleagues and proof-readers to make the necessary changes to your work so that the writing is clear, the ideas are cohesive and the reader is given indications where your argument is headed. Consider how you use your data as evidence to prove your points.
Final seminar or mock viva	If there is a final seminar or mock viva, submit your draft dissertation/thesis to the supervisor in plenty of time for them to review it well. Prepare a presentation on the findings of the research and how this relates to the research question.
Write the final draft	Incorporate suggestions, contributions and corrections offered in the final stages. Also begin to consider how chapters or certain sections may be rewritten to suit submission to possible journals for publication or conferences where a paper based on your work could be presented.
Submission due	Leave plenty of time to thoroughly check the document, ask faculty staff about printing requirements and conventions, contact the printers and submit.

Managing and Monitoring the Research Project

Once the research project starts it needs to be managed and monitored. Depending upon the time scale, you may need to think about setting yourself deadlines to coincide with the lists you have made for your milestones or critical path. Even the best plans can go wrong, which is why you need to monitor the project and be aware of anything that has the potential to influence your deadlines. Monitoring the project involves carefully matching the progress you are making to your research objectives. It also involves looking at and assessing the quality of your outputs. Sometimes it is useful to look at your work with 'fresh eyes' by coming back to it at a later date.

A research project may offer the first opportunity to interview and/or survey the opinions, ideas, experiences and knowledge of others. As such, special consideration needs to be given to the planning, conducting and catering for an individual or a group of research participants. The decision to survey via an online mode which perhaps uses a Likert scale (Likert, 1932) or to devise a series of structured or semi-structured questions will depend on your methodology and your research questions. Once the decision has been taken as to the style and type of data to be collected, the selection of participants is vitally important (see Chapter 11 for more guidance). Considerations for triangulating the data may mean that interviews will take place, for instance with a teenage patient, the assigned physician, a related health care professional such as an Occupational Therapist and the parent should the patient be under 18 years of age. The opinions taken from this group of stakeholders offer a holistic view of the nature of the situation and therefore each voice must be represented in the analysis and checked for reliability; the findings are to be written in the final draft.

Practical Tips

- Think about the purpose of your project and how this is reflected upon through your research question.
- Assess the relevance of the literature review to the hypothesis/research question.
- In research terms, think about the feasibility of your primary research and relate this to your time lines.
- Think about the accuracy of the data that you are likely to collect as well as the suitability of the venue you select for collecting the data.
- Relate everything that you do to the assessment requirements.

The data collection phase is one aspect of the process which will need to be carefully planned and controlled. Major tasks involved in this phase will probably be the writing of a series of structured or semi-structured interview or survey questions. There will be tension between avoiding bias or projected answers and the need to ask enough open questions to stay on the topic which will then provide information with which to answer the research questions. You can find more guidance on this in Chapter 9.

Similarly you will have to give attention to how you manage your relationships with participants. When planning to interview participants, for example, consider how this may impact on their time or whether the recounting of their experiences may trigger unpleasant memories and potentially cause psychological harm. Practical and logistical aspects of interviews range from deciding on a venue to how the information will be recorded, and these will need to be organised well in advance. Participants should be advised of how long the process will take and how to get to the venue. Should the research involve an online response, ensure that participants have access to reliable technology and that you are close to the computer room to trouble-shoot when necessary. If the interview is to be recorded, protocols regarding privacy, storage, transcriptions and intellectual property must be devised, discussed and followed. Simple aspects of 'hospitality', such as good lighting, ventilation, privacy, time between participant interviews, drinking water, and enough seating should all be considered and are aspects of the research which can be planned for and controlled. Further guidance on issues such as this can be found in Chapters 3, 9 and 11.

Case Study

Lauren

I took a child-centred methodological approach under the phenomenological paradigm. This involved data collection from semi-structured interviews with six children. I also incorporated photos and a ranking task into the interviews to make the process more child-friendly and see whether the findings from the tasks were reiterated/backed up by what they said during interview. Due to the nature of my question I also gained data from semi-structured interviews with two parent volunteers at the same school.

The biggest contributing factor in managing my research project has probably been living in the library (not quite but almost). It is only two minutes down the road, which has been very handy. I find the library is the only place I can sit down and feel productive and actually get something written or finished.

Since starting the research project I have attempted to continuously work on it, chipping away bit by bit (even if it was finding a journal and taking notes to include), just so I felt like I was always making progress. Luckily I have very few other commitments, so the majority of my time has been prioritised for my studies (my parents would say too much).

I do feel like I have lost my work/life balance during the past five months. But that is how I tend to approach things: all or nothing. This way, I have managed to stay on top of all my work to a standard I am happy with and knowing I can have my life back once it is finished. However, should I do it all over again this is something I would definitely want to change.

My main commitment has been working in a primary school one day a week, and I even found myself using my lunch time there to revise or read and note take for upcoming assignments. My other assignments have been fitted in around my research project, doing the majority of the background research in the evenings and then taking two weeks out at Easter from my dissertation to focus on completing the bulk of them. I did anticipate this would be hard as I usually struggle to divert focus from one piece of work to another knowing it is not finished. But they were actually a welcome distraction and knowing they are finished allows me to revert all attention back to the completion of my dissertation.

I really don't tend to plan, as I usually find myself disappointed when things don't go to plan. I have a diary and calendar which I couldn't live without. I made myself a work calendar which only featured Uni deadlines, meetings etc. This way I also set out days when I would work on various pieces/sections of work with estimated completion dates written in as well. But I followed this quite loosely and used it more for peace of mind knowing I had enough time to complete everything.

I make a lot of lists with things that need to be done and when, and get great pleasure in ticking them off.

Lauren's experiences indicate a determined and positive approach to her research. Knowing yourself as a learner, that is the strengths and weaknesses of your study behaviours, will assist you when conducting your project. Lauren's reliance on a diary, lists and calendar system are easy and simple planning tools which worked well to propel her closer to her targets. This honest account of her experiences reveals that researchers do what is necessary, and that may be placing a personal life in the background for the duration of the project. Lauren's experiences as a researcher have changed her; the comment 'However, should I do it all over again this is something I would definitely want to change.' indicates that she now has greater expertise and would be able to incorporate study into her life with greater ease. Possessing new skills, Lauren could now streamline certain aspects of the research process.

Key Points to Remember

- Constructing a research project is a very personal thing. We all have strengths and weaknesses. Think about how you can make the most of your strengths and minimise your weaknesses as you construct your research project.
- Make a list of the things that you need to complete in order to meet your assessment requirements and complete your project. Add some timings to this list and then work out your milestones, and possibly move this forward with a network or critical path analysis. If necessary use a spreadsheet to help yourself with this. Use this document to monitor and manage your progress.
- Things sometimes go wrong. As long as you are monitoring and managing your project, when things do not happen as you expect, simply alter or change your plan.

Further Reading

This is a helpful book for beginners in research:

Bell, J. (2010) *Doing Your Research Project: A Guide for First-time Researchers in Education, Health and Social Sciences* (5/E). Buckingham: Open University Press.

The following two books can help you further your understanding on methodologies which are key to managing your project:

Clough, P. and Nutbrown, C. (2012) *A Student's Guide to Methodology* (3/E). London: SAGE.
Rosenau, M.D. and Githens, G.D. (2005) *Successful Project Management: A Step-By-Step Approach with Practical Examples* (4/E). Hoboken, NJ: John Wiley & Sons.

References

Bruce, A. and Langdon, K. (2000) *Project Management*. London: Dorling Kindersley.
Burns, T. and Sinfield, S. (2008) *Essential Study Skills: The Complete Guide to Success at University* (2/E). London: SAGE.
Carmona, M. and Sieh, L. (2004) *Measuring Quality in Planning: Managing the Performance Process*. Abingdon: Spon Press.
Goldenburg, J. and Mazurskey, D. (2002) *Creativity in Product Innovation*. Cambridge: Cambridge University Press.
Likert, R. (1932) 'A technique for the measurement of attitudes', *Archives of Psychology*, 140(55).
Maylor, H. (2001) 'Beyond the Gantt chart: Project management moving on', *European Management Journal*, 19(1): 92–100.
McKenney, S. and Reeves, T.C. (2012) *Conducting Educational Design Research*. Abingdon: Routledge.
O'Leary, Z. (2010) *The Essential Guide to Doing Research* (5/E). London: SAGE.
Peters, T. (2003) *Reimagine! Business Excellence in a Disruptive Age*. London: Dorling Kindersley.
Richman, L. (2012) *Improving your Project Management Skills* (2/E). New York: American Management Association.

For additional online resources please visit the book's website:
https://study.sagepub.com/needhamandpalaiologou

6

WRITING THE PROPOSAL
KRISHAN SOOD

Chapter Aims and Objectives

This chapter aims to help you to:

- understand what a research proposal is and its importance;
- develop your skills in writing a research proposal;
- explore the different ways of writing a research proposal;
- examine some examples of research proposals so you can reflect on what is good practice.

Introduction

As part of the research process, you have to write the proposal, which this chapter is about. As mentioned in Chapters 1 and 4, research means finding out about things. Sometimes we call it enquiry or investigation or project as it involves writing the proposal, the actual research plan. Like a good business plan, you will be asked to write a proposal outlining why you want a bank, for example, to lend you money. The art is in giving as much convincing detail as possible in easy-to-follow steps that will make the bank manager give you the loan. You have to make the plan foolproof and this means that it has to be rigorous, and in academic language, to have emerged from the literature. To this extent your job is like that of a detective, to use as much evidence as possible to give shape and direction to these efforts.

There are different ways to write a proposal as part of your research process. Some researchers like to write their proposal in a linear, logical and step-by-step way. This means you have to use what is known as a deductive research methodology, linked to positivist paradigms (see Chapter 2) and often use quantitative approaches to data (see Chapters 11 and 12). Another approach is to have a more fluid and intuitive approach to your writing.

This is known as an inductive research methodology (see Chapters 2 and 9), often associated with interpretivist and postmodern paradigms, and frequently using qualitative approaches to data (see Chapters 9 and 10). You should not be alarmed by the terminology, however, as this has been explained in previous chapters of this book.

Let me start with the end in mind so that you are familiar with my thinking with regards how to write the proposal. Whatever approach you take, you will need to complete some or all of the following steps. What I suggest (by using a template that I have successfully used with my students) is that you are more likely to generate research writing that is 'informative, ethical, meaningful, persuasive and significant' (MacNaughton et al., 2010: 14). Each of these terms will be addressed throughout this book, so please read Chapters 2, 3 and 4 carefully as they form part of the integral approach to writing the proposal. For example, ethical research is based on informed consent, does not harm participants, attempts to benefit them and makes a positive contribution to knowledge and to the broader social good (see Chapter 3). The best quality cake, for example, is a mix of different ingredients carefully balanced and baked to perfection, as is a well written proposal.

An imaginative proposal is innovative and original and captures the imagination and taste buds of the reader! But take heed, we all had to start somewhere and learn from our mistakes until one day your peers judge your work to be worthy of publication. You will learn from others, get feedback from your peers, tutors and fellow students which will benefit from you bringing your creative skills to the fore when you undertake writing your proposal. As a budding or experienced researcher, it is important to remember that we all suffer the pain and frustration when we are on a quest for new knowledge or even to make sense of existing knowledge. Of greater importance perhaps, you will have an accurate record of a unique piece of purposeful research which you yourself have undertaken and documented.

The key elements of a research proposal

- Proposed title
- Provisional research questions (normally three or four)
- Key concepts on which your research proposal will draw
- Research approach
- Data collection tools and sampling
- Proposed method(s) of data analysis
- Ethics statement

(adapted from Student Handbook, University of Leicester, 2012)

Before I describe in some detail the above stages, which are fixed, linear and limiting as a research model, let me pose another research model which can be useful in developing the writing process. This is the *research spiral* which offers a more flexible, dynamic and fluid approach compared to a static model. The stages involved in the spiral are:

- choosing a topic;
- thinking about methods;
- reading for research;
- collecting data;
- data analysis;
- writing up; and
- then back to choosing a topic.

The beauty of this model is that the researcher can enter into the spiral at almost any point. I suggest you go to the original source of the spiral model to be self-critical of your own design and execution (Blaxter et al., 1996: 10).

In this self-repeating research spiral, we move away from a fixed process allowing for more flexible and open ways of thinking about the writing process. With this model, the process becomes open to change as you progress with your writing. For example, you develop your focus of research by reading around the topic, which should permeate every stage of this spiral process. At other times a piece of evidence may emerge from your observation of what a child has said, or some piece of writing that you have seen during your observations. These experiences may lead you to read and ask different and amended research questions. In these ways the spiral research model is useful because it can be entered at almost any point and helps you to remain open-minded about your writing process. As you develop your knowledge and understanding of the topic of interest that you are writing about, consider how each approach of the spiral process relates and how it might change the view and development of your research writing. Remember, thousands of articles, dissertations and theses are written and published. Yours is yet another one that advances the knowledge boundary a bit further. Don't think you will change the world overnight, as you will surely be disappointed. Treat your writing as a good modest contribution as well as being one of the most significant steps in your own education.

Academic Writing

Academic writing is riddled with anxiety as it is the most difficult part of doing research. We all have different rituals and ways to write. I think as the writing process is so private, you feel that by writing your thoughts out for everyone to read and judge will expose you. Even the experienced author goes through the same anxiety and this apprehension is natural. So the first step is to start writing, although that is easier said than done. So, draft a short piece and get help from your peers and from experienced people. What happens is that through much drafting and redrafting along the way all your hard work becomes excellent prose for all to read.

It is conveying the precise meaning that you wish to convey that is the hardest task in academic writing. Anderson (1993: 90) wrote that, 'unlike journalistic writing, academic writing is clear and orderly … there are no surprises … there is no climax … the reader should know what the paper is about from the first sentence'. So a conservative and measured account is often what is needed. Whilst this may seem restrictive it is probably wise to stick to this advice.

How to Write the Proposal

In writing the proposal 'what do I want to find out' and 'why' should be two bits of information that should be relayed to the audience. It is common sense and good practice to start with an outline. This is an overall plan of your journey, your ideas, your thoughts and stream of consciousness which provides a skeleton plan for your work. This is the pre-draft stage. The outline stage helps you to organise your ideas in a logical, clear way.

A good outline plan is made up of a single paragraph or two and forms the building blocks of prose. Use technical words only if they convey the meaning you want them to. Using an active voice is better than a passive one. For example, 'The teachers completed the questionnaire' rather than 'The questionnaires were completed by the teachers'. By looking at other people's writing, you will soon learn to use a variety of sentence structure patterns, which you can vary to construct a tight meaning.

Activity

Like a good photographic presentation where the pictures you show first are to capture people's attention, ask yourself what will be the order of presentation? How will you know if the audience is still with you? Apply this scenario to your writing.

What this scenario shows is that it is only after doing the presentation, or writing it first time, and getting feedback on it, that you will make improvements. Thus, the secret of good writing is to draft and redraft. Like good finished brickwork or painting or a ceramic vase, you only see the smooth and contoured object as the end (pretty) object. Another approach to writing the proposal is to re-read it after leaving it aside for a while. Some suggest re-reading it aloud as this tends to show up obvious mistakes. Ultimately, you have to be brave, and let a critical friend have a look to offer a useful and constructive feedback.

There are various sections that can be utilised when writing the proposal. This depends on what you are trying to convey. Whatever the convention used by you, follow it throughout the writing process. Let us work our way through an example.

Proposed Title

An outline is a skeleton plan and will include the title, descriptors for your literature search, your intended methodology and the deadlines you need to set to complete the preparation and fieldwork. You will only be able to construct the outline once you have done some supplementary reading in your area of interest, together with some reading about the sorts of methods for data gathering which are available to you. So the title gives a clear indication of the topic to be addressed. A good critical friend or small group discussion is sometimes helpful in deciding an appropriate title.

I gave the titles in the next activity box (below) to a group of postgraduate students and asked them to decide if they were do-able in the time frame normally allowed for their degree. But before they worked in small groups to dissect them, I gave them Bassey's (1999: 38) definition of what research is:

> Research is systematic, critical and self-critical enquiry which aims to contribute to the achievement of knowledge (and practice).

Although the definition is that of research, its words can be applied to developing the title. I asked the students to look at these titles and apply the three 'criteria' from the definition provide by Bassey (1999). I asked them, 'is the title too big or too small; too complex or too simplistic' and 'how would they modify it to take account of the criteria?' If they were taking a feminist perspective, what would they do? If they were looking at cross-cultural differences, what would their take be on these questions? If they were working towards justice, fairness and openness, what would their stance be? If they were to turn them into a research question that can be investigated, what would they do first, what questions would they ask and how would they go about investigating each? Getting the titles in to some kind of a shape for enquiry was the main task.

Activity

In small groups discuss: What makes a good research question, and therefore, a good title?

1. Are children's examination results related to the size of their school?
2. Is there life on Jupiter?
3. What happens inside black holes?
4. Are computer games good for children's mental health?
5. Do people in love gaze into each other's eyes more than people without a romantic attachment?

These questions generated lively discussions. With comments like:

For title 5 – 'what a stupid question!'

For title 3 – 'where do we start?'

For title 4 – 'this has huge scope to develop', 'what computer games exactly?', 'what does it mean by mental health?', 'how do we measure....?'

By the end of the session, there was a common understanding amongst the group of the need to focus the question into a meaningful, realistic title that could be made into a good research project. The need for objective evidence far outweighed the need for subjectivity and anecdotal evidence. They also suggested avoiding the use of emotive or emotional language in answering the questions, and here, the need for arguments requiring underpinning with theories was essential.

Provisional Research Questions (normally three or four)

This topic is also addressed in Chapter 4 of this book, so please read it alongside this chapter. First, however, let us just rehearse one or two key points about writing the provisional research questions. They are provisional because you may still be thinking about the topic, reading a bit more about the area of research or methodology or looking at current government policy on it. This takes time to reflect upon and make sense of, so it is a crucial first step in devising meaningful and clear research questions. In the end, these research questions must be of realistic size (i.e. possible to complete in the time frame that researchers normally have). They need to be tied closely to the title and aims of the research and you should start looking at a working title, no matter how 'large' and 'cumbersome' and 'challenging' it first appears. Through mind-mapping and using other learning tools, start to develop a line of thought/consciousness that develops the final working title. Along this investigation, you will discover what to discard and what is not possible in the time scale. So the end product is a distillation of a lot of thought, discussion and reflection. It takes time, but it is worth spending valuable time doing this activity.

Let us look at one example of how one student undertook the development of a title and research questions through email contacts.

Case Study

Julie (anonymised name) is headteacher of an international school abroad. She emailed me with a working title and aims of the project that she wished to do. She wrote:

> My initial thoughts were based around an initiative that our school's group has implemented, entitled High Performance Learning (HPL), which would have been based on leading this implementation into my school. This is what much of my reading had been based around, until I felt that in order to implement HPL, I would need to create a professional learning community at my school. I began looking at how this could be done by developing Action Learning Sets within the school.

I have since attended a Senior Leadership Programme led by our school's group, which included the positioning of our school in the local market. This is after all a key issue for us since we are fee paying, for profit and have competition in the local area. It also comes at a time when my school specifically is at a point when we are re-establishing its identity. My thoughts are that before I can introduce High Performance Learning to my staff, but before I can establish PLC into school, we need to go back to basics and establish who we are as a school, who people think we are and what makes us special/what can we do to make us stand out from all those 'similar' schools in the locale. This would then drive all those other areas. I have therefore taken several steps back to where I first began, but feel I wouldn't do justice to those other topics as I need a firm foundation on which to build – a strong, clear vision and mission.

Then through several email communications, Julie decided on her proposed title and subsequent research questions, but she also added the background information about the school setting. This contextual background is very helpful to make the reader aware of the situation and setting where the study will be conducted. Her proposed title was:

Getting the Message Across: Leading the Development of an Effective External Marketing Strategy Which Promotes the Unique Selling Point of Jairung International School *(anonymised name).*

Her provisional research questions were:

1. To evaluate existing research conducted with interested external parties with regard to school choice in city B.
2. To understand how Jairung International School is currently meeting the needs of parents with regard to the priorities identified from existing research and how this is externally marketed.
3. To develop a systematic and coherent marketing strategy which promotes the unique selling point of Jairung International School to interested external parties.

You will see from the title and the research questions posed that there has been much thinking and reflection to get to this point. The title, with its first part before the colon, suggests to the reader what the main aim is of the research. The part after the colon suggests how this will happen at the school being investigated. Maybe you can think of a title in this format. Some researchers think that the title should be short and to the point, others think that it should be fuller. Whatever the choice, its meaning should be clear at first glance.

One way to think about your title and its main aim is to imagine you are 'trapped' in a lift with your boss going up to the fifteenth floor. There is no escape! You want her permission to do the project, with maybe some funding to go with it or some time off to do quality research. You only have 30 seconds before the lift gets to the fifteenth floor. So make your case, make it punchy and convincing to get agreement.

Key Concepts on Which Your Research Proposal Will Draw

Julie's research proposal is based on management aspects of the school as she is head-teacher, concerned with looking at leadership and management concepts to improve school practice. Her main concepts were: leadership, management, school choice and marketing. Let us look at the term concept and conceptual framework. Anderson (1993: 46–47) identifies six types of knowledge:

- historical knowledge;
- axiological knowledge;
- theoretical and conceptual knowledge;
- prior research studies;
- reviews; and
- academic debates.

In focusing on theoretical and conceptual knowledge, for example, he indicates that this gives the structure within a particular field of inquiry and a skeleton to hang your ideas on. So when you look at prior knowledge you should see where appropriate theories and theoretical frameworks will help develop your ideas/topic.

Burton et al. (2008) also talk about the conceptual framework of a research study as a 'group of ideas, concepts and theoretical perspectives that give overall structure and coherence to a study' (2008: 37). Developing the conceptual framework will require discussions with fellow students, mentors, tutors and the emerging ideas from previous research findings that come from the literature. You will read in Chapter 7 about constructing the literature section. The aim of the literature section is to show that you have carefully looked at existing work in the field with insight and through a critical lens to make sense of what others in the field have found. In developing the conceptual framework, Burton et al. (2008: 39) offer a useful guide reproduced here:

- Compare and contrast different authors' views on an issue;
- Group authors who draw similar conclusions;
- Criticise aspects of methodology;
- Note areas in which authors are in disagreement;
- Highlight exemplary studies;
- Highlight gaps in research;
- Show how your study relates to the literature in general; and
- Conclude by summarising what the literature says.

Hartas (2010) summarises features of a 'good' literature review and she breaks down a critical literature review into four main steps.

1. Compare and contrast (here look at what people have said and what is similar or different);
2. Critical appraisal (here comment on the strength of the sources e.g. about the quality of research tool used or sample group and draw out the implications of differing ideas and views);

3. Analysis and synthesis (here comment on the first two stages and look at what are the agreements/disagreements and the implications and possible reasons for this);
4. Development of arguments (here summarise and draw out the implications).

Thomas (2013) offers some helpful tips on how to do your research project drawing on the idea of a design frame, an example of how to support and develop your research project. This is an important issue as having a good skeletal framework to your design proposal will make the proposal sound and fit for purpose. Giving dates and times to each stage of the proposal is a very good tip to develop as good time management will avoid undue stress at later stages.

When your initial conceptual ideas are completed, you should be familiar with key writings and research in your topic. You should know about the quantity and quality of this work, understand how this knowledge will shape your own research questions and you should now be able to refine your initial research questions (MacNaughton et al., 2010). This is what is known as a deductive approach. As new researchers, most have found this iterative process complex and unclear about what the term 'concepts' means. So consultation with a supervisor or research mentor may be invaluable at this point to get feedback on what is viable and what isn't. In summary, developing a clear understanding of the concepts is crucial, and through an iterative process, learning how to scaffold the later analytical framework.

Activity

How would you start developing your conceptual framework?

Key texts to be used – try to be as specific as possible at this stage

Julie used the following (only a few shown) array of texts using relevant books and journal articles, identified from other bibliographies, electronic databases, Google Scholar etc.

Bunnell, T. (2005) 'Strategic Marketing Planning in International Schools', *International Journal of Educational Management*, 19(1): 59–66.
Cohen, L., Manion, L. and Morrison, K. (2011) *Research Methods in Education* (7/E). Abingdon: Routledge.
Jennings, J.L. (2010) 'School choice or schools' choice? Managing in an era of accountability', *Sociology of Education*, 83(3): 227–247.
Li, C. and Hung, C. (2009) 'Marketing tactics and parents' loyalty: The mediating role of school image'. *Journal of Educational Administration*, 47(4): 477–489.
Mazzarol, T. (1998) 'Critical success factors for international education marketing', *International Journal of Educational Management*, 12(4): 163–175.

You can see from the list that the richness of your knowledge and understanding comes by trawling through a range of references. No one reference will suffice if you want to develop a critically reflective analysis. When you read, you are making meaning and connections with your own focus of study. Similarly, when you are writing the proposal, you are both authoring your own experience and deepening your understanding of others as you interpret ideas and develop a case for others to read, it is what Graue and Walsh (1998: 212) call 'shaping and contouring perspectives'.

Stake (1995: 123) gives us an example of how to organise a case study report, so please do have a look at that article. A case study report gives the reader examples of short dialogues, vignettes and fragments of interview as part of evidence. MacNaughton et al. (2010: 339–340) offer the following example which describes the 'feeling' of a place:

> The gate is accessible and invites us to enter. The wooden building has windows with curtains and, on the corner of the entrance, a round table decorated with flowers creates a home-like atmosphere. Wall panels, displaying carefully children's art work and texts, also present information for the parents. Some staff do the cleaning, others prepare the meal (smells of home-made food), and everyone is busy knowing what they are doing.

Vignette writing is an important process in providing evidence which gives the reader a mini-voice of a setting, a person or an event.

Activity

What are your plans for collecting different sources of information?

Research approach

This is Julie's approach to collecting the evidence, her methodology, and a sort of research story. Julie wrote that she will undertake action research, since:

I will be heavily involved in leading school improvement in this area and will have an influence on the outcome of the research. Existing research documentation will be analysed to inform the starting point of the research as well as background information pertaining to the group to which the school belongs. Background information of the vision and mission of the NAE group and how this is disseminated and put into practice within the schools in the group as our unique selling point. Analysis of research conducted by independent company 18 months ago, which was organised and arranged by the NAE group with regard to what dictates school choice for international families moving to/in City B. Further research by an independent group is due to be conducted within the dissertation timeline. An evaluation, through policy and procedure, of what Jairung International School currently provides in accordance with parental priorities for school choice as identified in the independent research and how this is currently marketed, through existing publications, DMP, events etc. A survey distributed to interested external parties to identify how implicit we are in conveying our unique selling point and how this can be further improved. Follow up interviews to be conducted with a sample of the surveyed group. Results of the survey and interviews, as well as evaluation of documentation used to inform the development of a systematic and coherent marketing strategy which promotes the unique selling points of Jairung International School.

Looking at the above example, you can see how important it is to reflect upon your personal story and situation and context. Good research will have your personality stamped on it and be deeply stimulating to you as well as of practical professional use. Personal enthusiasm and passionate interest for the topic will likely lead to the high levels of motivation needed to sustain your interest. We briefly turn next to some idea about methodology as a concept.

Methodology is about the principles and values, philosophies and ideologies that underpin your research (Clough and Nutbrown, 2002) and can be closely linked to the ideas explored in Chapter 2 on ontological, epistemological and axiological stances to be taken by the researcher.

Positionality is a term used to define and explain your role or position in your organisation. This may be, for example as a teacher, head of department, headteacher, SENCO or a doctoral student. Having an understanding about your positionality is helpful to the reader as they can visualise or contextualise where you stand in the research design and execution. It may have affected the relationship between researcher and participants and the research process, especially the kind of knowledge or understanding you are trying to produce. One can deliberate about positionality as offering you some advantage of having a close relationship with the respondents, or putting you in a trustworthy position, but it is actually about recognising the likelihood that you may have influenced the research outcomes. This can be positive or negative as it arguably allows you a greater possibility of prompting truthful answers to questionnaires and interviews and the research process.

The crucial point is that you need to have some firm grasp of your principles and values that will drive and inform your methodologies. An example cited in Roberts-Holmes (2014: 24–25) regarding child-centred and anti-racist methodologies illustrates this quite well, as reproduced below.

Katy's methodology

Katy's research project is closely connected to her social situation and hence is meaningful and important to her. Katy's research is motivated by her concern with issues of social justice for ethnic minority children in early years' settings. Her values and principles are a deeply held conviction about the injustice of racism, especially when directed towards children. Thus her methodologies underpinning the research are child-centred and anti-racist.

In writing about the process of data collection and sampling you need to be aware of a number of things. Firstly, describe clearly and concisely how you identified the potential sample group, known as the research sample or research population. At this point, the need to justify the choice of respondents has to be made. You can find out more about population samples in Chapter 11. At this stage you need to recognise a clear understanding has to be developed about the purpose of sampling from a larger population and justifying method. You will also need to demonstrate a critical awareness of potential ethical issues that need to be addressed and you can find guidance on this in Chapter 3.

I have mentioned that quite often research proposals and projects in education are small scale with data collection occurring over a short period of time. This means that either the sample size is likely to be small or few data collection methods are used to answer a research question. It is important to remember that 'small-scale studies are not smaller or less important versions of larger investigations' (MacNaughton et al., 2010: 210), so they too will need to be looked at critically.

Burton et al. (2008) make useful observations about two key issues prior to starting the data collection process. They are to do with 'gaining access to an organisation where evidence collection will happen and how to get through to "the gatekeeper"' (2008: 48–49). The gatekeeper is a powerful concept where entry into (and exit from) an organisation is strictly controlled and requires their permission to proceed. Gaining access means being very clear about who and where and when to approach the organisation. For those of you working in schools this will normally be the head teacher, but other gatekeepers appear in other educational settings. This means communicating as part of a covering letter or verbal introduction to the data collection. Cohen, Manion and Morrison, (2011: 339) offer a list of ideas about such letter writing. Here it is worthwhile sticking firmly to the ethical principle of informed consent (see Chapter 3) and forming 'trust-based relationships with gatekeepers and key informants' (Burton et al., 2008: 50).

Activity

Proposed method(s) of data analysis

Once the data collection process has been devised and organised, the next step of the research process is to look at how the data will be analysed. This requires use of the conceptual framework discussed earlier in this chapter. Julie undertook the following procedure:

Data from questionnaires will be analysed based on categorical responses and the frequency with which they occur. These will be expressed in table form. There will be some weaknesses that need to be considered with regards to the questionnaires – I will have no control in how many are completed and returned and whether these represent a balance of the external parties. Much of the documentation as well as the semi-structured interviews lends itself to qualitative data and initially is to be interpreted to gather an understanding of current practice and to provide information. In this instance, analysis will take place as the data is being collected and opinions will begin to be formulated.

Ethics statement

It is common practice to complete the ethics form/statement and get permission to proceed before embarking on a research project or developing your proposal. Ethical issues are addressed in Chapter 3, but an excellent free online source of information is the *Revised Ethical Guidelines for Educational Research* (2011) published by the British Education

Research Association (BERA). The key points to write about in the proposal are to ensure that ethical principles continuously permeate all aspects of research and that you reflect upon your responsibilities as an ethical researcher. This means being mindful and taking full care to ensure that before any participants give their informed consent and actually participate in research, 'they understand there is a *limit* to the anonymity and confidentiality that can be given to what they tell the researcher' (Roberts-Holmes, 2014: 50). Negotiating access with the gatekeepers to gain their consent and trust to carry out the research is an important part of writing. It is vital that gatekeepers, like headteachers, teachers, nursery managers or the parent, have all the relevant information about the research. In keeping with good practice and with the United Nations Convention on the Rights of the Child, the child needs to be asked to give consent, or 'assent' as it is known in these circumstances.. Roberts-Holmes (ibid.) notes that, wherever possible, you should gain informed consent from the children themselves. For students on degree courses this is an area to discuss with your supervisor to gain approval *before* undertaking any research, especially if any child protection issues arise.

In summary, the key ethical aspects to write about in your proposal are to demonstrate a strict adherence to ethical guidelines, clearly reported voluntary participation, informed consent (which means they have the right to determine what is in their own best interest) and the right to withdraw from the research without suffering any negative consequences (Burton et al., 2008: 56).

Summary

In this chapter I have argued that developing a proposal for your research project requires clarity and preparation regarding the scale, scope and your role as a researcher. This is a demanding first step, but worthwhile if you want to get some grip on the complex interactions of concepts, methodology and ethical issues. The crucial things to remember are 'what do I want to find out from my research before asking which method/methodology?' and 'how can I write a convincing story?' The focus is crucial and should arise from using theoretical perspectives to develop the research questions and help to determine data collection strategies. What you have to decide is which suits your interest, purposes and experience and then work methodically and systematically to develop a proposal. In considering your proposal don't forget to think about what is reasonable and manageable to do in the time available to you.

Activity

In writing the proposal, it is also important to undertake a time line of how the process will be managed. See if you can work out how much time will be allocated on your time line for data analysis; how much time will you allow for participant engagement and on background reading, for example?

Guidelines of Good Practice for Writing a Proposal

Here is a brief guide to get you started writing your proposal. This is one example of many that you will come across. Choose the one that fits the way you think and work best.

Good practice will describe the SETTING or CONTEXT of your study.
   You will need to:

- Describe the relevant features of the educational setting e.g. nursery, college, secondary/ primary school; number of staff; catchment area etc.;
- Explain your relationship with the setting;
- Draw attention to work reported in literature you may have read which would link theory to practice;
- Be aware of issues of confidentiality e.g. no setting or person should be mentioned by name.

Good practice will explain why the work is IMPORTANT for you:

- How will/did you benefit from carrying out this study?
- How will/did participants benefit from your work?
- What will/did the educational setting or other settings gain from this study?

Good practice will describe how you will/did IMPLEMENT your study:

- What new approaches and ideas will/did you use?
- What changes in practice will/did you hope to achieve?
- Who else was/will be involved?

Good practice will EVALUATE the IMPACT of your study:

- What did you find out and what was the impact of this activity on the quality of your own contribution to education?
- How are you measuring impact?
- How successful was this activity in promoting learning?
- What evidence was there to support your answer to the last question?
- Did this activity have any implications for other staff in this or other settings?
- Were you able to find additional information to support your work from books, journals, websites etc.?
- What questions came out of your study which may promote further Professional Development?
- What questions arose about ethical issues (if any)?

Good practice will SUMMARISE your study and suggest ways you can SHARE GOOD PRACTICE.

- What have you found out so far? (brief summary)
- If you were able to discuss this innovation with any other member of staff, what was their opinion?

- How will you share your ideas with others to improve teaching and learning?
- What potential value is there in your finding?

(Adapted from University College Plymouth St. Mark & St. John, 2010, personal communication)

A worked example of writing a research proposal

Planning the research proposal – the Positionality (who are you and what is your organisational context?)

Ruth Apple is Deputy Headteacher with a role as Assessment and Record Keeping Co-ordinator in a large urban primary school. She explores the idea of doing an investigation on record keeping with her supervisor because the headteacher feels it would be of use to the school, following an uncomplimentary link review the previous term, and would actively help Ruth in her job. Ruth has images of research proposal overload and wants something which helps with rather than adds to her workload. After discussion, the tutor and Ruth come up with the title:

'An analysis of how a whole-school policy on record-keeping may be developed and implemented in a large urban primary school'

The title reflects what Ruth wants and needs to do in school: analyse existing policy, devise appropriate management strategies for effectively developing a new whole-school policy and attempting to implement it.

Reviewing the Literature

If you are a student on a degree course, your initial meeting with your supervisor plus lecture notes, hand-outs and references will give you a good indication of where to start in terms of reading. The specific focus for your study will suggest key words or phrases (descriptors) which define and delimit the area you want to research; three or four descriptors should be enough.

Searching for what has been written about your area of study should be a systematic process. Most libraries now have online terminals to enable you to carry out catalogue enquiries. It is also worthwhile browsing the relevant periodicals on the shelves and online. General advice is for you to search systematically using key words which have been identified in your choice of title.

Ruth Apple began with 'primary schools', 'record keeping', and 'management'.

Having found appropriate literature you need to read it, keep records of what you have read, preferably using an index system, and organise your review in terms of major themes, issues and concepts. The written review should be an analysis of what has been written about the major areas of concern which affect your study. In your writing you will want to reflect these major themes using subheadings. Keeping careful notes about what you have read, together with distinctive quotations and references from relevant sources, should mean that writing the literature review section of the research proposal will be a question of simply expanding your notes and recording them in the recommended format and style.

> Ruth Apple found that the major themes related to the role of the co-ordinator, national and LA-level guidelines on record-keeping procedures, effective school-based curriculum development and the management of change. Because of what she intended doing in school, a large proportion of her notes was devoted to management approaches to planning for effective change.

Gathering Data: Which Approach?

Having conducted your literature review you should be in a position to state what data will need to be gathered for your particular research. You may need to take advice and guidance on small-scale research projects, dissertations and theses from your supervisor or critical friend.

Definitions – Case study and Action research

Case study: Given the limited time available, a case-study method offers you the opportunity to study a 'cross-section' of an organisation or other educational setting. You are focusing on a situation and attempting to analyse the various forces and influences which shape that situation. You are not attempting to generalise from the immediate environment, but are rather seeking an insight into why things have happened the way they have. In order to inform your study of events you will need to gather data from one or more sources to better explain the visible events.

Action research: This method begins with the problem or situation itself. The problem is first analysed in terms of possible management strategies, informed by theory. The research proposal becomes an analytical record of approaches taken and the effect on the original problem. Strategies are modified in the light of the effect they have on the problem. A feature of this method is that the process usually continues after the project, dissertation or thesis is complete. For the purposes of your research project an appropriate interim point is chosen which enables some evaluation of the chosen strategies to be carried out.

Ruth Apple was faced with the problem of needing to develop and implement a whole-school strategy in the light of a rather damning external review. Her reading suggested that effective change might best be promoted via a whole staff approach to the issue. She could, with the support of the headteacher, prepare a strategy for staff involvement and development based on a rational school-based curriculum development model drawn from the literature, adapted to suit her school situation.

Whichever approach you adopt, your proposal will need to record why you have chosen your approach in preference to others.

Gathering Data: Which Instruments?

Having decided upon a method the next stage is to choose the research instruments which best meet your needs. These also have to be considered and justified in terms of suitability and effectiveness. Your choice will be governed by considerations such as cost in terms of money and time, access to people and documents, the level of co-operation within the settings you investigate and, not least, the effect upon the setting of your 'stone-turning'. The essence of good research is that it is and is seen to be client-friendly. There are various instruments available to you such as the questionnaire, semi-structured interview, diaries, observation of meetings, policy documents. Discussion of each takes place elsewhere in this book.

Ruth Apple justified the use of Action Research as a method given the problematic nature of her study. She also considered that the most appropriate way to approach the problem was through a series of staff workshops, introduced and sponsored by the headteacher and led by herself. The data gathered for the purposes of the study included the existing school record-keeping policy and semi-structured interviews with the headteacher and two key stage co-ordinators on completion of the series of workshops.

Ruth would have like to have interviewed more teachers, recognising that there was some resistance to the initiative, but time constraints precluded this. The apparent limitations of her approach were made clear in her submission.

Presenting the Data

The data you present should be limited to that which has a direct bearing on your analysis. There is a temptation to present everything that you discovered in your research. Don't!! Try to present data in a clear and concise manner. Do not mix data presentation and data analysis.

Analysis of Data

Choosing which data to present is the first decision and you should only present the data which is most important or significant in terms of your enquiry. For the benefit of the reader you need to draw out those significant features and explain their importance. Your literature review should have identified the major themes related to your area of research, thus a second level of analysis is required. Your data should be examined in terms of those themes; in effect you are comparing your unique data to the existing body of theory and knowledge in your chosen topic. It is not enough to simply present the data, you have to place it in the context of the project as a whole and guide the reader through.

Conclusions

This section of the submission presents considerable problems for many students. Having introduced the proposed investigation, reviewed the literature, gathered, presented and analysed the data, there is a responsibility to draw the various sections together for the benefit of the reader. Here, there is an opportunity to make recommendations for future action based upon your research findings. The recommendations should be clear, realistic and specific.

Key Points to Remember

- Before you start your research proposal it is important to further your understanding of the key research terminology such as axiology, ontology, paradigms, the difference between various methodologies (see Chapter 2);
- Before you formulate your research ideas into a research proposal it is important to consider carefully the ethics of your project and make sure that there is no breach of ethical conduct with your sponsor or host university (see Chapter 3);
- Throughout this chapter by using several examples of real case studies, it has been demonstrated that a research proposal is important and needs to be constructed carefully;
- Remember that research has a purpose and this is to advance knowledge in the field you are planning to research so it is important to have examined the literature review before you formulate your research proposal.

Further Reading

Burton, N., Brundrett, M. and Jones, M. (2008) *Doing Your Education Research Project*. London: SAGE.
Roberts-Holmes, G. (2014) *Doing your Early Years Research Project* (3/E). London: SAGE.
Thomas, G. (2013) 'The Design Frame', Chapter 6 in *How to Do Your Research Project* (2/E). London: SAGE.

Useful Websites

- Researcher resources from British Education Research Association (BERA)
www.bera.ac.uk/researchers-resources/resources-for-researchers

A number of universities are publishing guidelines for research proposals so here are some good examples:

- The University of Sussex
www.sussex.ac.uk/ir/pgstudy/research_proposal

- The University of Glasgow
www.gla.ac.uk/colleges/arts/graduateschool/prospectivestudents/researchstudy/howtoapply/researchproposalssomegeneralguidelines

For students on degree courses please remember that each university might require different formats for the research proposal, so it is important to search the guidelines in your own university.

References

Anderson, G. (1993) *Fundamentals of Educational Research*. Hampshire: The Falmer Press.

Bassey, M. (1999) *Case Study in Educational Settings*. Buckingham: Open University Press.

Blaxter, L., Hughes, C. and Tight, M. (1996) *How to Research*. Buckingham: Open University Press.

British Education Research Association (2011) *Revised Ethical Guidelines for Educational Research*. Southwell: BERA.

Burton, N., Brundrett, M. and Jones, M. (2008) *Doing your Education Research Project*. London: SAGE.

Clough, P. and Nutbrown, C. (2002) *A Student's Guide to Methodology*. London: SAGE.

Cohen, L., Manion, L. and Morrison, K. (2011) *Research Methods in Education* (7/E). Abingdon: Routledge.

Graue, M.E. and Walsh, D. (1998) *Studying Children in Context: Theories, Methods and Ethics*. Thousand Oaks, CA: SAGE.

Hartas, D. (2010) 'Doing a Literature Review', in D. Hartas (ed.), *Educational Research and Inquiry: Qualitative and Quantitative Approaches*. London: Continuum.

MacNaughton, G., Rolfe, S. and Siraj-Blatchford, I. (2010) *Doing Early Childhood Research: International Perspectives on Theory & Practice*. Maidenhead: McGraw Hill and Open University Press.

Roberts-Holmes, G. (2014) *Doing Your Early Years Research Project* (3/E). London: Paul Chapman Publishing.

Stake, R. (1995) *The Art of Case Study Research*. London: SAGE.

Thomas, G. (2013) *How to Do Your Research Project* (2/E). London: SAGE.

For additional online resources please visit the book's website:
https://study.sagepub.com/needhamandpalaiologou

7

CONSTRUCTING THE LITERATURE SECTION

TINA BYROM

Chapter Aims and Objectives

This chapter aims to help you to:

- realise and provide the necessary thinking tools to assist you to write a literature section;
- develop a clear understanding on what a literature section is;
- begin structuring your literature section;
- deal with all the information you select;
- pull together all the information you have gathered from the relevant research on your topic.

Introduction

> The literature review [section] is one of the most important parts of any piece of academic writing. It is rather like the foundation upon which the rest of the work is built. Bricklayers never start building a house until a solid concrete foundation, with all the drainpipes, has been laid first. Once the foundation is laid, they can connect the rest of the house to it. In a similar way, all academic writing needs a base on which it can be fixed. (Oliver, 2012: 1)

The above quote emphasises the importance of the literature review/section to a piece of academic work as it frames, guides and provides direction for your entire study. When writing a literature section of a piece of work such as a dissertation there are a number of key things you need to think about. In the first instance you need to work out where you are at in terms of approaching the literature section itself. Students are sometimes fearful of writing the literature section saying such things like 'I feel out of my depth', 'I don't know where to start', 'I have no idea what I'm doing'. Whilst these feelings are understandable, writing the literature section of your dissertation or research project is an 'integral part of a research process' (Hartas, 2010: 96); it is simply the backbone of your work. It frames the study by presenting your reader with an idea of what your work will be about, what ideas already exist in the field and also what the essence of your argument will be. If you apply a systematic approach in dealing with literature, crafting the literature section of *your* dissertation or research project should be exciting and enjoyable as you uncover interesting ideas about a topic you are keen to explore.

It may be worth spending a few moments considering what a literature section is. The word 'review' is often used to describe a literature section, but this seems to be an inadequate term. Think about what you are doing with the ideas – you are doing more than reviewing them – you are using them to frame your own ideas and argument and preparing the foundations for your study (Hartas, 2010). The plethora of literature on literature reviews confirms that it is an active process. The language used in many texts (e.g. Hart, 1998; Machi and McEvoy, 2009) refer to 'doing', 'conducting', 'crafting', 'reviewing', 'critiquing', 'synthesising', 'surveying' and so on. In essence, when you are engaged with literature you are not passively working with it – you are actively picking it apart, working out its relevance to your own study and compiling your own argument from the synthesis work that you have completed. That is, through a systematic and active process, you are able to develop and present your academic voice through using the ideas of others whilst still assessing the value of those contributions. When you begin to think of the literature section in this way, it helps you to consider what it is not or what it should not be. It should not be:

- a list describing one piece of literature then another (descriptive);
- an opportunity for you to present everything you have read about your chosen topic (lack of direction and selection);
- based on dated sources that are not seminal texts (currency).

Fink identifies a literature section as being:

> A systematic, explicit and reproducible method for identifying, evaluating, and synthesising the existing body of completed and recorded work produced by researchers, scholars, and practitioners. (Fink, 2010: 3)

From this you can identify three clear stages involved when undertaking a literature section:

- identifying appropriate sources;
- evaluating and testing out their relevance to your work;
- synthesising information into a well-structured and coherent written argument.

The literature section can be summarised, therefore, as a piece of critical analysis which demonstrates your knowledge and understanding of the field within which you are studying. In that sense it has the following functions:

1. It illustrates where your work is located in relation to existing work in the field;
2. It frames your own argument;
3. It consolidates previous research into a structured piece of writing;
4. It helps to frame the research question.

It should be made clear at this point that a literature section should not be a place where you:

- answer your research question;
- get on a 'soap-box' and rant about your own views;
- write descriptively;
- produce a long list of what you have read about.

This chapter will provide a number of pointers for approaching literature which should help you avoid some of the pitfalls that can occur when putting a literature section together. It also offers some strategies which can help you manage the sources you may explore.

Where to Begin?

The first step is to think about the area you wish to explore. There is very little that has not been explored and you should see your work as adding to an existing body of knowledge (O'Leary, 2004; Burton et al., 2008). This thought should help you as you begin your search but also provide you with some comfort that you don't have to invent a new research area.

You also need to identify where you will draw your information from. The following are possible sources, although not an exhaustive list, from which you can gather information:

- article in a peer review journal
- article in a professional journal
- authored book
- chapter in an edited book
- textbook
- conference proceedings
- thesis or dissertation
- magazine or newspaper
- websites (but not Wikipedia, as it is not edited)
- official statistics

Thomas (2013) provides a useful summary of the relative benefits and pitfalls of various sources, particularly emphasising the issues involved with accessing non-peer reviewed sources. The use of electronic databases, whilst contributing to the ease of locating information (Burton et al., 2008) also presents some issues of which you need to be mindful. Ensure that you follow the appropriate referencing conventions for all sources, but in particular online sources, to ensure that you do not fall foul of academic misconduct/plagiarism (see Chapter 3 for more information).

Oliver (2012) advises the use of key terms in helping you identify sources for your work. Key words can be placed into search engines to help you identify the most appropriate sources for your chosen area, but you can also look at the list of references at the end of a source to see whether that could provide some useful sources for you (O'Leary, 2004). Once you have identified a particular source to use, you need to ask questions about the quality of the source you are using:

- Is this piece of literature based on a piece of research?
- Can I trust this source?
- What kind of research has been used?
- Was the study large or small scale?
- What is the research claiming – what conclusions are being made?
- Who has authored the work?
- Would the researcher have a vested interest in the results?

It may not be possible to answer all of the above questions, but they serve as a useful guide in helping you assess whether the literature you are exploring has any limitations that may impact on your own study. For example, in working out whether you can trust the source you may wish to find out whether the work has been peer-reviewed. Work that is peer-reviewed undergoes a rigorous process of being reviewed by other academics working in the field and may have been amended to reflect a detailed critique of it. Information from other sources may not have been through this process, however, so it is your job to weigh up the relative merits of the different types of sources you use.

To begin with you should have an idea of what area you would like to explore. You may have a research question, but this may still be in development. At this early stage, it does not really matter whether you have fully defined your question – you should be able to develop it further once you have read around your area in more depth. Let's look at Tricia's story:

Case Study

Tricia was interested in exploring the area of working-class students in schools. At the beginning of the process she was not entirely clear about the direction of her study but was intrigued by the idea that there seemed to be some differences in educational outcomes across middle and working-class young people. To help her refine the research question she looked at:

Department of Education (DfE) data on attainment;

Higher Education Funding Council for England (HEFCE) data on low participating groups in higher education (HE);

Academic journal articles and books recommended by her supervisor.

(Continued)

(Continued)

Whilst the statistical data interested Tricia, she was much more interested in the sources that presented narratives of young people's experiences of education as they made decisions about whether to go to university or into work. This led her to develop a research question: 'What are working-class experiences of education as they prepare to transition out of compulsory education?'

The key message here is that Tricia used the literature to reframe the direction of her study. It had moved from an interest in academic attainment differences across social class groups to their aspirations. The statistical information continued to be helpful in providing an overall picture of what happens but Tricia's interest and on-going motivation was based on the 'stories' that had been presented in what she read.

As a result of this process, Tricia entered a phase of filtering her literature – working out what was important to her study, that which was important but peripheral information and that which was irrelevant to her study. Whilst she could then focus her efforts onto the specific area she was exploring, she continued to ensure she had a sufficient range of texts to enable her to consider different perspectives and views that were evident in the literature (Coles and McGrath, 2010). She noticed that as she read, she could identify different themes and this formed the basis of how she organised her search. Machi and McEvoy (2009) provide a useful tool for this as illustrated in Figure 7.1.

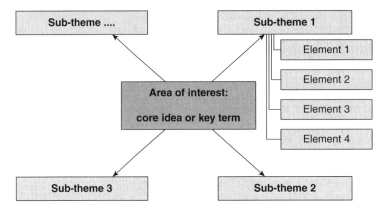

Figure 7.1   Tool for organising literature into themes (Adapted from Machi and McEvoy, 2009: 52)

In practice, this structure will enable you to clearly identify the specific focus of your research. For example, Ben wanted to look at the broad theme of Social Justice and Education, but did not have a clearly defined focus. He used the tool in Figure 7.1 to help him construct an overview of the literature to determine the specific area he would explore. As he continued to read he found four main themes emerging: academies; SEN and inclusion; educational outcomes; marketisation of schools. He was able to further extrapolate sub-themes on the area of educational outcomes (as illustrated in Figure 7.2) as he continued to read. This sub-theme then formed the main focus of his reading and engagement with the literature.

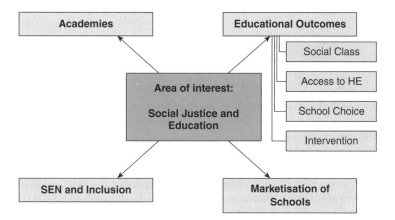

Figure 7.2 Tool for organising literature sub-themes (Adapted from Machi and McEvoy, 2009: 52)

At this stage Ben continued to be unsure of the exact research question he wanted to explore, but he had gone a long way in determining what the precise focus of his study would be. This often takes longer than most students expect, so be prepared for this part of the process to take time as you begin to unearth parts of the literature which will excite and motivate you.

Developing the Research Question

As you progress through the literature you should make notes of anything that interests you. This will help you to funnel down into something that is researchable. Your research question should literally 'tumble' out of the literature section. Because your literature section builds a case, and sustains an argument around the research you wish to explore, your question should naturally flow out of that case. In that sense, by the time your reader gets to the end of the literature section, your question should not come as a surprise. The following case study illustrates how this can be achieved.

Case Study

Polly used her literature section to explore the ways in which pupils permanently excluded from school end up experiencing other forms of disadvantage. She uses appropriately themed subtitles to help build her argument. The subtitles were as follows:

– Educational Exclusion
– Social Supports

(Continued)

(Continued)

– Institutional Habitus
– Working-Class Disadvantage

In each section Polly made a case which had the common thread of disadvantage running through. It therefore came as no surprise to the reader when she stated the aims of the project as being:

> *The literature discussed proposes many societal barriers and educational inequalities young people face, particularly for those of working-class origin. In accordance to this, recent times have revealed an increase of NEETs, proposing a lack of interest towards further education and getting into employment – due to the unreliability of the economy and job market. Therefore, this study proposes to explore the aspirations of young people, in particular pupils permanently excluded from education as they are probable to fall into the category of NEET (DfE, 2013b) obtain low or no qualifications (Castle and Parsons, 2006), and self-eliminate themselves from society because of earlier rejection (Bourdieu and Passeron, 1977). In particular the main foci are: to explore pupils' plans after compulsory education and the wider future, and pay attention to their experiences of the process of ending education, the support received and concerns for the future. In order to explore these foci, the following research question is posed: 'What can permanently excluded pupils tell us about their educational experiences and how these have informed their thinking about their future?'*

Polly has done a commendable job in ensuring the literature presented leads into her aims and research question. It is clear from the question that the aims of the project can be met: it all ties together and makes sense. It is also clear that Polly had been through a process of managing the information in her study: she was able to construct appropriate sub-themes within her literature section which helped her achieve coherence. This was not achieved by chance. Polly developed a systematic approach to managing the literature which we will explore in the next section. (For more information on developing your research question(s) read Chapter 4.)

Managing the Information

As you find sources to read you will need to keep a good record. An organised approach will help you to manage the sources so that when you need to refer to the information, you can find it quickly. There is nothing more frustrating when putting a literature section together, when you know that you have read something that would contribute positively to your argument, but you just cannot locate it. You may wish to invest in Refworks or Endnote which are online bibliographic software management systems and commercially available. They link into Microsoft Word, for example, with a 'cite while you write' function which helps you to integrate the sources into your argument as you go along. However, if you do not have access to tools such as Endnote or Refworks there are alternative ways in which you can manage your sources.

Source	Key Point	Relates to..	Key Quote	Page no.

Figure 7.3 Grid to structure literature

The grid I have devised (see Figure 7.3) not only helps you to synthesise and consolidate the reading that you do, it helps you to manage the literature. You could organise the grid into themes so that when you commence writing, you can easily access what you have read for each theme. The key concern is to ensure that your hard work in relation to the literature does not get misplaced. It is worth investing time into developing a method that you can manage and that works for you.

Another example of how to work with the literature is provided in Table 7.1. This structure helps you to consider the way in which the sources contribute to your own understanding of the issue/s under exploration. For each of the subheadings, you can identify key aspects of a text that help you shape your thinking about your research area, which can subsequently feed into the argument you develop.

The key difference between the first and second grids is the depth of critique. The first grid offers a descriptive level of information and does not require much analytical thought. The second provides much more detail and also illustrates how the text relates to other sources in this particular field. This approach will encourage you to think deeply and deconstruct the text in a way to highlight areas of tension (critiques of other definitions), limitations of the material (excluded from the definition), and understanding of the source (included in the definition). Thus it is a useful method for being able to cross-reference the content with other sources. This process of critique should enable you to form an argument of your own. The final column is a useful way of pulling out key quotes which can appear in your own literature section. You should use quotes sparingly, of course, and my advice would be to ask yourself whether you simply cannot put the information in a better way without losing some of its meaning/message. Where possible you should try to paraphrase rather than use direct quotes, but if you believe this will have a detrimental effect on the passage's meaning, you should quote it directly, remembering the specific conventions that apply to quoting existing material:

Quotes of more than two lines should be in a separate paragraph and indented from both the left and right;

Quotes of less than two lines should be integrated into your text with quotation marks appropriately placed.

Table 7.1 Completed literature section grid

Focus	Class Definition	Critiques of other Definitions	Included in Definition	Excluded from Definition	How Class is Used	Advantages	Disadvantages	Useful quotes
Explore the issues behind widening participation and how such moves have resulted in 'growing inequalities in higher education' (vii)	Use Registrar General's occupation rating scale to identify class positions 1, 2 and 3NM (middle class) and 3M, 4 and 5 (working class) but also allow for 'ambiguity about class positioning' (13)	Refer to Jackson and Marsden's 1962 study to highlight class fractions: 'sunken middle class' (5)	'Increasing complexities of class positionings' (6) Work that highlights disparities in access between top social group and bottom (6)	'...local habitus... sustained by active neighbouring and socialising' (111) as identified by Savage, Bagnall and Longhurst (2004) in Devine et al., 2005	Attempting to identify class in terms of 'practices and collective social processes' (16) in relation to higher education choice	Allow for complexities of class position and attempt to move away from binary categories in definitions of class	Class emerges as a collective during analysis of higher education choice – students are homogenised into the binary of working and middle class when describing their attitudes towards particular universities despite intentions to embrace a more in-depth stance on class analysis	'There is no uniformity of class conditions, practices and outcomes, but rather, different working class fractions with differing priorities in relation to risk, challenge and fitting in.' (x) **'...social class differences in access have remained intractable.' (1)**
Focus on different groups (gender, race, age) and how their 'degrees of choice' are 'shaped by their social class' (vii)	Use 'actual' parental occupations and type of housing and deconstruct both groupings for a more 'differentiated examination' (13) Also use both parents' occupation and education to construct their own 'composite [class] categorisation' (13)	Goldthorpe's 'service class' and raise the question of how it would be possible to distinguish them from other types of employees (15)	Differentiation of those with a longer familial history of being middle class (15) 'established middle class' and 'novitiate middle class' (15)					'...policy changes initiated in 1997 have made it more, not less, difficult for young people from lower social classes to attend university and this is borne out by the statistics..' (5)
Highlight the relationship between institutional habitus and working/middle class habitus to demonstrate why the middle class route to HE is less problematic than that of the working class	Service class differentiation: benefits of employment over and above salary (pension rights, increments, employment security and career opportunities) and degree of professional autonomy and managerial or administrative authority (15)		Utilise 'new developing sociology of social class that focuses as much on class processes and practices as on position in the labour market' (e.g. Savage, 2003 and Skeggs, 2004)					**'The old binary between working and middle class has never explained enough about the myriad ways in which social class is acted out in people's lives' (5)** 'Intra-class differences are based upon family history, capitals, skills and dispositions.' (15)

Whatever strategy you adopt for managing your sources, you will need to ensure that it supports your endeavour to consolidate, evaluate, critique and synthesise the material you read (Punch, 2009; McMillan and Weyers, 2010). In addition, if you ensure that this part of the process is conducted methodically it will save you much time later in the writing process (Walliman, 2011). It is obvious when students have not systematically approached the literature that informs their study and can often lead to a fragmented section that does not achieve coherence. In addition this can lead to the argument not being supported with sufficient evidence. Look at Luke's opening section in the case study below.

Case Study

The English education system has been an on-going debate since 1944, especially that of secondary education. Not only has it been subjective to the public, it has also been dramatically influenced by Educational Acts through the years. The system has always favoured the upper class families, finances being an influential factor on a child's education in more ways than one, this does not seem fair for the child as everybody should have an equal opportunity to succeed and lead a life that they choose. The system has progressed dramatically since the 1944 Education Act, there have been many different approaches that have been put across to help improve the system and allow us to gain a greater education. In 1944 it started out, in my opinion, as a system that favoured the middle class, regardless if you pass the 11 plus or not. The test would entail you looking at what one of three schools you would go to.

'Different types of school for different types of mind, was clearly modelled on a class-divided vision of education' (Ball, 2003).

It is very difficult to determine what this literature section is setting out to do. The first paragraph reads very much as a first draft, where ideas are being noted. There is no sense of direction or argument. The inclusion of Ball (2003) is not linked into the work in a coherent way as there is no sense of chronology and it is unclear whether Ball is in fact referring to the structure of education following the 1944 Education Act. There is little substance to this opening and also an apparent lack of understanding of the key themes that are being written about. There is also the issue that Luke has omitted to provide the page number for the quote he has included. Another example of a weak literature section, in this case study from Helena, is provided below.

Case Study

The term continuity, defined by Capel (2006) as 'a consistent line of development without any sharp breaks' (46). This statement is supported by Murdoch (2004) who states that Physical Education should 'be one logical, focused, seamless, smooth state of growth or

(Continued)

(Continued)

advancement' (287). Publications by the DFES (1987: 4) divulge that the introduction of the English curriculum also welcomed an aim that all children would undergo 'a broad and balanced curriculum whilst demonstrating continuity and progression'. More recent research into continuity within education by Capel (2013) suggests that 'communication between teachers which ensures the planned provisions of teaching and learning to facilitate pupils' continuous development' (CCCUC, 1998: 10).

In this example, in addition to the poor writing style, Helena moves from one author to the next without having completed any critical evaluation and synthesis of the material. There is an attempt to relate the material as she goes through an explanation of the term 'continuity', but this is not done in a way where her own authoritative voice is evident. It is very important, as you move through your argument, that you sustain an authoritative voice and that your argument is evident from the start of your literature section.

In this example from Helena there is also some confusion with the key terms being used. She does not adequately convey the different meanings between 'continuity', 'growth', 'advancement', 'progression' and 'continuous development'. Because these appear to be central to what is being said, it is important that the meanings are appropriately delineated in order that the reader can clearly identify what message is being conveyed. She is also not being consistent with her referencing technique.

It is equally important to ensure you start your literature section with a purpose – that is, start it convincingly with a strong argument achieved through the development of an authoritative voice.

Present the Argument from the Beginning

Your literature section should read like a coherent story and not a list of ideas that you have come across. In order to achieve this you need to *synthesise* and *analyse* the material you are reading (Coles and McGrath, 2010; Oliver, 2012). One of the main tasks you have when constructing your literature section is to draw your reader in – capture their interest in your work from the beginning. Take Lisa's beginning sentence in the case study below:

Case Study

There are a number of theories surrounding how educational and career aspirations are formed and developed. This research will be focusing on the educational and career aspirations of Year 9 children (age 13–14), within a mainstream, state maintained high school. The study explores the aspirations of 'middle class' students, which are determined based on their lack of eligibility for free school meals (FSM), which are funded by the government, for families who are receiving state welfare.

The writing here is very descriptive and vague. There is an unsubstantiated claim in the very first sentence: *'There are a number of theories surrounding how educational and career aspirations are formed and developed'*. The writing does not make it clear what the theories could be and indeed whether they are in fact 'theories'. As a result, this opening does not provide sufficient information to draw the reader in. There are also potential issues with the broadness of the project under exploration: educational and career aspirations have two large literature bases supporting them and for most writing projects it would be better to focus on one area. In addition, this opening alludes to the type of research that will be conducted despite being the opening of the literature section. Whilst this information is useful to the overall project, it is problematic to present it in the opening statement without having presented the argument that justifies using this age group and context. This information would more appropriately sit within the methodology section where the sample and research methods are discussed.

Following a meeting with her supervisor, Lisa was advised to re-visit this and construct a more focused and argument-based opening. That is, she needed to think about the 'issue' under exploration. The final re-working was as follows:

Case Study

The aspirations of young people have been identified as being influenced by social class (Bourdieu and Passeron, 1977). Whilst 'children of higher social class origins are more likely to aspire to high educational and occupational goals' (Valadez, 1998: 559), there is limited research that identifies the issues or difficulties that this group could face when thinking about their career goals and aspirations. Power et al. (2003) identify some of these difficulties and this research will build from this work.

In this final iteration (and there were many drafts in-between), the sense of argument is much clearer. Lisa clearly identifies what the research is about and uses literature to build the case for the study. Machi and McEvoy (2009: 62) argue that 'scholarly argument is not meant to overpower, but rather convince'. This can be achieved if attention is paid to the development of the argument, that is, the way in which your writing can be viewed as sustaining its message. The trick to this is to ensure that your themes flow from one to another and to avoid description.

Achieving Flow

Kamler and Thomson (2006) provide a useful framework for structuring your writing. Whilst their advice focuses on doctoral level writing, it can also be applied to all dissertations. They suggest that scholarly writing should be interesting and that it should move away from 'stodgy prose' characterised as 'soporific slabs of writing, formulaic, over signposted, bristling with brackets, crabbed and turgid, [and] generally just a very dull read' (Kamler and Thomson, 2006: 125). They also refer to the writing process as being formed by 'argumentative moves' (ibid.: 125). 'Moves' in this instance can be understood as being stages or steps in the argument that you are building. In establishing the 'argumentative moves' for your own work you need to clearly think through what it is you want to say and in what order you want to say it. In the same approach used by Kamler and Thomson (2006), Rich began to consider the order in which he wanted to explore the area of working-class young people's educational experiences. The following email exchange illustrates the difficulties Rich faced as he tried to bring all the information he had read together into a coherent argument.

Case Study

Rich's email:

I'm really struggling with my assignment again. The plan that I've got I'm rapidly losing faith in and beginning to panic. My question is still 'Is the education system failing young people from disadvantaged backgrounds?'

I really need help but don't know what to do and really worried I'm messing everything up. Any advice would be welcomed with open arms!

Tutor's reply:

We'll talk about this on Thursday – my first word of advice is – don't panic. My second is: go back to the crux of the argument – what would you like your assignment to say? Then construct the sentences that will help you develop and shape your paragraphs.

E.g. Is the education system failing young people from disadvantaged backgrounds?

Evidence suggests that young people from disadvantaged backgrounds do badly at school (use statistics in this section)

This issue has been an on-going problem for many years despite Government initiatives (highlight Government initiatives that have sought to address the problem)

This issue can be understood through Bourdieu's conceptual tools (highlight field – structures within schools that contribute to the problem; habitus – the alienation from education experienced by disadvantaged groups)

Summarise the key issues

With this structure you should have sufficient scope to write an insightful assignment – for 'field' – there is so much to write about which could actually take up more words than you have, so make sure you synthesise this area of your work.

Begin jotting notes on how you will support each section (e.g. section 1 – statistics – exam results; truancy; exclusion rates – highlight that these are different across the differing social group demographics). Then keep expanding until you can get some paragraphs out of it.

This short email exchange helped Rich to re-focus his argument and he subsequently went on to produce an interesting submission that successfully presented a number of complex theoretical ideas. In reaching this successful outcome, Rich had to focus his intention on the argument. He went through the process of writing out sentences that could be used to frame each section of his work in the way that Kamler and Thomson (2006) suggest. His first attempt was problematic as it did not fully capture the sense of direction for the argument, lending itself to a very descriptive and chronological account of working-class disadvantage in education as illustrated in the following case study section:

Case Study

Rich's proposed structure:

1. Children are 'born to fail' – Wedge and Prosser, 1973;
2. The tri-partite system continued to privilege middle-class young people;
3. The 1988 Education Reform Act created an education market place;
4. Exam results show that working-class young people perform less well than their middle-class peers at all stages of education.

As Rich discussed this structure with his tutor he soon began to understand the issues with this approach and began to re-craft the structure based on his tutor's advice:

Rich's revised structure:

1. Examination results illustrate that working-class young people do not achieve as well as their middle-class peers;
2. This 'problem' contributes to low participation rates of young people from disadvantaged backgrounds in higher education (HE);
3. Whilst Government policy has attempted to address the issue, it appears not to have been successful;
4. Bourdieu provides a theoretical perspective that enables us to understand the structural constraints within education that contribute to the issue.

Rich then began to craft and re-craft his work and successfully presented an engaging and persuasive argument that fully integrated a range of sources and the theoretical ideas of Bourdieu. He avoided the potential for description by focusing his attention on what he wanted his argument to say and by employing the techniques he had discussed with his tutor during tutorials.

Avoiding Description

Avoiding description is a key element of your writing. You will find that higher marks are awarded to work that is able to present an argument rather than that which merely describes existing ideas. The skill of turning descriptive writing into an argument requires practice and you will need to be committed to drafting and re-drafting your work many times (Basit, 2010). You may find this difficult and it can at times be difficult understanding what the difference is. The following example illustrates descriptive writing:

> In 1988, the Education Reform Act introduced league tables which consequently led to the marketisation of schools.

Once this statement is presented in a different way it can clearly establish a position where your voice comes through. The re-drafted statement offered below is much more persuasive than the descriptive writing in the previous example. You should identify what the 'issue' is that needs to be presented and work your sentence around that. In this example, the 'issue' was the impact of the 1988 Education Reform Act in developing an education quasi-market place. There is no sense of argument in the descriptive writing, whereas in the second, the 'issue' can clearly be identified: 'increased competition between schools'.

> The publication of league tables, following the 1988 Education Reform Act, has increased competition between schools, effectively turning education into a quasi-market.

The following case study further emphasises the way in which descriptive writing leads to a weak argument being presented.

Case Study

All parents are different and therefore have differing opinions of where their child should go to school. Gewirtz et al. (1995) looked at the overall market, choice and equity of education. The research looked at both demands and supply in terms of what parents wanted and how schools chose pupils in 'three overlapping local education markets in an English city – London' (Gewirtz et al., 1995: 21). Interviews were conducted with parents, teachers and members of the LEA involving ideas of choice, enrolment and school performance. In terms of demand there is a strong correlation between that of social class and educational background. Parents from a more privileged background were more in control of the process of their child's school choice and understood the public resources given to them to make an informed choice (Brighouse, 2000; Gewirtz et al., 1995). Despite these results it is important to note that this is not always the case as two children from the same social class may have either very involved parents; who know about the education system or parents who care less about their children's education.

Due to this, it is clear how 'educational inequality may be facilitated by school choice' (Brighouse, 2000: 113) as not only are the parents bothered by their children's education; pushing for their children to attend certain schools but these children are more attractive to schools because of their parents enthusiasm and involvement for them to succeed.

If we unpick this section we will see issues not only with description but many other aspects of academic writing:

- The first sentence, for example, makes the claim that 'all parents are different and therefore have differing opinions of where their child should go to school'. This claim is not substantiated and therefore has not been supported within the field within which the ideas are located.
- The second sentence begins descriptively by stating that Gerwirtz et al. (1995) 'looked at the overall market, choice and equity of education'. There is no argument being presented here. As a reader, I need to know what the issue is. For example, a more interesting statement might be 'Gerwirtz et al. (1995) identified a lack of choice and equity in educational choice since the marketisation of schools'. This then becomes more interesting and less ambiguous in meaning.
- The third sentence is out of place. There is no need to identify the research methods as part of the narrative/argument unless it is vital to the argument. That is, if you can identify a potential issue in relation to the findings that has been influenced by the way in which the research was conducted. In this example, the information appears unnecessary and does not develop the argument in any way.
- There is an attempt to critique the literature through the statement 'Despite these results it is important to note that this is not always the case as two children from the same social class may have either very involved parents; who know about the education system or parents who care less about their children's education'. There are punctuation errors in this section of writing but importantly, there is limited coherence. The statement is not supported through literature and comes across as very anecdotal. In academic writing this should be avoided.

Writing a literature section should be an enjoyable process – it enables you to understand the field within which you are working but also provides you with an opportunity to develop your own position on a particular issue. Whilst some of the process can be frustrating at times, approaching your literature systematically should help avoid some of the feelings identified at the beginning of the chapter. Let's look at some key points that will help you as you engage further with your area of interest.

Key Points to Remember

- 'There is no such thing as the perfect review' (Hart, 1998: 25). This should not only offer you a sense of relief, but it further emphasises the idea that there is no work that can be free from bias/judgement. As you begin to form your own argument, you are presenting your views and as such, your own writing will contain your values/judgements.

As you search through the literature be mindful of the range of sources you collect, question whether you are sticking to work that appears to fit with your own standpoint. If you do this you may not be able to construct a balanced argument that details contradictory views.

- Part of your job will be to weigh up the credibility of the sources you have identified: not all sources will carry the same level of credibility in the academic world (Thomas, 2013). Journal articles and book chapters go through a rigorous peer-review process and as such carry more weight than newspaper articles and some online sources. Our advice would be to assess the credibility of each source as you read it and consider whether the viewpoint needs to be focused on as you develop your argument.
- The process of identifying and deciding upon literature to be used in your literature section is not a simple one, because it requires interpretation of text – the critical uncovering of ideas and evaluation of fit: whether the work will feature in your argument or not. You need to take time with this. As identified above, you should be prepared to draft and re-draft your literature section – it will not come together overnight and it should not be rushed. You will not be able to do justice to your research area if you try to construct your literature section in a very limited time period.
- Your 'story' should have a beginning, middle and an end. You should outline the issues at the beginning (setting the scene for your dissertation; identifying the issue or problem to be explored) then move into the middle (explanation of the issue based on previous work) and the end (summarise the main issues, paradoxes, dilemmas and questions that have emerged as a result of the literature section).

Further Reading

Fink, A. (2010) *Conducting Research Literature Reviews: From the Internet to Paper* (3/E). London: SAGE.

Hartas, D. (2010) 'Doing a Literature Review', in D. Hartas (ed.), *Educational Research and Inquiry: Qualitative and Quantitative approaches.* London: Continuum.

Ridley, D. (2012) *The Literature Review. A Step-by-Step Guide for Students* (2/E). London: SAGE.

Useful Websites

Most universities publish guidelines for doing the literature review so for students on degree courses you can start by searching your university if they offer these guidelines.

Here are two examples:

- The University of Leicester
  www2.le.ac.uk/offices/ld/resources/writing/writing-resources/literature-review

- The University of Reading
  www.reading.ac.uk/internal/studyadvice/StudyResources/Essays/sta-startinglitreview.aspx

References

Basit, T. (2010) *Conducting Research in Educational Contexts*. London: Continuum.

Burton, N., Brundrett, M, and Jones, M. (2008) *Doing your Education Research Project*. London: SAGE.

Coles, A. and McGrath, J. (2010) *Your Education Research Project Handbook*. Harlow: Pearson.

Fink, A. (2010) *Conducting Research Literature Reviews: From the Internet to Paper* (3/E). London: SAGE.

Hart, C. (1998) *Doing a Literature Review*. London: SAGE.

Hartas, D. (2010) 'Doing a Literature Review', in D. Hartas (ed.), *Educational Research and Inquiry: Qualitative and Quantitative Approaches*. London: Continuum.

Kamler, B. and Thomson, P. (2006) *Helping Doctoral Students Write: Pedagogies for Supervision*. Abingdon: Routledge.

Machi, L. and McEvoy, B. (2009) *The Literature Review*. Thousand Oaks, CA: Corwin Press.

McMillan, K. and Weyers, J. (2010) *How to Write Dissertations and Project Reports*. Harlow: Pearson.

O'Leary, Z. (2004) *The Essential Guide to Doing Research*. London: SAGE.

Oliver, P. (2012) *Succeeding with your Literature Review: A Handbook for Students*. Maidenhead: Open University Press.

Punch, K. (2009) *Introduction to Research Methods in Education*. London: SAGE.

Thomas, G. (2013) *How to do your Research Project* (2/E). London: SAGE.

Walliman, N. (2011) *Your Research Project: Designing and Planning your Work* (3/E). London: SAGE.

For additional online resources please visit the book's website:
https://study.sagepub.com/needhamandpalaiologou

8

SELECTING APPROPRIATE RESEARCH METHODS FOR AN EDUCATIONAL CONTEXT

MARK CONNOLLY

Chapter Aims and Objectives

This chapter aims to help you to:

- make the link between your research question(s)/hypothesis and the methods you intend to use;
- distinguish between methods which will generate data in the form of numbers and words;
- identify the methods which are the appropriate tools for *your* research project;
- dismiss methods which are not appropriate for testing your hypothesis or answering your research questions.

Introduction

Where previous chapters of this book focused on designing your research project, this chapter concentrates on the actual techniques – the research methods – that you will need to bring this design to life. If we think of a research project as a new building, then, at this stage, you will have already drawn up the building plans – ontology, epistemology, methodology – and now you must make decisions as to which tools you need to construct your building (see Chapter 2). Many students, however, make the mistake of deciding on their method *before* they have a design in place and this is like buying a cement mixer to build your house while you were still considering using a wooden framed construction. It is important, therefore, that your methods follow your design and that the methods which you choose are the tools suitable for testing your hypothesis or answering your research questions. There is no point, for example, in choosing to use observations of a teacher's disciplinary strategies if you are interested in parental views of discipline within a particular school. Therefore, if you do not feel that your research question is formed or that your design frame is fully developed, then I recommend you go back to previous chapters of this book and refine your design before you start considering the methods discussed in this chapter.

While I outline a range of methods that you might want to employ within your research project, please be aware that this is not a definitive list and that you can use methods that are innovative and creative. Make sure, however, that any method you choose not only fits within your design frame, but, more importantly, answers your research question and is not chosen for its innovation and creativity alone (see the discussion of the term 'methodolatory' in the 'Practical Tip' overleaf).

Practical Tip

Your research question(s)/hypothesis are the horse and your methods are the cart – your methods must follow from the question you wish to ask or the hypothesis you wish to test.

For each method described in this chapter I will give an example of a recent student research project where some of the questions asked can be answered by the method under consideration.

Activity

Consider your hypothesis/research question(s). Do you think that this/these would be best answered or tested by:

- asking people questions (if so, to whom will you ask questions?);
- watching what people do (if so, who will you watch?);
- assessing what people have recorded in writing or in visual form (if so, what kinds of material will you use?).

In Chapter 2 of this book you have been guided in creating a design frame for your research project and have been introduced to concepts such as *positivism* and *interpretivism*. Even if you do not fully understand the philosophical underpinnings of these terms by now you should have a general understanding of how these relate to methods which usually generate numbers – *quantitative* – and methods which usually generate words – *qualitative*. Within this chapter I will keep the use of these terms to a minimum, as the representation of these approaches as polar opposites – and thus incompatible – can militate against effective research [n.b. the chapter follows Punch's (2009) call for a relaxing of the qualitative/quantitative distinction]. Rather than using the qualitative/quantitative categorisation, I will organise the methods you might use into three categories:

a) methods which generally generate words;
b) methods which generally generate numbers; and
c) methods which can generate either words or numbers.

Practical Tip

Only choose a method if it is the correct tool for answering your research question. In criticising research which privileges a certain method, Janesick (1994) blended the words 'method' and 'idolatory' to create the term 'methodolatry' to describe 'the slavish attachment and devotion to method'. (Janesick, 1994: 215).

The Generation of Words as Data

This section of the chapter will consider data collection methods which generally generate words as data. As you will see, however, this distinction is far from watertight: for example both interviews in the form of one-to-one questionnaires and observations are often used to generate numbers. However, on the whole, interviews, observations and documentary analysis do lend themselves to the generation of data in the form of words.

Interviews

Example: A student research project which used interviews as a tool for data collection

Research question: What are teachers', students' and parents' perceptions of the effectiveness and usefulness of Citizenship Education?

Interviews are quite often the method of choice within student dissertations and theses. One explanation for this could be that the interview is a method of communication that we are all already familiar with from the formal job interview to the entertaining celebrity chat show interview. This familiarity does not, however, mean that the interview is an 'easy' research method or that it answers most research questions. Neither of these assumptions is true: the interview needs to be well designed, thoughtfully prepared and sympathetically executed and only answers *certain* research questions. With this thought in mind, the interview *is* often the correct tool to gather data that will answer certain research questions and is a very effective tool for accessing participants' feelings, interpretations, beliefs or how they construct reality. In the example above, interviews will answer a research question such as: 'what are teachers' perceptions of the effectiveness of citizenship education?' However, an interview could *not* answer the question 'how effective is citizenship education?' It can only tell us, instead, what that interviewee's interpretation or perception of its effectiveness is (the results of this student's project, for example, found that while teachers thought that Citizenship Education had an impact on students' political and social awareness, both parents and students believed that it was wasting students' time).

A key strength – though also a potential weakness – in using interviews as a research tool is that they often rely upon face-to-face contact between the interviewer and the interviewee: a strength in this allows for the establishment of a rapport between the researcher and participant; a potential weakness in that such physical contact can impact upon the data gathering process. In a face-to-face interview your physical presence should allow you to observe the more subtle nuances with regard to both the verbal and body language that an interviewee uses, thus giving you greater insight into their perceptions and beliefs. How much attention you pay to these nuances depends on your research frame and design: will you be interpreting your interviewees' responses using an analytical technique that focuses on language, or are you simply interested in how the interviewee constructs his/her version of reality? In addition, through developing a rapport with the interviewee you can encourage him/her to be more forthcoming and fulsome in her/his responses. Establishing such a rapport can be difficult and often depends on the interviewer persona which you wish to adopt within your interview: are you pretending that you know nothing about the subject; do you wish to adopt the persona of a knowledgeable outsider; do you wish to engage with the interviewee as part of his/her group, and so on? This raises particular problems when interviewing children as they immediately view you, as an adult, as a figure of authority, thus militating against building an effective rapport (it is often better to interview children as a group – see Chapters 3 and 6 and below).

Open and closed questions

The primary difference between types of questions is whether they are 'open' or 'closed'. An open question allows for any response: an example of an open question relating to the research project above would be 'what are your opinions of the teaching of citizenship education in your school?' A closed question, on the other hand, limits the response a person can make: these can be limited to two choices in a yes/no question or a number of choices that have been set by the interviewer. Examples of these are: 'do you agree with recent changes to the citizenship curriculum? Yes/no'; or 'How supportive are you of recent changes to the citizenship curriculum? Very supportive, supportive, neither supportive nor unsupportive, unsupportive, very unsupportive.' While these types of closed question can allow for easy analysis and the generation of quantitative data, they disallow for nuance in the interviewee's response (an interviewee may want to clarify what 'changes' the interviewer is asking about).

Types of interviews

There are different types of interviews and many academics have offered typologies which explain these various approaches: Fontana and Frey (1994), for example, order interviews along a continuum relating to both the structure and formality of the interview type (see below).

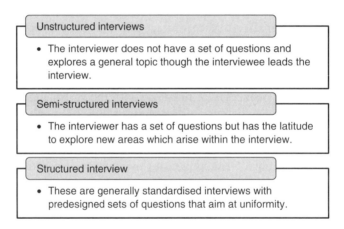

Figure 8.1 Adapted from the work of Fontana and Frey (1994: 363)

What distinguishes these types of interviews is the level of 'depth' that your research questions require: the structured interview has a tight set of predesigned, standardised questions which can offer a broad perspective but disallow an in-depth exploration; the semi-structured interview uses a predetermined set of questions but has the freedom to explore new avenues of enquiry; and the unstructured interview does not have a predetermined set of questions which allows the interviewee to explore issues as deeply as they wish. As with all data collection the choice of tool depends on the research question that you are asking.

Structured interviews

The structured interview is very close to the questionnaire in that the interviewee asks a series of pre-set questions relating to predetermined themes. These questions are asked to each respondent in exactly the same order with no variation or fluctuation, with the interviewer aspiring to adopt a completely neutral persona. Generally, these types of interviews are not recorded and the interviewer records the answer on a form that includes both the closed and open questions asked. This type of interview has strengths in that the responses are easily coded and analysed and response rates for this type of interview are often much better than those for administering self-completion questionnaires. As stated above, however, the fundamental attribute of an interview is that it allows for interpersonal, usually face-to-face, contact which can result in much richer data whereas the use of prescribed questions within a structured interview can work against the generation of this kind of data.

Semi-structured interviews

The semi-structured interview tends to be the most common form of interview used in qualitative research projects in education. You should not simply use this as a 'default' choice, however, without considering *why* it is that you have opted for this type of interview with regard to your design frame and research questions. If, for example, you are interested in how someone's upbringing conditioned their attitudes towards education, an unstructured life-history interview might be more appropriate. Thomas (2013) uses the colourful analogy that semi-structured interviews in these circumstances would be like asking respondents to be an artist, but only providing them with a painting-by-numbers kit. What often attracts students to this type of interview is that it combines some of the tightness offered by a structured interview with some of the latitude allowed by an unstructured approach.

The structure within this type of interview is provided by a set of questions – the interview schedule – that the interviewer wishes to explore (see Figure 8.1 above). Unlike a structured interview, this schedule is not prescriptive and is merely an indicative guide which you can deviate from if the interviewee leads you to an area which you have not yet considered. The schedule should include topics you wish to cover, initial questions, and possible follow-up questions and probes that you might use to elicit more detailed responses (see Figure 8.2 below).

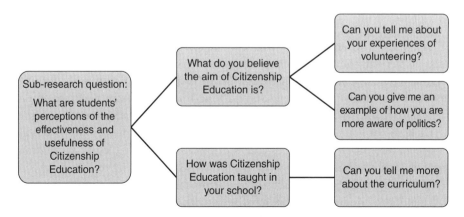

Figure 8.2   Using a spider diagram to design an interview schedule for a semi-structured interview

Unstructured interviews

There are a wide variety of unstructured interviews, but they all share certain characteristics: they do not use predetermined categories; they are not standardised; they are open ended; and they aspire to achieving deep responses from the interviewees. In many ways, this type of interview resembles a conversation rather than an interview in the traditional or everyday sense and consequently they are often also referred to as 'conversational interviews' (n.b. more information on their use is to be found in the next chapter). By using this type of interview you are acknowledging the complexity of the social world and people's interpretations of this: the interviewee will lead you and guide you through their interpretation of the world in all its complexity.

Practical Tip

Interviewing is the art of listening, not talking. Remember the Turkish proverb 'If speaking is silver, then listening is gold'. Often when researchers begin to transcribe their interviews they realise that they have been talking over the interviewee or constantly offering their ideas and opinions. It is important to remember that while you are talking you are not learning anything.

Of course, allowing the interviewee such latitude can result in the interview going in an unexpected and, at times, irrelevant direction. In addition, because this method is used to probe deeply into how a respondent understands the world and his/her position in it, the interviewer position can transfer into that of a trusted confidante and, at times, a counsellor, which raises its own set of ethical concerns: is the interviewee becoming upset, are you becoming upset, is the interviewee comfortable with the data being published and, if so, in what form? It takes a great deal of sensitivity to manage these issues effectively but, if this is achieved, then this type of interview can yield deep and meaningful data.

Group interviews and focus groups

A group interview is when the researcher conducts an interview with more than one person at a time. As with all methods you need to ask yourself the key question: 'how will using a group interview answer my research question(s) in a way that other forms of data collection will not?' Group interviews have a long tradition within educational research, where the researcher has utilised the dynamics of group interaction to access data that would otherwise not have been available. Often within a group people are more willing to make explicit their views, perceptions and opinions (social psychology has illustrated this in terms of 'risky shift phenomenon' where a group is more willing to take a risky decision than an individual would be). In the study on Citizenship Education considered within this section the student conducted group interviews with two sets of students within which they gave detailed, insightful and candid responses to her questions.

Although group interviews and focus groups are often used interchangeably, they have different aims. Group interviews are often a means to generate data quickly and conveniently and do not specifically aim to use or assess group interaction – thus the main dynamic is between the interviewer and the group. Focus groups, on the other hand, encourage, foster and facilitate interaction among the group and are often specifically interested in the actual dynamics of the group itself. Within this latter category of group interview the role of the researcher changes to being a moderator and facilitator of the group discussion and, as with individual interviews described above, the latitude that the facilitator gives to the group depends on the project's design frame and the research questions which s/he is attempting to answer. In general terms, just as semi- and unstructured interviews allow the interviewee to take the lead, within focus groups the aim is for the discussion to be led by the group (see, for example, Cohen et al., 2011: 433).

To facilitate such group-led discussion the interviewer/moderator can use a variety of stimuli to initiate and provoke discussion. These stimuli can be written, visual or oral: for example, in this research project the student used a short video about the perceived benefits of Citizenship Education to prompt a discussion amongst the students.

Case Study

Group interviews with children

Within policy (most notably Article 12 of The United Nations Convention on the Rights of the Child) there has been a growing recognition of the need to listen to children's voices. This has been reflected within educational research, where researchers have moved from a position of asking others *about* children to actually listening to what the children themselves have to say. This raises many issues both ethically and practically: in terms of ethics, how much capacity do children have to consent to participation; and, practically, what methods are effective while interviewing children? It has been common to cite the perceived 'problems' in researching children's opinions: they are easily distracted and have limited memory; they wish to give a response to please the adult whether it makes sense or not; they are prone to fantasy. However, these 'problems' may be to do with inappropriate methods employed by the researcher or the inability of the researcher to adopt a child-centred view of the world (Punch, 2002). For example, researchers in the field of health (Morgan et al., 2002) have argued that group interviews are an effective way to access children's ideas and opinions. While conducting group interviews with asthmatic children, Morgan et al. (2002) found that within the more natural group talk environment children tended to be more forthcoming and that the uses of prompts, especially visual prompts such as pictures and photographs, yielded rich data into the problems these young asthma sufferers experience.

Practical issues with interviewing

Although this issue will be explored more fully in the next chapter, once you have made the decision on the type of interview you wish to conduct you then need to turn your attention to the practicalities of carrying out this interview. The main questions that you need to consider with regards to the selection of your interviewee are:

- how will I gain access to these interviewees;
- how am I going to manage the interview process; and
- how am I going to record the interviews I conduct?

There are two questions that students on degree courses often ask their supervisor as soon as they have decided upon interviews as a research tool: the first is 'who should I interview'; the second is 'how many interviews do I need to conduct'? Unfortunately these are not questions to which it is possible to give a precise answer, but they should be able to give you some guidance drawn from both general principles relating to qualitative interviews and from the research questions that you wish to ask in your research project. The first principle is that, as a research method, interviews offer you depth rather than breadth, so you should select your participants based on their value to your study (the degree of depth or breadth you wish to achieve is derived from your research question which then informs the type of interview you may wish to carry out – see above). How you sample these participants again depends on the questions you wish to ask, but there are a variety of sampling procedures: you may want to interview participants with a range or extremes of opinion; you may sample by convenience – those who are available; you may let one participant lead you to the next – this procedure is known as snowball sampling. [For a more detailed account of these differing sampling procedures see Chapter 11 and Patton (2002)].

Whilst I have already discussed many of the key techniques in managing the interview process in terms of deciding on the persona you wish to adopt and developing a schedule of questions you wish to ask, it is also good practice to pilot the interview that you wish to conduct. This is simply a trial which will allow you to make adjustments and amendments before you proceed and part of this preparation involves deciding how these interviews will be recorded. Generally, structured interviews use a response sheet since the categories have been pre-determined, while less structured interviews are generally audio or video recorded. It may be useful to have a visual recording of a focus group interview to aid transcription or if you are interested in group dynamics. Be aware, however, of any ethical considerations in relation to both audio and visual recording, especially if your research involves children (see Chapter 3 for more guidance on this).

Practical Tip

Review your research question(s)/hypothesis. Can you answer or test these through the use of interviews? If the answer is yes then decide on what type of interview you think would be best suited to doing this.

Diaries

Diaries or reflective journals have been used extensively within education, particularly, for example, as a way of articulating implicit learning experiences while undergoing initial teacher training. As a research tool the diary performs a similar function by providing a space for the participant or researcher to both record events and to reflect upon his/her interpretation of the meaning and significance of the events that have experienced or witnessed. The anonymity offered by a diary can result in you having access to deep and sometimes intimate understandings of how a participant interprets his/her social world (Alaszewski, 2006). This can be a particularly effective tool when researching with children and young people as it removes the adult researcher from the research process and can empower the young person to reflect on his/her life. A particularly effective tool for researching with young people is the video diary, where young people are encouraged to record their thoughts and experiences over a period of time. [For a detailed account of both the potential and the challenges – ethical and practical – that such an 'emancipatory' approach offers, see Chapter 3, and Holland et al. (2008).

Observations

Example: A student research project which used observations as a tool for data collection

Research question: How do male and female teachers' and parents' perception of risk impact upon outdoor education lessons?

Observations have been a favoured research technique within both general social research and social research with an educational focus. While interviewing might be described as the art of 'hearing data', observations can be described as the art of 'seeing data'. How you wish to 'see' this data depends upon the approach that your research project has taken and the questions that you have asked. As with the approaches to interviews outlined above, observations can be categorised with regard to the type of structure you wish to use within your observation: do you wish to systematically record certain predetermined activities or behaviour (this would require structured observation); or do you wish to watch and record elements of a social scene which you may or may not be participating in (this lends itself to an unstructured approach to observation)?

Structured observations are often categorised as a quantitative research method – though not exclusively so – since the structure allows for the generation of numbers. In the study above which investigated risk, gender and outdoor education, this student developed an observation schedule and recorded the number of times male and female teachers warned children of danger while taking part in Forest School activities. To conduct her research in this way she had to identify what linguistic constructions constituted warnings of danger and then simply tick these off during a series of Forest School lessons. This form of observation is known as *frequency count recording* e.g. male teachers made six warnings per session, while female teachers made two warnings per session. If this student was interested in children's gendered risk-taking she might have identified tree climbing as a risk-taking behaviour and observed the amount of time that boys and girls spent doing this while in the forest. This would be categorised as *duration recording* e.g. boys spent 13 minutes tree climbing while girls spent 7 minutes. Alternatively, she may have used an *interval recording* technique. To do this she would have to decide on the time interval she wished to break the observation into (e.g. 30 seconds); the students she wished to observe (e.g. boys in the class); and the type of behaviour she wished to observe (e.g. risky play). If the Forest School session lasted one hour (120 possible observations) and the boys participated in risky play in 10 observations then the student could conclude that the boys entered into risky play activity 12 per cent of the lesson.

A qualitative approach to observation lends itself to a much less structured observation design frame. Unlike the examples given above you would not pre-determine or decide in advance the categories or classifications before entering into the research setting. This type of observation is often termed participant observation as the researcher attempts to understand the social world from the inside and is thus participating within this social setting. The use of the term 'participant' often confuses students as they only associate it with research where the researcher has direct involvement in the social scene. To clarify this it is useful to draw upon the distinctions outlined by Wolcott (1988) with regards to levels of participation:

- the first level is that of 'complete-member-researcher' where you are a member of the group or social scene you are observing;
- the second categorisation is that of 'active-member-researcher' where you are not part of the group, but you are participating in their activities; and
- the third category is that of 'peripheral-member-researcher' where you are neither a member of the group nor participating in the group's activities.

This, of course, raises fundamental issues with regard to the role of the researcher when conducting observational research, in particular in relation to how involved s/he will be in the social scene that is being observed. When educational research takes place in the classroom, for example, it would be impossible for the researcher to enter the room unnoticed and adopt a 'complete-member-researcher' position (apart from types of action research where a practitioner is assessing or researching his/her own practice).

Practical Tip

Review your research question(s)/hypothesis. Can you answer or test these through the use of observations? If the answer is yes, then decide on who or what you might observe and what type of observation you think would be best suited to doing this.

Documentary analysis

> **Example:** A student research project which used documentary analysis as a tool for data collection
>
> **Research question:** How are European policies in relation to SEN interpreted within British, Scottish and Welsh educational contexts?

While the focus of much social research is on the spoken word, there is a wealth of written words that are often underused: Coffey and Atkinson (1996) highlight the fact that researchers often produce accounts of literate social worlds as if they were without writing, while Prior (2003) celebrates the written word as having as much value as the spoken word in the analysis and understanding of social action.

This is particularly true with regard to researchers working in the area of education where national government, local government and educational settings all have a wealth of documents which could be an accessible and rich source of data for any research project (n.b. most official documents are easily and freely available on the Internet).

There are a number of approaches to the use of documents within a research project. Some projects – especially those with a policy focus – can be conducted using documents exclusively: the student research project example above traced chains of policy in relation to SEN and inclusion from a European to a national (British) and then devolved (Welsh and Scottish) governmental levels. However, within research projects, documents can be used in conjunction with other research methods. In the project outlined above, for example, documentary analysis could inform interviews with headteachers and teachers in relation to their SEN policies or inform observations of how these policies are interpreted and implemented within the classroom.

The types and variety of documents that can be used within a research project are wide-ranging and certainly not confined to policy: other sources of documentary data includes biographies, diaries, letters, notes, institutional or corporate memoranda, minutes from meetings, emails, blogs or web pages. In addition, documents are not confined to the written word but can include audio and visual evidence such as pictures, photographs, newspaper reports, radio/television recordings and interactive websites. The most useful categorisation for the student researcher is to think of documents as being either personal (diaries, emails, photographs); private (institutional memoranda, minutes from meetings); or public (government reports, newspaper articles). Of course the value of documents – as with all social research – rests in assessing their quality as a data source. To assess this you need to first verify the document's authenticity (is it genuine?); next you must consider whether or not it is credible (are there errors or distortions which compromise its accuracy and integrity?); following this the representativeness of the document must be assessed (is it typical of the documents within its class?); finally you need to consider the document's meaning (can the document be understood and what is it attempting to say?).

> ## Activity
>
> Review your hypothesis/research question(s). Can you answer or test these through the use of documentary analysis? If the answer is yes then decide on what documents you might use and how you will access these.

Research Methods Which Only Use Numbers

This section of the chapter will consider research methods which only use numbers as a data source. Although you might expect the collection of such quantitative data to be through the use of survey instruments such as structured interviews/observations and questionnaires, the possibility exists (see below) for questionnaires to contain words as well as numbers. As Thomas (2013: 189) contends, there is a tendency to treat numbers as being 'superior envoys of truth'. While this should be resisted – as with words they are merely conduits for knowledge – there is a wealth of numerical data freely and easily available to the student researcher which could answer many interesting and important research questions. Questionnaires are explored more fully below and also in Chapter 11. In addition to the information provided above, therefore, relating to the structured interviews and observations this section will look solely at the use of secondary data.

> **Example:** A student research project which used secondary data analysis as part of its data collection
>
> **Research question:** What is the relationship between boys' and girls' month of birth and academic achievement in a South Wales primary school?

Secondary data analysis

From a practical perspective there are a number of advantages in using pre-existing sets of data:

- it costs little in terms of money and time;
- this data allows you to access information on a large and diverse population to which you would otherwise not have access; and
- the data should be of the highest quality.

There are, however, issues with regard to using data that has been collected by others: primarily – as with all methods – this involves a consideration of the appropriateness of this data for answering the questions that you have asked in *your* research project as this data will, in all likelihood, have been gathered to explore other concerns and answer other research questions.

Some secondary data sources in the UK

The Department for Education (DfE) (www.gov.uk/government/organisations/**department**-for-**education**): *the DfE provides a wealth of data on students' results, participation, academic progress as well as information on schools and work. The devolved governments of Wales (http://wales.gov.uk), Scotland (www.scotland.gov.uk) and Northern Ireland (www.deni.gov.uk) all have similar data for their populations.*

Economic and Social Data Service (ukdataservice.ac.uk): *this service provides access to a wide range of secondary data and is free to academic users.*

Neighbourhood Statistics (www.neighbourhood.statistics.gov.uk): *this resource collates data on particular geographic areas and the characteristics of the population who live there.*

www.secondarydataanalysis.com: *this is an additional resource which accompanies Emma Smith's excellent guide to using secondary data in educational research (Smith, 2008).*

The world has much data like this which offers exciting possibilities for the educational researcher. This data can be generated at a 'local' level within a particular school or local authority or it can be at a national or indeed international level: Smith (2011) gives the examples of the Pupil Census; the Millennium Cohort Study; and the Programme for International Student Achievement (PISA).

In the example above the student used data that had already been collected within the school to answer her first research question. As part of a mixed methods project the student also used interviews as a data gathering tool. Smith (2011) advocates the use of data within such small-scale projects and advises that analysing such data is relatively straightforward even for those she calls 'stats-phobic'. The examples Smith gives to illustrate this are: a mixed methods research project into life in a Sure Start project which used data from the UK National Census to access demographic data on the area in which the research project was taking place and the characteristics of those taking part and not taking part in the project; and a study into student experiences of taking a gap year using data available in the Youth Cohort Study.

Research Method Used for Generating Data in the Form of Words/Numbers

The methods considered previously in this chapter generally produce data solely in the form of words or number; the methods considered in this next section of the chapter can generate data as both words and/or numbers.

Example: A student research project which used questionnaires as part of its data collection

Research question: What are parents' opinions of the Foundation Phase curriculum?

Sub-questions:
- Are parents supportive of the Foundation Phase curriculum?
- Why are parents supportive or not supportive of the Foundation Phase curriculum?
- What changes do parents suggest should be implemented to improve the Foundation Phase curriculum?

Questionnaires

As with all research methods, when deciding on using a questionnaire you need to keep your research questions in mind. The questionnaire is very effective in generating data from a large sample of people in a relatively short period of time: its strength is thus breadth rather than depth.

Activity

Consider the research project above. Which of these questions do you feel could be best answered in a questionnaire? What types of question would you need within the question-naire to answer these research questions?

In the research project above a questionnaire could be a suitable method for assessing the opinions and attitudes of a wide variety of parents towards the Foundation Phase curriculum. A question relating to satisfaction levels with the Foundation Phase curriculum would generate data to answer this question, for example:

- 58% of parents are very satisfied;
- 20% of parents are satisfied;
- 12% of parents are neither satisfied or dissatisfied;
- 10% of parents are dissatisfied.

Where a questionnaire would have limitations would be in answering the 'why' question which requires a method that offers depth within the answer – there could be an open question within the questionnaire asking why people had the opinions they had, but this might generate additional qualitative data which required further analysis (see Chapter 11 for more guidance on questionnaires in general and this issue in particular).

Preparing a questionnaire

If you decide that a questionnaire *is* the appropriate method for testing your hypothesis or answering your research question(s) then you need to carefully plan its structure so that you can generate data that will give you answers to your questions. I always advise students to create a tree diagram to ensure that there is a close alignment between their main research question, their sub-research questions and the questions they will ask in their questionnaire.

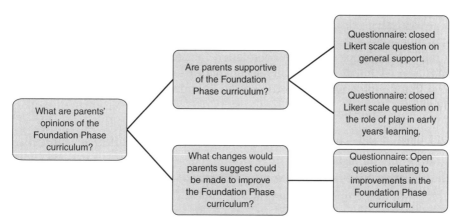

Figure 8.3   Using a tree diagram to generate questions

The first question you need to ask yourself relates to the research population to which you are distributing your questionnaire. Have you, for example, decided that you want to divide this research population into subcategories: in the study above if the researcher wished to find out the differences between fathers' and mothers' responses, the first question on the questionnaire needs to be related to the parents' gender.

Here are a series of tips to consider when devising a questionnaire:

- Good advice on constructing your questionnaire is the acronym 'KISS' – Keep It Short and Simple.
- Only ask questions that relate to your research questions. Whilst the participant's age, gender and social position may be relevant, do not include these types of questions unless you are specifically interested in these subcategories (again see Chapter 11 which discusses the use of variables such as these). However, be sure that you do include these questions if they are key to your study (I recently reviewed a questionnaire for a student whose research question related to boys' and girls' reading habits, yet there was no question relating to the gender of the respondent).
- Make sure your questions are not ambiguous – remember, unlike an interview, you will not have the opportunity to clarify any of your questions once they have been asked.

In the example given above in relation to the Foundation Phase one of the questions my student asked was a closed question 'do you visit your child's school often?' This is ambiguous because one person's understanding of visiting the school often differs greatly from another person's. A more precise question would have been: do you visit your child's school: daily; more than once a week; weekly; more than once a month; monthly; more than once a year; yearly; never?

- Avoid both leading questions and negatives (especially double negatives) within your questions. If you were running the project example above and asked the question, 'What pleases you most about the Foundation Phase curriculum?' then you must ensure that you also ask the question 'What are you least pleased with in the Foundation Stage curriculum?' otherwise this could be construed as a leading question. A question with a confusing double negative would be 'Do you believe that children who have not taken the Foundation Phase are not as well prepared for study in later life?' A much simpler version of this question would be, of course: 'Do you believe that children who have studied the Foundation Phase are better prepared for study in later life?'

You need to draft and then pilot your questionnaire. By going through this process you will eliminate any ambiguities or errors within your questionnaire design. If we take the research project we have been discussing in this section in relation to the Foundation Phase curriculum, two of the questions that the student originally included within her questionnaire were the open questions: what aspects of the Foundation Phase curriculum do you value most; and what aspects of the Foundation Phase curriculum do you value least? When she piloted this questionnaire she discovered that parents were unable to answer these questions because they did not have the requisite prior knowledge.

As will be seen in more detail in Chapter 11, questions which generate numbers are one of three types:

- forced choice
- multiple choice
- opinion/attitude

Consequently, in the example here the researcher modified this question so as to provide aspects of the curriculum and asked participants to list these from most to least important (probably by using an attitudinal scale), thus getting more useful data.

In doing this, of course, she was limiting the possible responses, but maximising the amount of data that did not require further interpretation. In other words she would be getting numbers rather than words. If she had used an open text box question, asking for the parental views, then she ran the risk of either getting too little or too much qualitative data. Open text boxes in questionnaires are therefore not recommended, unless you are prepared to risk getting little (or no) data or giving yourself the task of conducting further analysis of words.

| **Practical Tip** |

Piloting your questionnaire

A pilot study gives you the opportunity to pre-test your questionnaire. This is an essential part in the questionnaire design process as it allows you to:

- clarify ambiguous questions or instructions;
- test the length of time it takes a respondent to complete the questionnaire;
- assess whether or not the questions are giving a range of responses;
- edit the questionnaire in line with any feedback given to you by your respondents.

If you feel that you have to make major changes to your questionnaire as a result of this pilot, then you may want to edit your questionnaire and then re-pilot it, thus refining your research tool so that it effectively answers your research questions.

Maximising your response

When constructing your questionnaire, always keep the participant in mind (remember that they are giving you their precious time and that they may have little or no knowledge or, in some cases, even interest in the area that you are researching). Normally, the easier a questionnaire is to follow, the higher your response rate will be. Just as in interviews, where I advised you to begin with questions to make the respondent feel at ease, make sure that you do not begin your questionnaire with questions that will make the respondent feel uncomfortable. It is best, for example, to leave open-ended questions to the end of the questionnaire (if you decide to use them). Always attach a brief letter of explanation with your questionnaire, outlining what your project is and giving the respondent an indication of how long it will take to complete; ensure that this is easily understood and written in a friendly tone which avoids all academic jargon. (Again see Chapter 11 for further guidance on how to maximise your response.)

Key Points to Remember

- Do not consider your methods *before* you have finalised your design frame.
- Make sure that the method(s) you choose answer your research question(s).
- Consider the practical issues of using the research method that you have decided upon.
- Pilot your method to refine its use.
- Consider other research projects that have used the method(s) you are considering in the area that you are researching.

This chapter aimed to offer an overview of methods that are available in an educational context. Chapters 9, 10, 11 and 12 that follow aim to discuss in detail these methods to offer theoretical information as well as practical examples on how to use these methods and how to analyse the data you collect.

Further Reading

For an introduction to research methods you can further your reading with the following:

Menter, I., Elliot, D., Hulme, M., Lewin, J. and Lowden, K. (2011) *A Guide to Practitioner Research in Education*. London: SAGE.

Punch, K. F. (2009) *Introduction to Research Methods in Education*. London: SAGE.

If your research involves young children this book will help you to design, select and undertake your research:

O'Reilly, M., Ronzoni, P. and Dogra, N. (2013) *Research with Children: Theory and Practice*. London: SAGE.

Useful Websites

- National Foundation for Educational Research (NFER)
  www.nfer.ac.uk/schools/developing-young-researchers/how-to-choose-your-research-methods.cfm

- Palgrave Study Skills
  www.palgrave.com/studentstudyskills/page/choosing-appropriate-research-methodologies

- University of Plymouth – Research Methods in Education
  www.edu.plymouth.ac.uk/resined/resedhme.htm

References

Alaszewski, A (2006) *Using Diaries for Social Research*. London: SAGE.

Coffey, A. and Atkinson, P. (1996) *Making Sense of Qualitative Data: Complementary Research Strategies*. Thousand Oaks, CA: SAGE.

Cohen, L., Manion, L. and Morrison, K. (2011) *Research Methods in Education* (7/E). London: Routledge.

Fontana, A. and Frey, J.H. (1994) 'Interviewing: The art of science', in N.K. Denzin and Y.S. Lincoln (eds), *Handbook of Qualitative Research*. Thousand Oaks, CA: SAGE, pp. 361–376.

Holland, S., Renold, E., Ross, N.J. and Hilman, A. (2010) 'Power, agency and participatory agendas: A critical exploration of young people's engagement in participative qualitative research', *Childhood*, 17(3): 36–37.

Janesick, V.J. (1994) 'The dance of qualitative research design: Metaphor, methodolatory, and meaning', in N.K. Denzin and Y.S. Lincoln (eds), *Handbook of Qualitative Research*. Thousand Oaks, CA: SAGE, pp. 209–219.

Morgan, M., Gibbs, S., Maxwell, K. and Britten, N. (2002) 'Hearing children's voices: Methodological issues in conducting focus groups with children aged 7–11 years', *Qualitative Researcher*, 2(5): 6–20.

Patton, M.Q. (2002) *Qualitative Research and Evaluation Methods*. Thousand Oaks, CA: SAGE.

Prior, L. (2003) *Using Documents in Social Research*. London: SAGE.

Punch, K.F. (2009) *Introduction to Research Methods in Education*. London: SAGE.

Punch, S. (2002) 'Research with children: The same or different from research with adults?', *Childhood*, 9(3): 321–341.

Smith, E. (2008) *Using Secondary Data in Educational and Social Research*. Buckingham: Open University Press.

Smith, E. (2011) 'Using numeric secondary data in education research', British Educational Research Association online resource. Available at: www.bera.ac.uk/resources/using-numeric-secondary-data-education-research. Accessed 11 April 2013.

Thomas, G. (2013) *How to do your Research Project* (3/E). London: SAGE.

Wolcott, H.F. (1988) 'Ethnographic research in education', in R.M. Jaeger (ed.), *Complementary Methods for Research in Education*. Washington, DC: American Educational Research Association, pp. 187–249.

For additional online resources please visit the book's website:
https://study.sagepub.com/needhamandpalaiologou

9

COLLECTING QUALITATIVE DATA
YU-HAO KATE LIN

Chapter Aims and Objectives

This chapter aims to help you to:

- understand the characteristics of qualitative data;
- differentiate different roles of researchers in data collection;
- select appropriate participants of study;
- familiarise yourself with the purpose, process, techniques and limitations of interviews, observations and documents as three of the commonly used qualitative data collection methods;
- assess interviewing, facilitation, observation and note-taking skills;
- develop guidelines or criteria for conducting semi-structured interviews, focus group and participant observation;
- understand effective ways to manage a range of qualitative data sources; and
- evaluate the reliability and validity of data collection methods and the principles of triangulation.

Introduction

The design and process of empirical material collection is one of the key components to determine the integrity of research. Decisions and practices made throughout the data collection process are influenced by the research inquiry and interpretive paradigm of a study and influence the analysis and interpretation of the data as well as the evaluation of the research quality. Accordingly, being aware of a range of inquiry methods and practical strategies to collect qualitative data and how to use them effectively to gather relevant data for an understanding of the phenomena being investigated is the major focus of this chapter.

Nature and Types of Qualitative Data

- Qualitative data are varied and divided into three main forms including texts, images, and sounds which are not presented in numbers or digits (Ryan and Bernard, 2000). Textual data involve descriptions of, for example, attitudes, perceptions, perspectives, assumptions or judgements of individuals or groups about specific themes in question. For instance, researchers are able to go far beyond 'snapshots' of 'what' or 'how many' and discover more details about 'how' and 'why' things happen. Another feature of qualitative data is that they focus on naturally occurring and ordinary events in real life settings to explain why certain thoughts and behaviours occur in specific social, cultural and physical contexts. This is described here as a 'constructionist' approach to research.
- In sum, qualitative data are rich and holistic and situated to locate meanings of people's lived experience or place events, processes and structures of lives in the social world around them at a specific point in time (Miles and Huberman, 1994).

Role(s) of Researcher in Data Collection

As a researcher you could be seen as an 'outsider' when you do not have any relationship with the community being investigated and thus have a different mindset and behaviour from members within that community. On the contrary, you are seen as an 'insider' when carrying out an investigation in a community to which you belong. In this respect, you share the values, life customs and behavioural manners of other members within that community and may well possess to some degree shared or similar opinions about situations or issues.

I suggest, however, that no educational researcher is a complete outsider or insider to specific settings being investigated as a constructionist researcher is not a blank sheet when entering the field of an inquiry. For instance, you may develop particular interests in certain social phenomena according to your personal experiences and also understanding of the phenomena gained through the background of your academic training and study of the field. That is to say, your prior knowledge constructed from previous experiences and the examination of the literature affect the formulation of interview questions or the focus of observations (Rodwell, 1998). It is important to recognise the implications of each role (Griffiths, 1998). For example, one criticism is that outsiders are sometimes exploitative and disrespectful and cannot understand and represent the experiences of the subjects of their inquiry properly (Bridges, 2002). To avoid possible drawbacks, the following principles are suggested (Bridges, 2002: 86):

- sensitive and reflexive understanding of the experience of others;
- respect for others as persons;
- listening to others in conditions of respect and care;
- mutuality of benefit and gratefulness for the relationships; and
- openness to criticism and the exposure of prejudice.

Based upon these principles and their research and interactions with informants, it is then up to the researcher to make judgements of what they perceive to be 'truth'.

Selection of Informants

Subsequent to defining your research purpose, themes in question, a bounded system (such as an elementary school in a Taiwanese educational context) and units of analysis, the following questions need to be considered and are dependent on the choice of sampling:

- What types of information are to be gathered?
- Where and when to collect data?
- From whom to obtain relevant data?

Unlike 'probability' (or 'non-purposive') sampling, which depends on selecting random and statistical representative samples to produce confident generalisations from the samples to a larger population (Cohen et al., 2011), 'purposive sampling' is based on a pre-determined purpose and samples are accordingly selected to include participants of interest and exclude those who do not suit the purpose. Sample sizes depend on resources, time available and the objectives of the study. This type of sampling technique helps you to select 'information-rich cases' for in-depth study (Patton, 1990; also see Creswell, 1998) and is suggested for adoption for naturalistic or qualitative inquiry (Lincoln and Guba, 1985; Miles and Huberman, 1994).

'Opportunistic sampling' is another technique helping you to identify significant activities to observe and questions to ask during the data collection process if you are doing case studies (Patton, 1990: 169–183). This type of sampling involves readily available respondents who are convenient for the researcher to focus upon and usually involve rich cases capable of in-depth study. Ongoing analysis of collected data, interpretation of critical incidents and review of the relevant literature along with an open and sensitive mind enable you to capture and enquire into those naturally occurring incidents and opportunities more thoroughly.

In constructionist research, in which social reality is put together and develops meaning, methodological design and decisions can emerge and change gradually as data collection proceeds (Erlandson and Harris, 1993). Within this research the focus is on how participants construct their world and their everyday lives. This explains why you may not be able to anticipate exactly what would happen in your chosen site. In other words, those unforeseen, but relevant, events or behaviours could not be taken into account in the design of data collection. Your recognition of the complexity of the context being investigated and your understanding of that context and multiple realities collected throughout the investigation may help you to be aware of what is appropriate to answer research questions and thus to look for ways to accumulate more relevant evidence by purposive sampling.

Methods of Collecting Qualitative Data

Research methods refer to techniques and procedures used in the process of data collection and analysis to obtain vivid information and in-depth understanding (Oliver, 2004; Cohen et al., 2011). For naturalistic (or constructionist) inquiries, methods allowing open-ended and inductive styles of questioning and observation are suggested as being more suitable (Lincoln and Guba, 1985; Erlandson and Haris, 1993; Rodwell, 1998). Researchers are encouraged to use a range of appropriate, practical, creative and adventurous methods to answer their research questions by investigating complex phenomena. For example, in looking at how teachers' pedagogical beliefs are embodied in the classroom, observations and informal conversational interviews can be adapted to find out how those beliefs are unpacked as classroom activities and practised in context.

In the following sections, three of most commonly-used methods for collecting qualitative data are discussed: interviews, observations and documents.

Interviews

In this section you will be given guidance on three of the most common types of interviews undertaken in qualitative research – the semi-structured, informal conversational and group interviews. It is also possible to use a structured interview, but these tend to consist of closed or attitudinal questions which do not allow the participant to express views and are, in essence, verbal questionnaires. Although such interviews have their place in educational research they are not explored here and more information on their use can be found in the previous chapter. Here we concentrate on semi-structured, informal conversational and group interviews in order to:

1. Describe functions, uses and limitations of semi-structured, informal conversational and group interviews (sometimes referred to as focus groups);
2. Outline steps for conducting a semi-structured interview and a group discussion;
3. Select appropriate samples of interest;
4. Draft an interview schedule and a focus group guide; and
5. Identify good facilitation, questioning, probing and note-taking skills and also ways to organise data to be gathered through interviewing and discussion.

An interview approach seeks to generate knowledge in relation to a topic of interest and situates data in their social settings through the process of interchanging viewpoints among people of interest (Kvale, 2007). Therefore the interview is often viewed as the most appropriate method to adopt where research aims to explore:

1. individuals' perceptions of structures and processes within a social unit (such as a school); and
2. meanings of specific phenomena to individuals (King, 1994).

Semi-Structured Interview

A semi-structured interview contains open-ended questions and aims to relate theoretical perspectives with real life circumstances by encouraging interviewees to reflect on and discuss their interpretations of interview themes (Scott and Usher, 1999; Cohen et al., 2011).

Prior to the interview, themes of a semi-structured interview are normally formulated in the light of research questions and literature review. For example, if investigating teachers' perspective on a school's support for their continuing professional development, interview questions could be organised by themes regarding appraisal and reward systems, initiatives and strategies to support professional learning and development of professional communities. Those themes can then be organised into a semi-structured interview schedule to ensure the coverage of important issues and also to allow flexibility to address individually initiated concerns throughout the interviewing process (Drever, 1995; Hitchcock and Hughes, 1995; Berg, 2004).

Focused interviewing actively involves probing in order to stimulate the respondent to elicit rich data in a way that does not involve too much intervention from the interviewer. There is also always a danger that an interviewer provides too strong a reflection of self within the data (Bernard, 2011). Main questions under each theme can be formed in a logical sequence with probes and prompts to avoid confusion and flow the interviewing process naturally since the order of questions affect interviewees' thinking and influences what they say (Fielding and Thomas, 2001).

It is worthwhile to give a proposed semi-structured interview schedule a trial run under realistic conditions and find out how the pilot participants interpret the questions and subsequently make modifications accordingly (Drever, 1995; Mertens, 1998; Pole and Lampard, 2002). Convenience, access and geographical proximity could be the criteria for pilot participant selection. Even though data collected from piloting will not be used and analysed, it is essential to explain what your research is about and how it will be conducted so that pilot respondents are able to situate themselves in context. In sum, piloting your interview schedule provides you with opportunities to practise in advance, enables you to gather various viewpoints from different angles and builds up your confidence.

Conduct of Semi-Structured Interview

Depending on your research objectives and questions, the same interview topics and sequence could be used for different groups of interviewees to increase the comparability of responses (Patton, 1990). The length of interview varies depending on the availability of individual respondents' time or interactions between interviewees and interviewers. Before each interview, it is necessary to explain the purpose of the interview, assure confidentiality and ask permission to record or make notes (see Robson, 2011 and Chapter 3 of this book). Interviewees should be able to choose their preference of recording the interview which is normally either through use of a digital recording device or by note-taking so that they feel more comfortable and relaxed throughout the whole interviewing process (Hitchcock and Hughes, 1995). To obtain detailed information in the course of the interview, the following tips help you to get interviewees to talk as freely and openly as possible, including:

- listening more than speaking;
- asking questions in a straightforward, clear and non-threatening way;
- avoiding using cues to lead certain responses; and
- showing your enjoyment.

Furthermore, effective use of probes and prompts helps to direct interviewees towards what they know but have not yet mentioned, or can be used for clarification and explanation of what they have already said. Table 9.1 provides some examples:

Table 9.1 Examples of effective probes. Mack et al. (2005)

Direct Questions	Indirect Probes
• What do you mean when you say...? • How did this happen? • How do you feel about...? • What happened then? • Can you tell me more? • Can you please elaborate? • I am not sure I understand X. Would you explain that to me? • How did you handle X? • How did X affect you? • Can you give me an example of X?	• Neutral verbal expressions such as 'uh huh,' 'interesting' and 'I see.' • Verbal expressions of empathy such as 'I can see why you say that was difficult for you.' • Mirroring techniques or repeating what an informant has just said such as 'So you were 19 when you had your first child.' • Culturally appropriate body language or gestures such as nodding in acknowledgement.

Informal Conversational Interview

The informal conversational interview is viewed as the most open-ended means to gather viewpoints (Patton, 1990). Thus, an interview schedule would not be necessary for informal conversational interviews since it is not feasible to predict what incidents would naturally occur as an investigation goes along (Patton, 1990; Berg, 2004). For instance, when investigations require researchers to do site visits for an extended period of time such as longitudinal or case study research, researchers tend to constantly analyse data collected, reflect on the data collection process and review the literature. As a result, certain issues and emergent themes may be realised which are not addressed in predetermined interview or focus group schedules. In this case, the use of an informal conversational interview is practical to capture viewpoints on those emergent critical incidents. That is to say, the informal conversational interview could be seen as an emergent design example and the length of this kind of interview varies depending on participants' experiences of and involvement in the circumstances. Similar to the conduct of semi-structured interviews, the purpose of the interview, the assurance of confidentiality and the informed permission to record, plus the adoption of particular behaviours and the offer of the interview transcripts need to be indicated at various stages of the informal conversational interview.

Focus Group

The terms 'group interview' and 'focus group' appeared to be synonyms; nevertheless, 'focus group' is viewed as an adjunct to group interview (Denscombe, 1998; Cohen et al., 2011; Robson, 2011). Unlike the 'group interview' focusing on the interaction between an interviewer and a group, a 'focus group' emphasises the interaction among a group of six to ten individuals to share their viewpoints on specific topics and themes of focus (Morgan, 1997). Pre-screening sex, age and marital status, educational backgrounds, ethnic group and culture or level of expertise is helpful to select participants with homogeneous character-istics. However, focus groups may not be appropriate for acquiring information on highly personal or sensitive topics.

Similar to when conducting other types of interview, a focus group discussion starts with an introduction of you and the purpose of your study and subsequently moves on to the explanation of the value and importance of the group's opinions and how the information will be used in the study. Moreover, the introduction needs to address ground rules and duration and conveys the expectation that everyone will contribute, all contributions will be valued and remain confidential and how the discussion will be recorded. Be warned, however, that transcribing group discussions is time-consuming especially if it includes dif-ferent voices, so you may wish to use video recording. Alternatively it would be ideal to have an interviewer and one note-taker facilitating focus groups so that the interviewer could pay as much attention as possible to discussions. The note-taker notes key words, participant quotes, and who says what, observes body language and also manages time and any recording device used.

Within the group you will play a role as a moderator with effective probing techniques to guide informal, fluid and relaxed discussion, encourage participants to talk freely and reveal their thoughts and feelings about the research topic and themes. Focus group ques-tions tend to be open-ended and thus the discussion may be loosely structured. Skills to manage group dynamics and discussion time are crucial in facilitating focus groups. To help with that, here is a focus group discussion guide to illustrate the process, and stress at the beginning the importance of everyone's voice being heard.

- Adapt or rephrase questions to a specific community of participants;
- Make repeat questions sufficiently detailed and open-ended;
- Start with easy questions and put objective, descriptive, less personal questions before subjective, value-oriented, personal ones;
- Be flexible about the sequencing of questions where appropriate;
- Summarise key messages before moving on to another question or topic;
- Use humour where appropriate to help people relax;
- Make sure that conversation occurs naturally and is not going around in a circle;
- Deal with those dominating the discussion and encourage participants to dialogue with one another;
- Give sufficient time to think and allow participants to complete their thoughts and sentences;
- Redirect people when they are not speaking from their own experience;
- Be sensitive about body language and maintain appropriate eye contact with participants;
- Avoid sharing your own opinion;
- Avoid lecturing;
- Avoid trying to force participants to reach consensus.

Activity

Think of the major functions of the semi-structured interview, informal conversational interview and focus group. Analyse the advantages and limitations of each. Filling in the Table 9.2 is helpful to externalise your thoughts.

Table 9.2 Choice of interview approach

Types of Interview	Major Functions	Advantages	Limitations
Semi-structured interview			
Informal conversational interview			
Focus group			

---| **Practical Tip** |--

Validating interview data

The notion of member checking is necessary subsequent to any form of interviews – offering transcripts, your interpretations of responses and conclusions drawn from data analysis to respondents in order to validate interview data.

Keeping a record of your interview is also recommended. Table 9.3 is an example of how you could keep a record of interviews being conducted.

Table 9.3 Overview of interviews

Types of Interview		Respondents							
		T1	T2	T3	T4	T5	T6	P	SCTL
Semi – Structured Interview	*Date & Time*								
	Length								
	Venue								
	Schedule Used	Semi-structured interview schedule – A						Semi-structured interview schedule – B	
	Recording Technique	Digital recorder							
Informal Conversational Interview	*Date & Time*								
	Length								
	Venue								
	Schedule Used	Based on informal conversational interview questions							
	Recording Technique	Digital recorder & digital video camera							
Focus Group	*Date & Time*								
	Length								
	Venue								
	Schedule Used	Focus group interview question							
	Recording Technique	Digital recorder & digital video camera							

Notes: interviewees' names are encoded according to the Grade they teach, 'P' means the 'Principal' and 'SCTL' means the 'Section Chief of Teaching and Learning' of a case school.

Observations

Observation is commonly employed as the means to understand 'live' situations in physical, human, interactional or programme settings by looking at and reflecting on them (Patton, 1990; Morrison, 1993; Cohen et al., 2011). It provides holistic, 'thick descriptions' of, for example, education systems and processes and records practices. It is a useful but time-consuming data collection method in studies of practice in educational settings.

Observation can be in a structured, semi-structured or an unstructured manner depending on sampling techniques. For example, time sampling is used when you set a designated amount of time and observe what is happening. Alternatively event sampling, known as experience sampling, allows you to note down what is happening in ongoing experiences and events which may vary over the course of an extended period in their naturally occurring settings (Reis and Gable, 2000).

Qualitative observation is classified into three basic types (Angrosino, 2005), including:

- *Naturalistic observation* which is conducted in natural settings without awareness, manipulation or intervention;
- *Participant observation* which involves a researcher participating in situations in a natural setting and/or manipulates the environment;
- *Laboratory observation* which takes place in a controlled setting, such as experiments, with and/or without participants' awareness and a researcher's involvement.

In this section of the chapter you will be given guidance to:

1. Distinguish between different types of observation and in particular:
   a) Describe the function and uses of participant observation;
   b) Differentiate various roles researchers play in participant observation and how the level of their involvement imposes certain limitations on research;
   c) Select appropriate sampling techniques for participant observation;
2. Draft observation guidelines;
3. Identify effective skills and useful tools for note-taking and data organisation; and
4. Recognise the possible uses and value of composing a research journal.

Activity

To address the research question '*How do teachers infuse thinking skills in their instruction and interaction with pupils?*' please consider whether observation is an appropriate data collection method. If so, please answering the following questions and draft an observation checklist or guide:

- What type of observation will be more effective for me to employ?
- What potential themes and scenarios will I be observing and find?
- What will I be observing?

(Continued)

(Continued)

- Who will I be observing?
- How will I observe?
- Where and when can I observe?
- What will my role and degree of involvement be throughout the data collection process?
- How will I gather, record and organise observational data?
- Will I be keeping a research journal? If so, what will be included and how often will I review and reflect on the content?

Participant Observation

Participant observation is a commonly adopted approach in educational research. It allows you to immerse yourself as an observer and/or participant in an educational setting and the quality of observational data depends on your ability to catch meaningful moments or incidents (Lightfoot, 1983). Such immersion leads to so-called 'persistent observation' assisting you to experience things as an insider and get insights into those events in order to understand contextual characteristics and factors meaningfully so that the analysis and interpretation of the empirical data will not appear to be superficial (Denscombe, 1998; Robson, 2011).

Your role and level of involvement in participant observation are complex and may impact on the reliability of data collected. For example, in a study looking at teachers' continuing professional development in a school setting, the researcher could participate in professional development workshops passively to observe forms of interaction between workshop leaders and teachers and play a role as 'participant-as-observer' when providing feedback. This requires the researcher to not only play different roles, but also use a number of techniques, skills and his/her five senses (i.e. taste and smell, as well as touch, vision and hearing) to collect data. Some limitations indicated are that recorded data cannot provide holistic descriptions of individuals, groups or events. Researcher biases could result from sampling based on personal beliefs about what is relevant and important. Interpretation of observational data may thus represent a subjective view of multiple realities based on researchers' understanding and experiences (Scott and Usher, 1999; see also Chapter 6 of this book for a discussion on researcher positionality). That is to say, qualitative observational data relies on memory, personal discipline and the diligence of researchers.

Table 9.4 illustrates a range of flexible positions in a continuum of participatory involvement (Gorman and Clayton, 2005: 16):

Table 9.4   Role of observer and degree of participation and limitations

Role of observer	Level of involvement	Limitations
Complete observer/ unobtrusive observer	*Non Participation* No level of involvement or interaction with insiders.	- In-depth understanding of behaviours in insiders' own worlds is not allowed. - Building rapport and asking questions for new information are restricted.

Role of observer	Level of involvement	Limitations
Observer-as-participant	*Passive Participation* Little level of involvement or interaction with insiders.	• Opportunities to immerse in situations are limited. • Misunderstandings and misconceptions of researchers' roles may be caused.
Moderate membership/ peripheral membership	*Moderate Participation* Balance between insider and outsider roles in the way that researchers interact with insiders and engage in, but not participate in activities observed.	• Researchers' fear of being subjective as interpreting data may be caused. • Level of participatory involvement may be intentionally restricted by researchers.
Participant-as-observer/ active membership	*Active Participation* High level of involvement in major activities but not ready to embrace values, goals, skills or customs as members.	• Objectivity may be limited. • Role as an observer may be switched to an informant.
Complete membership	*Complete Participation* Prior integration with insiders and thus full involvement in activities.	• Findings revealed and arguments made may not be convincing. • Researchers may not be able to capture specific behaviours or significant incidents as they have 'gone too native' to recognise them.

Adapted from Adler and Adler (1994); Gorman and Clayton (2005)

Observation Guides

Developing an observation guide prior to data collection is helpful in the way that it identifies what you will be looking for in each case. It is also practical to trial a developed observation guide or checklist enabling you to practise and make necessary adjustments. The following box is an example of guidelines for classroom teaching observation shared between a researcher and teachers being investigated:

Example: Observing teaching

The purpose of observing your teaching is to explore how you synthesise and interpret your knowledge into classroom instruction. It is also beneficial for me to gain a better understanding of your teaching circumstances. I would like to observe you once a week for two hours from September 2004 to January 2005. I will take notes while observing you and the observational notes of each lesson will be made available for you at the beginning of the following week, which can also be used as a reference if you wish to discuss your teaching issues and problems with other teachers. I will not attempt to influence your teaching when in your classroom. Therefore, my location in your classroom will be negotiated with you. The data recorded from the observation will be confidential and only used for this research. The interpretation and use of the information will be shared and agreed with you prior to its being published as a research thesis. Your name will not be mentioned in any circumstances or in any conversations with other teachers.

Activity

Develop a list to identify the sort of information that you would include in your guidelines for classroom teaching observation such as that above. Think about how the guidelines you develop would influence your approaches and preparations for the observation.

Recording Observations

It is useful to decide how to effectively and objectively record all accounts and observations. A narrative system such as observational forms and field notes is more economical compared with video recording and may make participants feel more comfortable (Simpson and Tuson, 1995). Table 9.5 is an example of how to organise observational data collected.

Table 9.5   Overview of observations

Types of observation		Date(s)	Length	Venue	Recording Technique
Observation of Class-room Teaching	T1		80 mins		Observational form
	T2				
	T3				
	T4				
	T5				
	T6				
Observation of Action Learning	Set Meetings		1 hour		Using a digital recorder and a digital video camera
			1 hour		
			1.5 hours		
			2 hours		
			2 hours		
			1.25 hours		
			2 hours		
			1.75 hours		
			1 hour		
			1 hour		
Observation of Professional Development Activities	Educational Seminars		2 hours		Field note
	Peer Observation & Group Discussion		40 mins + 1 hour		Observation form

Types of observation		Date(s)	Length	Venue	Recording Technique
Observation of School Meetings			40 mins + 1 hour		
			40 mins + 30 mins		
			40 mins + 40 mins		
	Professional Workshops		2 hours		Field note
	Morning Meetings		30 mins		Observational form
			30 mins		
			45 mins		
			1 hour		
			15 mins		
			40 mins		
			40 mins		
			35 mins		
	Administrative Affairs Meetings				Field note
			2.5 hours		Observational form
	Curriculum Planning Meetings		2 hours		Observational form
			1.5 hours		

Improving Your Note-Taking Skills

Taking notes on what you have observed and on what participants say is necessary regardless of whether the observation is digitally recorded. The amount of detail and the quality of description are crucial to record observational data. These notes serve as a backup when recording fails but also capture non-verbal clues such as body language and facial expressions. Everyone has their own style of note-taking and format of notes. The list below, however, provides you with an overview of elements to be included in observational notes as follows:

- venue, date and time;
- descriptions of the setting and informants;
- scripts and summaries of behaviours occurring in relation to key areas of focus;
- expanded notes with sub-themes, examples and insights.

Considering the amount of qualitative data you will need to manage and organise, it is useful to review observational notes straight after the observation so that you can refresh your memory about the scripting or recall some critical occurrences which have not been noted. Simultaneously, you could note down insights into contexts, relationships and behaviour, thoughts and connections reflecting main and sub-themes of the study, which could be kept in a so-called research journal, diary or log (see below).

Reflexive and Reflective Journals

The notion of 'human as instrument' requires researchers to be sensitive and flexible when interacting with data encountered in the data collection process. For instance, your prior knowledge may be gradually expanded and modified when confronted with unpredictable issues in the research process. It was McAdams (1997) who raised the question about the problem of modern identity. He viewed the self as a reflexive project that an individual can work upon so that, like a work of art, an identity is a product or a project. Thus the self is something that an individual works upon in everyday life and develops over time, with many layers and the potential for possessing inner depth. Additionally, his/her identity (or multiple identities: see e.g. Alcoff and Potter, 1993; Reinharz, 1997) as a researcher including roles, values, ideas, knowledge, motivation and prejudices may to some extent influence the research process. Nonetheless, such identit(ies) may bring about bias in different stages of research. To minimise and avoid researcher assumptions and biases shaping the data collection process, keeping a reflexive journal to record the daily (or weekly) research schedule, insights and reasons for methodological decisions and to reflect upon a researcher's values, interests and growing insights with regard to the research is also recommended (Lincoln and Guba, 1985; Erlandson and Harris, 1993). In this sense keeping a reflexive journal is a very personal thing as it provides insights into the relationship of the mindset and former experiences of the researcher against the research being undertaken.

Keeping a research diary to track changes made and to monitor personal growth throughout the research process is a powerful way to:

1. Think about your own identities and roles at the different stages of the process;
2. Capture sense perceptions and tacit understandings of phenomena; and accordingly
3. Expand and modify your constructs when confronted with unpredictable issues.

That is to say, tacit forms of personal knowledge involved in the meaning and decision-making processes will be externalised explicitly and they will also monitor the personal growth of the researcher.

A reflective journal is used as a means to capture participants' growth and knowledge for meaning making and reflective thinking on specific events and experiences (Francis, 1995). It can also be used as a means of professional development. For example, in teacher education, the composition of a teaching diary could provide tangible evidence of mental processes of individual teachers, making their thoughts visible and concrete by means of interacting with, elaborating on and expanding ideas and articulating connections between new ideas and what they had already known (Kerka, 1996). In this sense a reflective journal enables a researcher to record the progress of their own learning. It is a document that grows with the learner or, in this case, the researcher, in a way that encourages reflection and self-directed learning. This could be seen as another form of qualitative data as it can be used to validate the learning process, for the purpose of interpretations of data and also to support presentation.

A list of guidelines for writing a reflective journal with explanations helps to give participants an orientation of what they are expected to write about. Two issues need to be communicated with participants to avoid unwanted outcomes. First, it is identified that some people write their journals descriptively rather than reflecting on meaningful and relevant events and experiences due to the fact that either the guidelines do not motivate reflection or they do not know how to write reflectively (Paterson, 1995). Second, there is a drawback in that some journal writers just write for others, but not for themselves, i.e. they write what they think others wish to see (ibid.). A reflective journal helps the researcher to provide connections between their research, thoughts, ideas and personal learning journey and in qualitative research this helps to bring out their understanding of actions and behaviours as well as to identify questions.

Documents as Sources of Qualitative Data

Data collected through interviews, focus groups and observations could be seen as primary sources; however, secondary sources are also relevant to look at to support the analysis and arguments of research findings. Yin (1989, 2003) classifies the sources of documents into *documentation* e.g. letters, meeting minutes, progress reports, etc. and *archival records* e.g. service records of clients, organisational charts and budgets, maps and diaries (see also Hitchcock and Hughes, 1995). Such secondary documents can foster your understanding of contextual characteristics and causal relationships leading to background meaning to support the analysis, interpretation and audits of data. Wellington (2000) defines the degree of access to documents from closed or restricted to those that are openly published. Assuming access, therefore, it can be possible to undertake qualitative research through such sources.

Managing Qualitative Data

Multiple sources of qualitative data need to be recorded and stored systematically. You could categorise them by research methods with back-up files labelled with date, time and place. The following activity allows you to think about how you will manage your data.

Activity

Think about a research project you have completed or are about to design. Consider data collection methods you have applied or are planning to employ at different stages and how those data are recorded and filed by completing the following table:

Table 9.6 Choosing data collection methods

Stages	Data Collection Methods	Record of Data
Pre-stage	Composition of a research diary	
In-stage		
Post-stage		

Reliability and Validity in Qualitative Research

Evaluating the quality of the research process you are undertaking is essential and you will need to demonstrate that appropriate principles and procedures have been used to ensure the reliability of research methods and the validity of conclusions (Silverman, 2005). Reliability in qualitative research relates to the evaluation of data collection methods which should be consistent and not distort research findings (Denscombe, 2002; Silverman, 2005). Specifically, reliability in this context is concerned with the degree of fit between what research records as data and what actually happens in the natural setting being investigated (Bogdan and Biklen, 1992).

Nevertheless, the above perspective does not denote the necessity of uniformity since two researchers investigating the same phenomenon may emerge with dissimilar findings (Cohen et al., 2011). In a similar vein, Walker (1993: 177) specifies that case study research focuses on *collecting definitions of situations* (that is, multiple realities) which are open to various interpretations. Such multiple realities constructed by individuals are changing and therefore it is less meaningful to take reliability into account in the evaluation of qualitative research (Kirk and Miller, 1986; Walker, 1993). Accordingly, Seale (1999) suggests low-inference descriptors (that is, recording data as concretely as possible) as a means to strengthen the reliability of collected data to allow the audience to formulate their own interpretation based on those reliable data.

Alongside reliability sits the notion of validity. Although validity is more often associated with forms of scientific research, because it involves assessing whether the research measures what it was intended to measure, it also helps the researcher to seek truth from the process of research (Golafshani, 2003). Instead of the form of precise measurement expected within quantitative research, within qualitative research validity comes from an assessment of the less definable trustworthiness, rigour and the overall quality of the process in a way that differentiates good from bad research.

Triangulation

> Triangulation is not a tool or a strategy of validation, but an alternative to validation. The combination of multiple multi-methodological practices, empirical materials, perspectives, and observers in a single study is best understood, then, as a strategy that adds rigor, breadth, complexity, richness, and depth to any inquiry. (Flick, 1998: 229–231).

Triangulation is commonly viewed as a means of using more than one source of information to validate findings and conclusions drawn and thus achieve a high level of accuracy. Triangulating data will facilitate you to maintain a critical attitude towards multiple realities being investigated and to increase the degree of convergence. It will enable you to seek out similarities and differences of various experiences and perspectives and consequently to develop convergent findings. Four types of triangulation are identified and summarised as follows (Patton, 1990; Stake, 1995; Denzin and Giardina, 2006):

- *Triangulation of Methods:* that is, to employ different research methods to collect data and subsequently to compare or integrate them to answer research questions.
- *Triangulation of Data Sources:* that is, to compare or cross-check the consistency of collected data derived at different times, spaces or respondents.
- *Triangulation of Investigators:* that is, to compare or integrate multiple interpretations of the same phenomenon given by different researchers.
- *Triangulation of Theories:* that is, to use different theoretical perspectives to look at the same phenomenon to develop more appropriate insights or interpretations about the phenomenon.

In terms of validity, triangulation supports processes that improve the validity of the research process. However, Lincoln and Guba (1985) distinguish the differences between positivist elements of validity such as 'internal validity' which are much more about measurement, to use the concept of 'trustworthiness' for qualitative data. Each aspect of trustworthiness has a parallel with criteria used in quantitative research:

- *Credibility* which parallels internal validity, i.e. how believable are the findings?
- *Transferability* which parallels external validity, i.e. do the findings apply to other contexts?
- *Dependability* which parallels reliability, i.e. are the findings likely to apply at other times?
- *Confirmability* which parallels objectivity, i.e. has the investigator allowed his or her values to intrude to a higher degree? (Bryman, 2012: 390)

The concept of trustworthiness thus sits more comfortably within qualitative research and researchers are advised to examine the strength of their data in this manner.

Key Points to Remember

- Qualitative data including texts, images and sounds are varied and situated in specific settings at and/or within a certain point of time to contextualise meanings of experiences, viewpoints, events, processes and structures of lives.

- Role(s) researchers play in investigations are complex as it is recognised that their prior knowledge and experiences are involved in and influence research design, data collection, analysis and interpretation processes.
- Along with an open and sensitive mind, 'purposive sampling' allows flexibility to identify 'information-rich' incidents relevant to themes in question and 'opportunistic sampling' enables the capture and investigation of those naturally occurring incidents and opportunities more thoroughly.
- Semi-structured interviews allow flexibility and reflectivity; however, the key to effectively gathering relevant information is learning how to question and probe.
- Focus group discussion encourages a group of individuals with similar characteristics to interact and share their viewpoints on specific topics and themes of focus, which requires skilled focus group facilitators to moderate conversations.
- Participant observation allows you to immerse yourself as an observer and/or participant to catch meaningful moments or critical incidents and to interpret observational data appropriately; however, limitations resulting from researcher and sampling biases need to be considered when developing observation checklists or guidelines.
- Piloting or trialling interview and focus group schedules and observation checklists or guides provides opportunities to practise in advance, enables you to gather various viewpoints from different angles and build up your confidence.
- Summarising field notes along with your insights and reflection, as well as identifying your preferred, effective ways to organise a wide range of qualitative data, are crucial to enhance the validity of the data and reliability of collection methods.
- Using multiple sources of information to triangulate is necessary to validate findings and conclusions drawn.

Further Reading

Denzin, N.K. and Giardina, M.D. (2006) 'Introduction: Qualitative inquiry and the conservative challenge', in N.K. Denzin and M.D. Giardina (eds), *Qualitative Inquiry and the Conservative Challenge*. Walnut Creek, CA: Left Coast Press.

Gubrium, J., Holstein, J., Marvasti, A. and McKinney, K. (2012) *The Sage Handbook of Interview Research*. London: SAGE.

For more on child observations:
Palaiologou, I. (2012) *Child Observation for the Early Years* (2/E). London: Learning Matters.

Useful Websites

- Gill et al. (2008)
  www.academia.edu/746649/Methods_of_data_collection_in_qualitative_research_interviews_and_focus_groups

- SAGE web page on research methods
  www.methodspace.com

References

Adler, P. and Adler, P. (1994) 'Observational techniques', in N. Denzin and Y. Lincoln (eds), *Handbook of Qualitative Research*. Thousand Oaks, CA: SAGE, pp. 377–392.
Alcoff, L. and Potter, E. (eds) (1993) *Feminist Epistemologies.* New York: Routledge.

Angrosino, M.V. (2005) 'Recontextualizing observation: Ethnography, pedagogy, and the prospects for a progressive political agenda', in N.K. Denzin and Y.S. Lincoln (eds), *The Sage Handbook of Qualitative Research* (3/E). Thousand Oaks, CA: SAGE, pp. 729–745.

Berg, B.L. (2004) *Qualitative Research Methods for the Social Sciences* (5/E). Harlow: Pearson Education.

Bernard, H.R. (2011) *Research Methods in Anthropology: Qualitative and Quantitative Approaches* (5/E). Walnut Creek, CA: Alta Mira Press.

Bridges, D. (2002) 'The ethics of outsider research', in M. McNamee and D. Bridges (eds), *The Ethics of Educational Research*. Oxford: Blackwell, pp. 71–88.

Bogdan, R.G. and Biklen, S.K. (1992) *Qualitative Research for Education* (2/E). Boston: Allyn & Bacon.

Bryman, A. (2012) *Social Research Methods* (4/E). Oxford: Oxford University Press.

Cohen, L., Manion, L. and Morrison, K. (2011) *Research Methods in Education* (7/E). Abingdon: Routledge.

Creswell, J.W. (1998) *Qualitative Inquiry and Research Design: Choosing Among Five Traditions*. Thousand Oaks, CA: SAGE.

Denscombe, M. (1998) *The Good Research Guide for Small-scale Social Research Projects*. Buckingham: Open University Press.

Denscombe, M. (2002) *Ground Rules for Good Research: A 10 Point Guide for Social Researchers*. Buckingham: Open University Press.

Denzin, N.K. and Giardina, M D. (2006) 'Introduction: Qualitative inquiry and the conservative challenge', in N.K. Denzin and M.D. Giardina (eds), *Qualitative Inquiry and the Conservative Challenge*. Walnut Creek, CA: Left Coast Press.

Drever, E. (1995) *Using Semi-structured Interviews in Small-scale Research: A Teacher's Guide*. Glasgow: SCRE.

Fielding, N. and Thomas, H. (2001) 'Qualitative interviewing', in N. Gilbert (ed.), *Researching Social Life* (2/E). London: SAGE, pp. 123–144.

Flick, U. (1998) *An Introduction to Qualitative Research*. London: SAGE.

Erlandson, D.A. and Harris, E.L. (1993) *Doing Naturalistic Inquiry: A Guide to Methods*. Newbury Park, CA: SAGE.

Francis, D. (1995) 'The reflective journal: A window to pre-service teachers' practical knowledge', *Teaching and Teacher Education*, 11(3): 229–241.

Golafshani, N. (2003) 'Understanding reliability and validity in qualitative research', *The Qualitative Report*, 8(4): 597–607.

Gorman, G.E. and Clayton, P. (2005) *Qualitative Research for the Information Professional* (2/E). London: Facet.

Guba, E.G. and Lincoln, Y.S. (1989) *Fourth Generation Evaluation*. Newbury Park, CA: SAGE.

Griffiths, M. (1998) *Educational Research for Social Justice: Getting Off the Fence*. Buckingham: Open University Press.

Hitchcock, G. and Hughes, D. (1995) *Research and the Teacher: A Qualitative Introduction to School-based Research* (2/E). London: Routledge.

Kerka, S. (1996) *Journal Writing and Adult Learning*. ERIC Document Production Service, No. ED 399413.

King, N. (1994) 'The qualitative research interview', in C. Cassell and G. Symon (eds), *Qualitative Methods in Organizational Research: A Practical Guide*. London: SAGE, pp. 14–36.

Kirk, J. and Miller, M. (1986) *Reliability and Validity in Qualitative Research*. London: SAGE.

Kvale, S. (2007) *Interviews: An Introduction to Qualitative Research Interviewing* (3/E). Thousand Oaks, CA: SAGE.

Lightfoot, S.L. (1983) *The Good High School*. New York: Basic Books.

Lincoln, Y.S. and Guba, E.G. (1985) *Naturalistic Inquiry*. Thousand Oaks, CA: SAGE.

McAdams, D. P. (1997) 'The case for unity in the (post)modern self: A modest proposal', in R. Ashmore and L. Jussim (eds.), *Self and Identity: Fundamental Issues* (Rutgers Series on Self and Social Identity, Volume 1), pp. 46–80.

Mack, N., Woodsong, C., MacQueen, K., Guest, G. and Namey, E. (2005) *Qualitative Research Methods: A Data Collector's Field Guide*. North Carolina, USA: Family Health International.

Mertens, D. (1998) *Research Methods in Education and Psychology: Integrating Diversity with Quantitative & Qualitative Approaches*. Thousand Oaks, CA: SAGE.

Miles, M. and Huberman, A. (1994) *Qualitative Data Analysis* (2/E). London: SAGE.

Morgan, D. (1997) *Focus Groups as Qualitative Research* (2/E). London: SAGE.

Morrison, K. (1993) *Planning and Accomplishing School-centred Evaluation*. Ely: Peter Francis Publishers.

Oliver, P. (2004) *Writing your Thesis*. London: SAGE.

Paterson, B. (1995) 'Developing and maintaining reflection in clinical journals', *Nurse Education Today*, 15(3): 211–220.

Patton, M. (1990) *Qualitative Evaluation and Research Methods* (2/E). Newbury Park, CA: SAGE.

Pole, C. and Lampard, R. (2002) *Practical Social Investigation: Qualitative and Quantitative Methods in Social Research*. Harlow: Pearson Education.

Reinharz, S. (1997) 'Who am I? The need for a variety of selves in the field', in R. Hertz (ed.), *Reflexivity and Voice*. Thousand Oaks, CA: SAGE, pp. 3–20.

Reis, H. and Gable, S. (2000) 'Event-sampling and other methods for studying everyday experience', in H. Reis and C. Judd (eds), *Handbook of Research Methods in Social and Personality Psychology*. New York, NY: Cambridge University Press, pp. 190–222.

Robson, C. (2011) *Real World Research* (3/E). Chichester: Wiley.

Rodwell, M. (1998) *Social Work Constructivist Research*. New York: Garland Publications.

Ryan, G. and Bernard, R. (2000) 'Data management and analysis methods', in N. Denzin and Y. Lincoln (eds.), *Handbook of Qualitative Research*. Thousand Oaks, CA: SAGE, pp. 769–802.

Scott, D. and Usher, R. (1999) *Researching Education: Data, Methods and Theory in Educational Enquiry*. London: Cassell.

Seale, C. (1999) *The Quality of Qualitative Research*. London: SAGE.

Silverman, D. (2005) *Doing Qualitative Research* (2/E). London: SAGE.

Simpson, M. and Tuson, J. (1995) *Using Observations in Small-scale Research: A Beginner's Guide*. Glasgow: SCRE.

Stake, R. (1995) *The Art of Case Study Research*. London: SAGE.

Walker, R. (1993) 'The conduct of educational case studies: Ethics, theory and procedures', in M. Hammersley (ed.). *Controversies in Classroom Research* (2/E). Buckingham: Open University Press, pp. 163–195.

Wellington, J. (2000) *Educational Research: Contemporary Issues and Practical Approaches*. London: Continuum.

Yin, R. (1989) *Case Study Research: Design and Methods*. Thousand Oaks, CA: SAGE.

Yin, R. (2003) *Case Study Research: Design and Methods* (3/E). Thousand Oaks, CA: SAGE.

For additional online resources please visit the book's website:
https://study.sagepub.com/needhamandpalaiologou

10

ANALYSING QUALITATIVE DATA

TREVOR MALE

Chapter Aims and Objectives

This chapter aims to help you to:

- develop an understanding of how to analyse qualitative data – particularly text;
- recognise that there is a strong link between data collection and data analysis;
- undertake content analysis and develop coding techniques for data handling;
- deal with a potential for bias that is commonly to be found in qualitative data handling;
- explore the benefits of computer assisted analysis and investigate some relevant software;
- present your data in a meaningful and helpful way;
- ensure your conclusions are justified by the evidence you have collected.

Introduction

Qualitative data are distinguished by the way in which they are based on the intensive study of as many features as possible of one or a small number of phenomena in the search for meaning (Miller and Brewer, 2003). Instead of condensing information, therefore, it seeks to build understanding by depth. Qualitative methodologies tend to 'generate large volumes of data resulting in potential problems associated with analysis' (Robson, 2002: 476). Basically this means you end up with a lot of stuff!

In this chapter I am going to examine the process of managing qualitative data analysis, first by examining the challenges offered by a project in which I am involved at the time of writing (see Case Study Part 1). There are two of us in the research team, but we are working so closely together that the task could have been undertaken by a sole researcher which I anticipate will apply to most people reading this chapter. Working in a team of researchers brings with it the need to create a shared understanding of the phenomenon and constant discourse in order to ensure alignment of research activities to maintain consistency. Collaborative qualitative research 'requires a kind of rigor that an independent researcher might not be aware of or need' (Weston et al., 2001: 381). If you are approaching a qualitative research project as part of a team, you are advised to undertake reading in addition to this chapter. It is assumed here that you will be acting as a lone researcher.

At this stage of the book I am expecting you to have read the previous chapter on qualitative data collection, and to have realised that the data do not exist in a vacuum and that there is a strong link between data collection and data analysis. It is quite common, for example, for the initial reaction of the researcher to shape the subsequent data collection process as new ideas and understanding emerge from the interactions you will have with participants in your enquiry. Consequently it is important that you look at qualitative data collection techniques first as your engagement with the participants could (and perhaps should) shape that stage of your research. The significance of that knowledge should become clearer as I take you through the rest of this chapter.

The Relationship Between Data Collection and Data Analysis

Typically in qualitative research, data analysis effectively begins at the same time as data collection. It is commonly agreed that there are three approaches to qualitative data collection: *content analysis*, *grounded theory* and *narrative analysis*, although if you undertake further reading you will find there are many other types of associated data collection which often relate to a specific research tradition such as ethnomethodology, discourse analysis and semiotics. Whilst these are important they are specialised approaches which, again, will need further reading if they are of interest to you as a researcher. In this chapter emphasis will be on content analysis and grounded theory as in most instances in small-scale research projects researchers are unlikely to undertake narrative analysis as the required processes can be complex and demanding.

A good working definition of the purposes of qualitative data analysis is that it allows you 'to make sense of data in terms of the participants' definitions of the situation, noting patterns, themes, categories and regularities' (Cohen et al., 2011: 461). The common approach in dealing with such data is to present it as text which can subsequently be reduced to codes and categories, in effect 'turning qualitative data into quantitative data' (Ryan and Bernard, 2000: 777). The assumption used in the rest of this chapter, therefore, is that you are seeking to analyse text which you have generated or to which you have direct access. Text 'is a window into experience' (ibid.: 790) which has to be presented in such a way as to demonstrate the commonalities of participants. As described in the previous chapter this is an approach that can include the use of pictures, audio/video recordings or observations, all of which are presented ultimately, however, as text.

A simple working definition of content analysis is to count the number of times various words, items or phrases are to be found in the text. In contrast grounded theory, in its purest sense, does not anticipate anything in advance of data collection and generates codes or categories from the data (Charmaz, 2006). As should be becoming obvious by now, however, I do not intend to marginalise the processes of data collection and analysis in this chapter and will, instead, seek to identify ways in which you can present conclusions that are based on evidence you produce through the data you generate or employ. At times this will mean I may be crossing theoretical boundaries, an approach that may irritate some purists, but one that I consider will help you to achieve a high degree of rigour in your conclusions.

In the case study I provide as an example (in Case Study Parts 1 and 2) you can see that the researcher(s) does not come to the situation without prior knowledge or, in this instance, prior experience of the situation being examined. This is probably true of all qualitative enquiry as the researcher is part of the activity. This is one of the essential differences between quantitative and qualitative research in that there is a strong potential for bias, both in the way data are viewed and the way in which the researcher can influence the behaviour of those being studied. There is also the fact that prior knowledge exists which is relevant to the situation whether it is theory, other similar research or personal experience.

Case Study

Part 1

This is the investigation of a school which has shown remarkable and consistent improvement since the appointment of the current headteacher some 16 years previously. As researchers we are familiar with the school having accumulated data during the previous year through semi-structured interviews (three) with the headteacher, with five members of the senior leadership group and two members of the governing body plus a focus group interview with members of the School Council. The purpose of that enquiry was to evaluate the working relationships and leadership behaviours at this level.

Consequently in establishing our research approach for this new line of enquiry we had some idea of what we were likely to see and sought to understand the way in which the school had improved through the experience of people who had been closely associated with it throughout the period. Thus we were able to construct a semi-structured interview protocol which, with the odd exception, we generally undertook together. We planned three visits to the school, each spread over three days, to conduct the interviews.

In the case study we had a good idea of what to expect, having already undertaken substantial enquiries within the school. We also had extensive knowledge of educational leadership and school improvement processes. Consequently it was difficult to come to this new inquiry without prior knowledge. Grounded theorists seek to avoid assumptions and expectations, preferring instead to examine the data in the search for patterns (Charmaz, 2006). This leads to a process of *open coding* which results in the identification of categories which emerge as the data is examined. These codes can be applied by the researcher or can be words or phrases contributed by participants which are known as *in-vivo* codes. In this process the data are therefore explored sympathetically, in order to ensure that the analysis is not biased. In other words the researcher is seeking to ensure that the only influence on the findings is the actual data collected.

Quite frankly I find it hard to accept grounded theory in this way and consequently argue that it is almost impossible not to influence the data collection or data analysis when you are an interacting participant. What needs to be done is to ensure, as far as possible, that you counter the potential for bias by seeking verification of the data during the analysis, preferably with the participants, although you can also compare your findings with other similar research. In the case study we did expect to find certain things as a consequence of our previous knowledge and experience so were able to identify some categories of data before we began the round of data collection. These are known as *a priori codes* i.e. codes that have been identified beforehand, in this case from both examining theory and because of our prior exposure to the school (see Chapter 2).

The process of data collection can often thus becoming an influencing factor as each activity informs you as a researcher and shapes the next stage. This is an iterative process – that is, you learn from each piece of data and usually become better equipped to ask more focused questions as you continue the enquiry. This is quite legitimate in my view as it matches the purpose of qualitative research which is to understand what is happening in that context. Consequently as you progress through the investigation you may have a set of questions that become increasingly sophisticated as they become more focused by the findings. In the case study I present here as an example, data collection so far has been through two intensive sets of interviews each spread over three-day periods, but separated by a couple of months. As co-researchers we know that we have been both reflexive and reflective in that process which, in turn, has allowed us to become ever more precise with our questioning. In other words what has been said to us in one interview has often been used in subsequent interviews in attempts to clarify our understanding and classify responses. We were able to say to participants, for example, something like 'when we were talking to Simon the other day he was telling us that there was a period when the corridors were no-go areas for staff. Was this true for you? [Yes]. Tell us what it was like for you.'

Here you can see that we have used the outcomes from earlier interviews as a code by which we are not only accumulating the number of times something happened (content analysis), but also shaping our questioning in the search for depth of understanding. This blurs the edges of the two principal approaches to qualitative research that we are examining in this chapter – content analysis and grounded theory. I am, in effect, arguing for an approach which combines the two in order to attain meaning. It is an approach which could be described as 'codified common sense' (Robson, 2011). Thus in our efforts to understand what is happening in the school we employ an iterative approach which makes use of findings to inform our subsequent data collection.

In short, therefore, I am trying to encourage you to avoid labelling your research approach and instead make effective use of the data to shape your enquiry as it progresses. It is my advice not to be tempted to define your research process too closely as this can become a hostage to fortune. Avoid bold statements like 'this is grounded theory' and give yourself some flexibility by saying something like 'this study makes use of techniques and approaches commonly associated with grounded theory'. Such an approach will give you the opportunity to explore the issue you have chosen without being confined to a particular approach. If, for example, you were to use the same questions throughout your enquiry in an attempt to enumerate the responses you run the risk of missing key issues and instead produce 'conclusions that can often be seen as trite' (Silverman, 2011: 85). As can be seen the development of codes (whether *a priori* or emergent) can shape further data collection as your research continues. This is because qualitative research is a process, not an event, and it is virtually impossible to separate yourself from what you are seeing unlike, say, a laboratory experiment. The key issue for you to recognise at this stage, therefore, is that there is a strong connection between data collection and data analysis.

Data Reduction and Coding

The consequence of qualitative research is often that you can quickly accumulate a vast amount of data. Look at Part 2 of the Case Study and you will see what a task we face. The primary task of researchers looking to analyse such quantities of data, therefore, is to make it manageable through a process of *data reduction*. This will aid in the recognition of patterns, themes and regularities, which characterise inductive analysis (Richards, 2006). This process will require you to generate *codes* which can then be developed into categories where similar issues are grouped together.

Case Study

Part 2

After two visits to the school we had accumulated a total of 33 interviews, each of which lasted about an hour. These were audio recorded and transcribed by a commercial agency which undertook the task as we requested, which was to record what was spoken and to ignore repetitions, interruptions and extraneous noises. By the time we had the first draft transcripts we had accumulated just over 235,000 words.

This was to be supplemented by documentation that was in the public domain, such as inspection reports, press cuttings and material to be found on social networking sites (such as Friends Re-united).

In addition we had been provided copies of private correspondence between one of the governors, the previous headteacher and the local authority which amounted to a further 10,000 words. There are numerous inspection reports still to examine as well as 16 years of press cuttings in what is a high profile school.

At the time of writing we are planning at least one more three-day visit where we hope to extend our collection of interviews even further and especially to include parents and other representatives of the local community.

A first step is to look at how you can make the amount of text manageable. Decisions will have been made in the design stage of your project as to how you will record events and the contribution of participants and there is a common tendency to end up with far too much material. On the other hand if you try to be sparing you run the risk of missing important contributions. Remember that what you are trying to do is to understand the circumstances and not to impose your own view on the data. Consequently you have to strike a balance between raw data and useable data. Raw data is what you have at the end of the collection process which, as you can see from our case study, can be enormous (and messy). This needs to be converted, cleaned up, coded and classified.

Converting raw data: your original material needs to be put into a format that not only allows you to explore it, but also to make it transferable. A key factor in qualitative research is *verification* i.e. people other than yourself, preferably the participants, need to confirm your understanding matches theirs. One way of doing that is to put your findings into a mode of communication that allows them to see what you have seen and confirm or deny your understanding of their world. Take, for example, interviews which have been recorded – these both need to be confirmed as accurate and to be put into a format which allows for analysis. Commonly, therefore, interviews are transcribed – in other words they become text. Similarly if you have asked participants to draw pictures these need an explanation that is independent of you. It may be that you choose to gain this verification through personal conversation, but this can be time consuming and invasive for the participants. It may be better, and more efficient in terms of personal time, to provide the participants with a copy of the text you produce following your interaction with them and ask them to check it for accuracy of understanding.

Converting raw data is commonly done through the use of text as this also allows for analysis that is independent of you and transparent. There are many words of caution here, however, as the process of conversion is expensive. The transcription of recorded interviews is extremely time consuming, for example, with audio recordings typically requiring as much as seven or eight times as long to transcribe as they did to record, and video recordings taking much longer still as there is so much more happening. In the case study we provide, you can see that we have a huge amount of text as a result of transcribing the interviews, but we have been able to employ a commercial service. If we were to undertake this work ourselves the task would be impossible without devoting enormous amounts of our time. You may like to consider, therefore, alternative ways such as producing a summary. I always like to digitally record interviews as I do not trust myself to remember what has been said and, equally, I find it difficult to hold the conversation and make field notes at the same time. Sometimes, however, digital recordings may not be possible in which case it is vital to make notes of the meeting as soon as possible afterwards. Another way of dealing with audio/video recordings is to play them back and just make notes of key issues rather than a full transcript. The important thing is that you have a record of the meeting which you can share with the participant(s).

Cleaning up the data: A key element of producing such records is to ensure that they are coherent and concise. This is the next stage of data reduction where you seek to take out meaningless or repetitive data. In the transcription of the interviews we conducted in the case study, we seek to return to the participant an edited version of the transcript which has not only taken out errors and repetitions, but has also removed much of the social discourse which is so necessary for a conversation, yet is not needed for representing what they have said about the focus of our questions. We then ask our participants to read the edited transcript and advise us of any errors or things they would like to be omitted (usually something they wish they had not said). We then have an agreed transcript which will allow us to go on to the next stage of data handling which is coding. Their agreement is also a key factor in terms of data verification. It should be noted that there are other ways in which verification could be achieved in a more time-efficient manner, such as holding a joint meeting with several participants in order to evaluate how well you understand their context. Indeed, in this case study we may well do that at some stage in the future when we consider we are ready to draw conclusions.

Coding: This is probably the most important stage of qualitative data analysis. The process of coding is a way of quantifying the data to see what themes exist. In the initial stages of your analysis every word and line of text effectively can represent a different category (or code) in providing first impressions of the data. At this stage you should be aiming to get familiar with the data and all good qualitative researchers seek to know their material well before they start analysing. As painful as it may be (given the volume of words you may have generated or seek to explore) you should aim to read the text, if possible several times. It is advised that this initial stage of interpretive analysis requires the researcher to remain 'close' to and 'immersed' in the data set and to avoid the temptation to start coding or jumping to broad categorisations of data prematurely (Charmaz, 2006). Once you are familiar with the data you can expect to see patterns emerging and these are the first stages of coding, a vital part of qualitative data analysis. Silverman (2011) provides sound advice in suggesting that you should start by making a detailed analysis of a small section of your data. He refers to this as *intensive analysis* which, he proposes, 'will give you a good initial grasp of the phenomena with which you are concerned' (2011: 62). He recommends these initial findings can then be tested by applying them to your whole data set, a process of *extensive analysis*.

There are several stages in the development of codes and these have already been partly discussed above. As a reminder, ideas that exist before you start data collection are known as *a priori* codes; these are supplemented by *emergent* codes – that is you see patterns and regularities in your data that you can put together as thematic units of analysis. These may be entire texts, chunks of text, responses to questions or grammatical segments. What you are trying to do with the development of codes is to ensure that any subsequent claims being made should fit the data and ensure negative instances have not been discounted (Silverman, 2011). This is a vital part of your analysis as without it you run the risk of misrepresenting the data. Some of the poorest reporting of research happens when the only aspects of data reported are those that conveniently fit the argument being offered. Good quality qualitative research is that which deals with the data in its entirety. The use of selective quotes, for example, is only justifiable when they are representative of a trend or pattern of responses.

As indicated above, codes are either *a priori* or *emergent*. Emergent codes are those to be found in the data which make use of the core element of grounded theory which is *open coding*. This is why the process of immersion in the data is important as the identification of these codes is something which is not always clear cut and requires interpretation. In the box on p. 185 I provide information about the use of computer software to analyse your data, an area to which you should give your attention if you are handling large quantities of data, but nothing replaces an inductive approach to the data. In an earlier study of mine, for example, I was trying to identify the most appropriate mode of support for beginning headteachers in England and asked participants of a self-completion survey to provide an open text response to the question 'What level of support would be helpful during the first two years of headship?' (Male, 2004). I got a variety of responses that not only included various versions of the word 'mentor', but also included phrases like 'professional support' and 'support from an experienced headteacher' all of which I was able to put together as examples of mentoring. In the final analysis this was by far the most common factor identified by the participants, but many of these instances would have been lost if I had not developed my codes in sympathy with the data.

In effect this process is an example of open coding although it could also be offered as an example of the next stage of analysis when dealing with emergent data, which is *axial coding*. Axial coding is used to link individual open codes into categories or clusters which will eventually be developed into theoretical themes and concepts (Charmaz, 2006; Richards, 2006).

A key function of the iterative data collection processes I have outlined in this chapter is the use of *memos*. Their use is strongly recommended by most handbooks of qualitative research as a means by which you can start to label your data. In other words you make a note (or memo) as to what occurs to you as you either generate or subsequently begin to analyse the data. In time these ideas may coalesce into a pattern or simply remain as phenomena. The gathering together of bits of data in this way leads to fewer categories of data and allows you the platform to develop cognitive maps. This process is explained more fully below in the example provided of mind mapping in Figure 10.1.

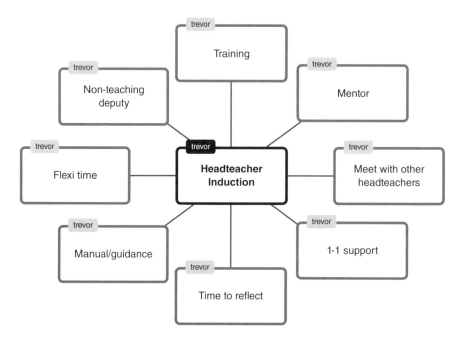

Figure 10.1 Mind mapping. Example 1

In this example I have used a simple mind mapping piece of software called Popplet to demonstrate how I could have presented my memos from the first look at the data emerging from the survey I undertook on headteacher induction (this software is readily available for free download to most computer operating systems. In this case I used Windows, but it works just as well on iPad). In truth I did not use this software at the time of my original data analysis as it did not exist at that time. Instead I used a pencil and a piece of paper in the first instance, but quickly then moved on to the more sophisticated method of using highlighter pens! I had received just over 1,400 handwritten responses to a self-completion questionnaire and had laboriously copied all the responses to my three open questions into a spreadsheet. As I had got over 90 per cent responses to the first two questions about support for beginning headteachers and 65 per cent responses to the third, very open, question 'What other comments would you like to make?' I had ended up with a lot of words to analyse (just over 73,000 words – 135 pages). Fortunately for you, nowadays even a simple text search on word processing software has reduced such a task exponentially, so long as you have identified the words or phrases you are searching for! You can find out more about computer support for qualitative data analysis below, but do remember what I told you earlier – get to know your data. Without that firsthand knowledge you run the risk of missing important findings, so do not be too reliant on software.

Computer Assisted Qualitative Data Analysis Software (CAQDAS)

As you can see from the example I provide above of data handling in the days before computers much activity had to be undertaken in order to recognise the occurrences of different codes. In other instances this might have involved producing multiple copies of the text in order that examples of codes could be grouped together. All such activity was laborious and the challenge of such tasks has been considerably reduced by computer software. Whilst I recommend you should make use of appropriate software to help your analysis I also suggest you need to consider the following issues before embarking on the use of specialist software:

- *First think about how you collect the data. Some audio recording software programmes or apps have a note-making facility which allows you to add a memo as you record. Clicking on that memo later will take you directly to the part of the recording so you do not have to search for it. Check out your apps store first as some of these recording programs are free.*
- *Investigate speech recognition software as this has the potential to change your data to text with minimal effort. Similarly look at the potential of using optical character recognition (OCR) software if you are looking to convert documents into word processing files.*
- *Now look at the potential of your standard word processing software for storing, organising and managing your data. Simple word searches can be used to find instances of coded data and 'cut and paste' techniques can bring that coded data together very simply.*
- *The key question to be asked then is 'Do I need to invest resources into using specialist software?'*

(Continued)

(Continued)

This last question is a critical one. In the first instance there may be a financial cost in terms of software purchase or licensing, although it may be that your employer or, if you are a student, your institution has that software available to you as part of a corporate package. There is still the hidden cost, however, which is your time. Using a new software program will require you to learn it, understand it and become proficient *before* you can see the benefits. If you are doing a small-scale or single piece of research you need to undertake a cost-benefit analysis of your time before committing yourself to that task. Remember that ultimately you will be judged on the quality of your data analysis rather than the way in which you handled the data, so do not lose sight of your main task. The medium should not be the message!

If you decide to look at specialist software for qualitative data analysis that takes you beyond the capabilities of your word processing software they fall into five categories (Weitzman, 2000):

- *Text Retrievers*
- *Textbase Managers*
- *Code-and-Retrieve Programs*
- *Code-Based Theory Builders*
- *Conceptual Network Builders*

Text Retrievers find all instances of words and phrases in the text and generally include features for content analysis. *Textbase Managers* assist with organising your data and making appropriate sub-sets. *Code-and-Retrieve Programs* allow you to apply codes to passages of text in order to later retrieve and display the text according to your coding. *Code-Based Theory Builders* go beyond code-and-retrieve programs to support theory building. *Conceptual Network Builders* allow the researcher to create graphic representations of the relationships among drawings. Not surprisingly software programs are being developed rapidly to accommodate many, if not all of these features. A simple Internet search will quickly lead you to a range of free/open source or proprietary software programs. The key message to remember, however, is that no software program will analyse your data for you – the definition of codes is still your responsibility. What the software will do is take away some of the laborious tasks from the analysis of qualitative research in much the same way as a calculator made arithmetic so much easier.

The key point in this section of the chapter is to see what issues of commonality emerge from the data, whether it is individual words, phrases or sentences. These need to be grouped together, to be classified into patterns, themes or even theory. Again seek to use software to help you with this (unless you prefer working with pieces of paper).

Classification: The last stage in the process of data analysis is *selective coding*. Here you are finalising the reduction of data into categories and classifications which demonstrate themes or even theory. In the following example I have shown how I might have used another example of mind mapping software to show how emergent ideas can be brought together to show (and justify) their relationship and allow the identification of themes.

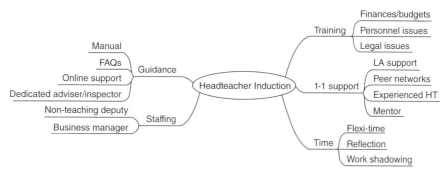

Figure 10.2　Mind mapping. Example 2

The theme of 'training' identified in the survey of headteachers I undertook is represented in Example 2 as having three aspects: finance/budgetary, personnel issues and dealing with legal issues (Figure 10.2). The sample had been stratified so I could represent these issues across maintained schools in England, thus allowing me to also report the number of times these issues had been relevant to beginning headteachers in the various sectors of the school system. What you will see in the example box below is how I am trying to represent the data quantitatively in order to demonstrate the significance of the findings. To show these findings I counted how many times headteachers from each subset of the sample population cited a particular aspect of training in relation to the total number of requests for further training. In the first example, therefore, 65 headteachers from secondary schools had identified the need for further training of which 15 had stated 'finance' as a specific need.

Training issues identified for beginning headteachers

There were more varied responses amongst the respondents who cited the need for **further training** during the first year of post. In terms of specific skills, the most frequently cited area was **finance** (secondary = 15 mentions out of 65; nursery = 3 mentions out of 16; special = 8 mentions out of 56; infant = 36 mentions out of 153; infant with junior = 72 mentions out of 346; junior = 9 mentions out of 62). **Personnel issues** (including help with underperforming teachers and subsequently capability procedures) was the next most important skill cited by respondents (secondary = 7 mentions out of 65; nursery = 1 mention out of 16; special = 5 mentions out of 56; infant = 18 mentions out of 153; infant with junior = 31 mentions out of 346; junior = 4 mentions out of 62). Requests for **more training and support with the law and legal information** were less obvious (secondary = 8 mentions out of 65; infant = 8 mentions out of 153; infant with junior = 19 mentions out of 346; junior = 3 mentions out of 62). No respondents from nursery or special schools identified this as a specific training need.

(Male, 2004: 162)

Whilst this is a very useful way of recognising repeated words or phrases, it is still important to remember you have to deal with negative instances of data as well as those that fit those categories. One way of dealing with such instances of outstanding data is to evaluate their significance. If only one person from 100 participants, for example, made a contribution that was substantially different from the rest you might be tempted to dismiss that finding as insignificant on numerical terms alone. It may still be a significant contribution, however, and worthy of mention in your final classification. One such example from my analysis of responses from headteachers to open questions in my survey was the infant school head-teacher who was the only participant to mention children:

> With the ever-changing role of headteachers it is vital not to lose sight of the true purpose of the job which is the education of the children.

I consider such a statement as impossible to ignore, yet it did not fit any of my defined categories. Consequently I had to include it! At this stage it really is for you to judge how best to deal with data that does not fit, but the advice is not to ignore it.

Data Display

Qualitative data typically consist or large amounts of text, even after applying codes and identifying categories, themes and patterns. Seek, therefore, to organise and display your findings through use of tables, charts, matrices and networks.

In the following example I have condensed the raw data from the open question in my headteacher survey 'What level of support would be helpful during the first two years of headship?' through the processes of open and axial coding and displayed the findings as percentages recorded for each of the identified variables of headteachers (in this case the phase of school). These percentages were determined by corresponding mentions of a single topic against the total number of responses recorded for all items mentioned in the categories used. So, for example, secondary headteachers deemed 'mentoring' to be the single most important element of support needed for the first year in post, with 90 mentions out of a total of 225 recorded responses to this question. Headteachers from all other types of schools also deemed mentoring to be highly important with those from nursery making 15 mentions out

Table 10.1 Type of support during first two years of headship (Male, 2004: 163)

Type of support	% of mentions					
	Sec.	Nursery	Special	Infant	Inf./Jun	Junior
Mentoring	40	28	31	27	31	31
Training in specific skill areas	29	30	36	39	33	35
Peer group support	7	9	6	7	8	8
Induction programme	9	9	6	4	4	4
Work shadowing	5	11	4	7	6	7
LEA support	6	9	10	5	8	4.5
Reflecting on practice	2.5	2	3	1	1	2
Specific training during deputy headship	-	-	4	9	9	9

of a total of 52 responses, those from special schools making 48 mentions out of a total of 155 responses, those from infant schools making 107 mentions out of a total of 393 responses, those from infant with junior schools making 320 mentions out of a total of 1,043 responses and those from junior schools making 54 mentions out of a total of 177 responses. A similar mode of analysis was applied to all other types of support mentioned thus allowing me to display overall findings in a simple and clear manner (see Table 10.1).

Given the way in which qualitative data can be developed into quantitative findings it is relatively easy not only to display it as tables, but also as charts, matrices and networks.

Conclusion Drawing

The approach which recommends that instances of qualitative data are enumerated surprises many people as it seems contrary to the nature of the research paradigm, but it is necessary to ensure that any conclusion you reach from the data has to be supported by the evidence. A simple test to apply to such conclusions is to ask the following question: 'Given the data, is that the only conclusion I could have reached?' If the answer is 'no' then you will need to explain why you chose that conclusion above other possible conclusions. The key criterion you are seeking is *rigour*, which means making sure that what you are presenting in your final analysis is represented by the data. In coding the data you are establishing the mechanism by which you can make substantive conclusions.

Qualitative researchers, it is suggested, 'appear to have little difficulty in making sense of their data and generating conclusions' (Robson, 2011: 479). In order to make sure your conclusions are justifiable, however, you are recommended to look at the work of Miles and Huberman (1994), commonly accepted as the gurus of coding, who provide a list of 13 tactics for generating meaning (see box below).

Tactics for generating meaning

1. *Noting patterns, themes and trends*.
2. *Seeing plausibility*. Do the trends, patterns and conclusions make sense?
3. *Clustering*. Grouping events, places, people and processes together if they appear to have similar patterns or characteristics.
4. *Making metaphors*. Metaphors are rich, data-reducing and pattern-making devices which help to connect data with theory.
5. *Counting*. Helps to enable you to see what's there by counting frequency of occurrence of recurrent events.
6. *Making contrasts and comparisons*. Establishing similarities and differences between and within data sets.
7. *Partitioning variables*. Splitting variables may help in finding more coherent descriptions and explanations.
8. *Subsuming particulars into the general*. Linking specific data to general concepts and categories.
9. *Factoring*. Attempting to discover the factors underlying the process under investigation.

(Continued)

(Continued)

10. *Noting relations between variables*. Using matrix displays and other methods to study inter-relationships between the different parts of the data.
11. *Finding intervening variables*. Trying to establish the presence and effects of variable intervening between observed variables.
12. *Building a logical chain of evidence*. Trying to understand trends and patterns through developing logical relationships.
13. *Making conceptual/theoretical coherence*. Moving from data to constructs to theories through analysis and categorisation.

(Miles and Huberman, 1994: 245–256)

Making use of these criteria should help you produce data that are meaningful.

Key Points to Remember

- Data collection and data analysis are strongly linked with early impressions and findings shaping subsequent data collection – this is an iterative process and is quite legitimate. Most people studying degrees in Education will probably only use *content analysis* and *grounded theory* in the analysis of their data. It is common to use both approaches.
- Normally data has to be transferred into text so that you can demonstrate its meaning to other people.
- Wherever possible you are trying to turn qualitative data into quantitative findings through the use of codes which bring together aspects of the data to demonstrate patterns or even theory.
- Codes can be developed prior to data collection (*a priori*) or as a result of viewing the data (*emergent codes*). The names or descriptors you give the codes can be personally developed or arise from the data (*in vivo*).
- You need to recognise how you can influence both the data collection and its subsequent analysis (*potential for bias*). Look to verify your findings and conclusions with your participants as achieving that understanding is the core purpose of qualitative research.
- Qualitative research tends to produce immense quantities of data which need to be reduced to manageable volumes. Raw data needs to be converted (if it is not already text) and cleaned up before coding and classification begin.
- Converting raw data into text can be enormously expensive in terms of time and resources. Look to use time efficient ways of gathering and summarising data.
- Remember there is no substitute for knowing your data when you are developing the codes for categorising and classifying your findings – good analysis begins with you being very familiar with the data.
- Deal with all the data, including the bits that do not fit your codes or aspirations – account for negative instances in your findings.
- Seek to classify your findings through combining data in the processes of *axial and selective coding*. Use of mind mapping software can be helpful in this process.
- Now seek to display your data in a way that makes it accessible, making use of tables or matrices.

- Make sure when you draw conclusions that they are justifiable – if the data do not immediately support that conclusion make sure you are ready to explain why you have chosen that conclusion.

Further Reading

Cohen, L., Manion, L. and Morrison, K. (2011) *Research Methods in Education* (7/E). Abingdon: Routledge.

Punch, K. (2009) *Introduction to Research Methods in Education*. London: SAGE.

Silverman, D. (2011) *Interpreting Qualitative Data* (4/E). London: SAGE.

Useful Websites

- Analysing Qualitative Data
  http://learningstore.uwex.edu/assets/pdfs/g3658-12.pdf.

- Analyse This! Learning to Analyse Qualitative Data
  http://archive.learnhigher.ac.uk/analysethis/main/qualitative.html.

- Introduction to Qualitative Data Analysis
  http://onlineqda.hud.ac.uk/Intro_QDA/.

References

Charmaz, K. (2006) *Constructing Grounded Theory: A Practical Guide through Qualitative Analysis*. London: SAGE.

Cohen, L., Manion, L. and Morrison, K. (2011) *Research Methods in Education* (7/E). Abingdon: Routledge.

Male, T. (2004) *Preparing for and Entering Headship in England: A Study of Career Transition*. University of Lincoln: Unpublished PhD Thesis.

Miles, M. and Huberman, A. (1994) *Qualitative Data Analysis: An Expanded Source Book* (2/E). Thousand Oaks, CA: SAGE.

Miller, R. and Brewer, J. (2003) *The A-Z of Social Research*. London: SAGE.

Richards, L. (2006) *Handling Qualitative Data: A Practical Guide* (2/E). London: SAGE.

Robson, C. (2002) *Real World Research*. Oxford: Blackwell.

Robson, C. (2011) *Real World Research* (3/E). Chichester: Wiley.

Ryan, G. and Bernard, R. (2000) 'Data management and analysis methods', in N. Denzin and Y. Lincoln (eds), *Handbook of Qualitative Research* (2/E) Thousand Oaks, CA: SAGE, pp. 769–802.

Silverman, D. (2011) *Interpreting Qualitative Data* (4/E). London: SAGE.

Weitzman, E. (2000) 'Software and qualitative research', in L. Denzin and Y. Lincoln (eds), *Handbook of Qualitative Research* (2/E). London: SAGE, pp. 803–820.

Weston, C., Gandell, T., McAlpine, L., Wiseman, C. and Beauchamp, C. (2001) 'Analyzing interview data: The development and evolution of a coding system', *Qualitative Sociology*, 24(3): 381–400.

For additional online resources please visit the book's website:
https://study.sagepub.com/needhamandpalaiologou

11

COLLECTING QUANTITATIVE DATA
TREVOR MALE

Chapter Aims and Objectives

This chapter aims to help you to:

- identify when it is appropriate to use quantitative research;
- find ways to make sure data is in the form of numbers which can be analysed statistically if required;
- manage the process of choosing, and managing potential participants and keeping them interested and engaged;
- make sure your research questions are valid and reliable;
- design a research instrument to collect your data and get a high response rate;
- recognise the difficulties of using a questionnaire as well as the benefits;
- explore the benefits of online survey instruments.

Introduction

There is often a temptation when approaching research to seek evidence that demonstrates beyond reasonable doubt that there is a truth which can be shown through the collection and analysis of quantitative data. Such an approach differs from other methodologies in that interpretation of the world is to be shown in numbers rather than words or other symbols. This may be because of a perception, to twist a phrase, that there is safety in numbers. Certainly there is comfort to be had from citing numbers as your evidence.

Few things look more convincing, for example, than being able to say something like: '93 per cent of all 14 year old girls think Beyoncé is a great singer'. Consequently a considerable number of new or inexperienced researchers often start the conversation about their planned investigation with the infamous phrase 'I think I will do a questionnaire'. More seasoned and experienced researchers often shy away from the collection of quantitative data, however, as there are inherent challenges within such an approach that signal danger to them. It is my intention in this chapter to explore those challenges in order to help you undertake your research in such a way that you end up with meaningful and useful data.

Collecting quantitative data means being able to ask questions that can be answered in such a way that data can be presented as numbers. Inevitably this means you have to define questions that reflect real issues and are meaningful to possible participants. Typically you would expect such questions to be answered without further interpretation and you would be looking to collect sufficient amounts of data to be able to represent the population you are sampling. The key challenges facing you in such a task are:

- identifying the population sample;
- choosing questions to ask;
- designing a research tool to present those questions;
- managing the data collection process; and
- informing the population of the results.

Identifying the Population Sample

A sample is the segment of the population selected for the investigation (Bryman, 2012). So, who are the people you want to ask questions? You cannot ask the entire population of the world so you will have to select the group you intend to investigate for a particular purpose and that selection will have to be representative. Imagine, for example, as a student on a degree course that you wanted to find out how many people in your university (academic staff and students) had personal digital devices (e.g. iPads, digital tablets or mobile phones with Internet connection) and considered themselves capable of using them to support learning. In this case your population is all academic staff and students within the university which can amount to several thousand potential participants.

In such an investigation it would be possible to ask them all, providing you have the means to collect such a large amount of data (we will explore this more fully below when we look at online surveys), but it is more likely that you will want to select a representative sample. Let's start with your research question(s) as this might provide many clues as to who you want to ask. Here it is fairly obvious that as the researcher you suspect or have good reason to believe there will be a difference between academic staff and students, probably both in terms of ownership of such devices, and in their perceived capability to use them in support of learning. Your research question might be, therefore:

Are academic staff and students (in xxxx University) equipped with and capable of using portable digital devices to support learning?

This is, in fact, two questions: what equipment do they have and how capable are they perceived to be in using such devices to support learning? For now, however, you just need to concentrate on how many of the two large groups of people would be representative. In other words how many people do I need to ask questions in order for me to be able to say anything that is typical of those populations? For whatever number you think of you will need to ensure that you get sufficient data to be able to undertake some meaningful statistical analysis, otherwise there is no point in conducting quantitative data collection. There is no set rule about this, but generally it is considered that statistical analysis is meaningless on a sample size consisting of fewer than 30 people. Consequently you have to get data from at least 30 people before you can apply any statistical test that can demonstrate significant findings. So let's imagine you choose a sufficient number of potential participants to make sure you have got data from at least 30 people.

That task, in itself, is a challenge, as you may have to ask your questions to many more than 30 people as they may choose not to reply, especially if your research tool means you do not have to be there when they answer the questions. Avoid that possibility for a moment, however, and for now work on the assumption that you have data from 30 academic staff and 30 students. Do those people represent the population of the university? The chances are they do not, because you have not defined any other categories of the population. In research terms such categories are known as *variables*.

In this planned investigation your first variables are: *academic staff* and *students*. Your immediate task, if these remain your only variables, is to decide how many of each category are representative. Normally the rule is that the smaller the total population the higher percentage of possible participants is needed. In a typical university, however, you might expect there to be several hundred academic staff and several thousand students. In this case it would be legitimate to have a lower percentage of the population identified as potential participants and be reasonably assured that your sample would be representative. Indeed with a population of several thousand students it would be reasonable to collect a large number rather than a percentage, so something like 10 per cent of academic staff and a thousand students would give you much data that could be considered representative. Unfortunately for you, however, it is not always as simple as that as the broad variables of academic staff and students may both need to be further categorised in order to ensure representation. Using research terms again these are the population *strata*.

The population always has different characteristics (strata) and your research may need to report on such differences. Both sets of potential participants, amongst other things, will be of a different gender and age, will have a variety of experience in the university and will belong to various faculties and departments. Consequently you may want to know whether your population sample is representative of all such categories. In that case, therefore, you will be looking to have a *stratified sample* of the population and whilst this may make your selection more difficult it should improve your data and allow for subsequent comparisons between chosen variables.

Finally, in this section, you need to make a decision as to how you choose your population sample in order to try and eliminate (as far as possible) skewed data. Your data may be skewed if you have over-representation of some people within your variables and one simple way to deal with this is to employ a random selection process amongst all potential participants. Let's assume you have identified, for example, a potential population of 2,000 first year undergraduate students that has an appropriate balance of chosen variables (e.g. gender and faculty representation), but you only wish to sample 400 of them; then you need to devise a way that each potential participant has a fair and equitable chance of being chosen. This could be the selection of every fifth name in an alphabetical list, for example, or names chosen at random (there are computer programs that can do that for you). The end result is that you will then have a *stratified random sample*, which is a very good position to be in if you want to claim your data is representative.

Once you have made you decision about the population sample (remembering, of course, that you could try to survey the whole population if you have an appropriate research tool) you can return to where you probably started which is to choose what questions you want to ask.

Choosing Questions to Ask

The first rule to apply here is to make sure there is good reason to ask the questions you plan to include in your investigation. It is simply not good enough to come up with a range of questions that do not have an underlying rationale. There are two such sources: either other research or relevant literature has signalled this is an aspect of life where these questions are relevant or you have devised a hypothesis which you wish to test. In good quality academic research these are commonly to be found together. In other words your research question(s) must have credibility, with each subsequent question asked of your sample having an identified or suspected reason for it to be asked.

If you are a student about to do your dissertation, for example, you should be looking to make sure your literature section relates to the questions you plan to ask. If we go back to the possible research I outlined above about the use of personal digital devices by academic staff and students in a university, you should be able to see immediately how easy it is to get confused (in that case by asking two questions in the same sentence). Questions should only ask one thing at a time and allow participants to make a response as indicated. The research planned in this instance had two strands – what equipment did they have and how capable did they feel of being able to use this equipment to support learning? These overarching questions now need to be broken down into separate questions that will investigate the issue thoroughly.

At this point you might want to do yourself a favour and see if anyone else has asked similar questions in the past that you can use, especially if those questions have rigour. It is quite legitimate to use an existing set of questions rather than developing your own provided you give appropriate credit to the author(s) of those questions. Many academic researchers will happily send you a copy of their questions, for example, if you agree to cite their work appropriately. The reason you may want to use an existing set of questions is that they may have been developed so they have high levels of *validity*. This concept is central to the use of questions in quantitative research and questions should have internal and external validity.

Definitions

The technical terms for aspects of internal validity are:

- *Content Validity* (do the questions measure the content they were intended to measure?)
- *Construct Validity* (do the questions measure hypothetical constructs or concepts?)
- *Face validity* (do the questions appear to measure what the instrument sets out to measure?) (Creswell, 2013)

A good quality set of questions will be measured against these criteria. If we take face validity, for example, it is possible (usually through piloting) to measure how many times people recognise the question in the same way as intended. A positive response of more than 7 out of 10 is usually an indicator of a high level of correlation. If you see a set of questions that have been used before by another researcher and they indicate a correlation of 0.7 (or higher) this signals that the question is usually recognised by participants in the same way as the researcher intended. It is possible to report on the internal validity of questions in other ways that do not include numbers such as, for example, a detailed account of how the questions were constructed or a description of the relationship between the question and relevant theory. Similarly the data could have external validity, in that there is a prospect of generalisability, again a concept with more than one aspect:

- *Concurrent Validity* (do results correlate with other results?)
- *Predictive Validity* (do scores predict a criterion measure?) (Creswell, 2013)

The key point here for you as a potential researcher is that if you decide to develop your own questions you will have to evaluate them in these categories of validity in order to justify their use.

Another key issue in the development of questions is the concept of *reliability* which is a common term used in the language of research. In its simplest form reliability means that administering the questions in another setting is likely to produce similar results. The issue of reliability is central to success in terms of:

- *Question Consistency* (how far questions remain consistent across constructs)
- *Test Stability* (whether individuals vary in their responses when the instrument is administered a second time)
- *Consistency in Test Administration* (whether errors were caused by carelessness in administration or scoring) (Creswell, 2013)

Again a feature of good questions is the extent to which these aspects of reliability have been measured, so principles similar to those identified for validity are relevant here. Where there is evidence of high levels of validity and reliability the emergent data is strengthened substantially. So when looking to administer a set of questions in support of your own research, you should investigate these concepts from either the work of another researcher or through your own mechanisms.

Designing a Research Tool to Present Those Questions

There are several ways for you to collect quantitative data which are generally referred to as surveys. You could, for example, conduct a telephone survey or produce a questionnaire for face-to-face meetings with participants. Such approaches are labour intensive and most researchers opt for a self-completion questionnaire as being their preferred data collection tool. In all these examples, however, the researcher is looking for responses to the same questions from their participants and this is where the data collection differs from that to be found in qualitative approaches where the researcher can adapt, amend or explain the questions they pose. Whilst it is possible to do this when in personal communication with participants in a survey, basically the quantitative researcher is looking for a response to a set question in order that data can be accumulated appropriately. Objectivity is thus supported through the use of common questions that limit the effect of researcher 'contamination' (Scott, 1996: 57). Traditionally, in research terms, questionnaires are seen as cost effective, convenient and generalisable. Large amounts of data can be collected relatively quickly, usually allowing for a wider geographical spread than other data collection techniques. Self-completion questionnaires are invariably the choice of researchers in this domain as they fulfil most, if not all, of the above criteria.

The task of questionnaire construction should not be underestimated. In using this approach most effort has to be expended on developing the questionnaire as, once it is functional, data collection is relatively easy by comparison. The process can take several months if you are starting from the beginning, needs lots of attention to detail and a great deal of testing. Now you can see why I suggest it is sometimes a good idea to use one that has been trialled, tested and shown to be robust. Take the Myers-Briggs Type Indicator (MBTI), for example, which is a *psychometric* questionnaire designed to measure preferences in how people perceive the world and make decisions (Myers et al., 1998). Based on the theories of psychologist Carl Jung, work on this questionnaire was started in World War II (1939–45) and first published in 1962. Whilst the inventory is not without a number of critics it is commonly judged to be robust with good levels of validity and reliability. Consequently those researchers who make use of the MBTI can avoid many of the challenges faced in constructing a questionnaire from scratch. Sadly for most readers of this book, however, the MBTI is not available without special training and can only be used under licence.

This is typical of many questionnaires – they are not available free of charge or can only be used with special permission or under licence. Fortunately, however, there are multiple sources who will give you free access to questionnaire templates and, in some instances, limited free use of their services. Major IT companies such as Microsoft and Google, for example, have tools and templates available which you can use freely. Alternatively you can investigate companies such as SurveyMonkey or SurveyExpression who will give you access to templates and a limited service free of charge. If you are a student it is also worth asking whether your university subscribes to a service like Bristol Online Surveys (BOS) which has full authoring and data handling facilities.

None of this takes away the need to evaluate the validity and reliability of the questionnaire you intend to use. Going back to the MBTI, for example, the intended outcome is to classify participants in terms of their preferred way of understanding the world. One major criticism, amongst a number of other critiques, is that it is possible for a participant to be given a different profile within a relatively short period of time. So for some participants who were re-tested, even within a few weeks of the original test, it was demonstrated that their profile had changed (Krznaric, 2013). The key issue for you, as a researcher, is to recognise that *all* research is open to criticism and you must report on both the strengths and weaknesses of whatever data collection tool you use. On a general level, for example, there is the view that questionnaires often enjoy a status that is 'falsely prestigious because of their quantitative nature' (Robson, 2011: 125). In making this statement Robson argues that findings are seen as a product of largely uninvolved respondents whose answers owe more to some 'unknown mixture of politeness, boredom and their desire to be seen in a good light than their true feelings, beliefs or behaviour' (Ibid.).

But let us go back to the research challenge I identified earlier of finding out about the use of personal digital technologies in the university. The purpose of collecting quantitative data is for you to be able to report numerically on your findings and interrogate those numbers in order to create *descriptive statistics* and *inferential statistics*. You will find out more about statistical analysis in Chapter 12), but in order to obtain that data you will need a series of questions that will provide you with demographic data about your population sample and will demonstrate their responses to various key issues. Questions fall into three categories:

- forced choice
- multiple choice
- opinion/attitude

A *forced choice* question is where you have to choose between options; a *multiple choice* question allows for several responses; a question relating to *opinion* or *attitude* normally requires participants to record their response on a scale.

Forced choice questions are commonly used in gaining demographic data, but can also be used when researchers are looking for a definite response. Online survey instruments typically use either a radio button or a drop down list for such questions. In the case of the research into academic staff in the university, for example, you would probably want to know their age (demographic data), so a simple forced choice question might look like that in Figure 11.1.

Your age
○ 21–25
○ 26–35
○ 36–45
○ 46–55
○ 55+
○ Other *(please specify)*:

Figure 11.1 Example of a forced choice question

Similarly, and still using forced choice questions, you could use a grid to find out aspects of their use of various technologies or their perceived competency. In this case for each question there is only one answer (Figure 11.2).

How would you rate your own skill level in using these technologies?	Competency			
	Expert	Some skills	Limited skills	This does not apply to me
a. A computer (desktop or laptop)	○	○	○	○
b. Laptop computer or notebook	○	○	○	○
c. iPodtouch or iPad	○	○	○	○
d. Word-processing	○	○	○	○
e. Spreadsheets	○	○	○	○
f. Diagrams or mind maps	○	○	○	○
g. Presentation software	○	○	○	○
h. Email	○	○	○	○
i. Internet for research	○	○	○	○
j. Digital image editing	○	○	○	○
k. Digital video editing	○	○	○	○
l. Music production and editing	○	○	○	○
m. Making podcasts	○	○	○	○

Figure 11.2 Second example of forced choice question

In researching other aspects of the use of technologies by academic staff you might want to make use of multiple choice questions in order to be able to report the extent of usage. In this case you may have developed a list of portable digital devices in order to see how extensively academic staff are equipped personally (Figure 11.3).

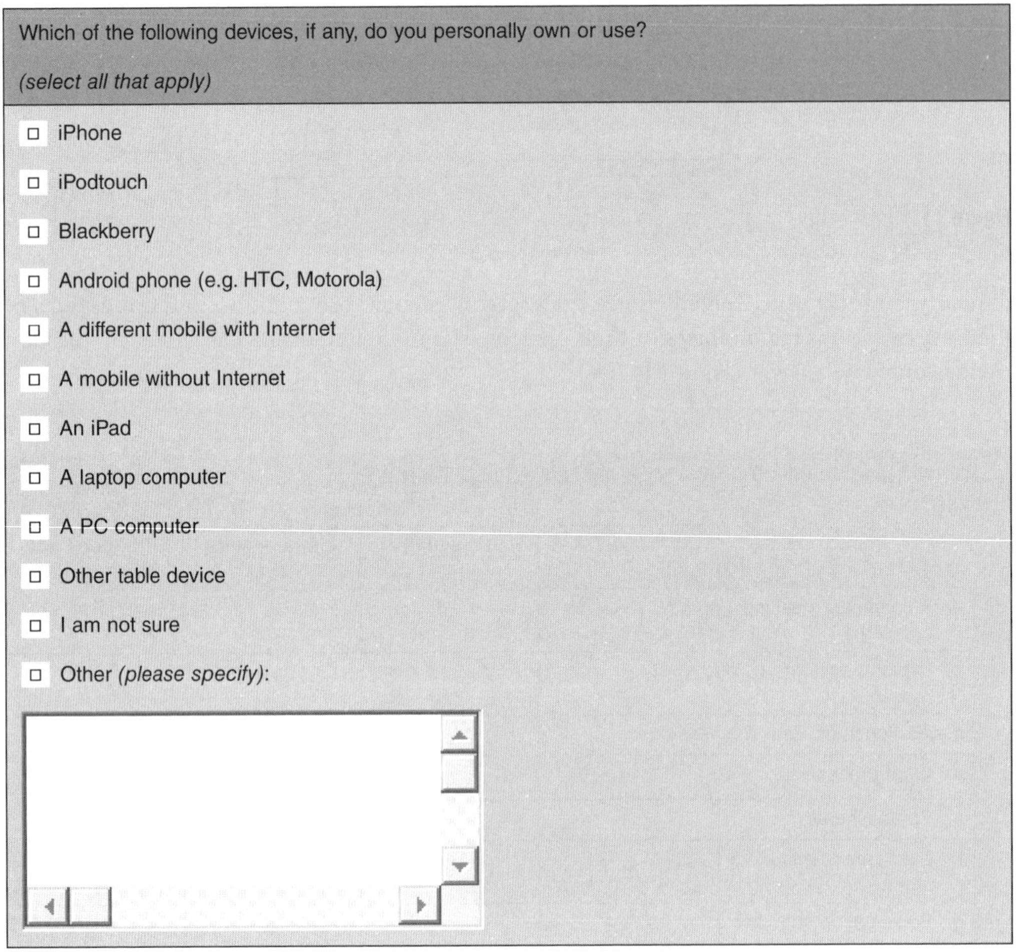

Which of the following devices, if any, do you personally own or use?

(select all that apply)

- ☐ iPhone
- ☐ iPodtouch
- ☐ Blackberry
- ☐ Android phone (e.g. HTC, Motorola)
- ☐ A different mobile with Internet
- ☐ A mobile without Internet
- ☐ An iPad
- ☐ A laptop computer
- ☐ A PC computer
- ☐ Other table device
- ☐ I am not sure
- ☐ Other *(please specify)*:

Figure 11.3   Example of multiple choice question

In all the above examples it can be seen, therefore, that in using online survey instruments you can build data relating to both demographic data and overviews of usage quite quickly. As you should be able to imagine, there are many questions that could be similarly constructed. By now, however, you might be wishing to find out how your participants feel about the use of such technologies and for that you need an opinion or attitude scale. In the following example (Figure 11.4), use is made of a four point scale in terms of agreeing with a series of statements.

How far do you agree with the following statements about enhancing learning with technology?	Level of agreement			
	Strongly agree	**Agree**	**Disagree**	**Strongly disagree**
a. I would like to make student learning opportunities more dynamic	○	○	○	○
b. I would like to be able to capture aspects of teaching sessions which the students can use later	○	○	○	○
c. I would like to be able to allow student input into learning opportunities (through use of mobile technology)	○	○	○	○
d. I would like to be able to create discussion groups	○	○	○	○
e. I would like to be able to create tools for staff-student collaboration	○	○	○	○
f. I would like to be able to create tools for student–student collaboration	○	○	○	○

Figure 11.4   Example of using an attitudinal scale

The use of scales is a very common feature of questionnaires, but there are decisions to be made regarding how many points there should be on that scale. There are many different scales that could be employed, but one of the more famous is known as a *Likert Scale* which is a scale from negative to positive, with a mid-point that is neither negative or positive (Likert, 1932). Most commonly this will be a five-point scale presenting a choice, for example: *Strongly Agree – Agree – Neither Agree nor Disagree – Disagree – Strongly Disagree*. The reason I mention this particular scale is to illustrate that whilst such an approach may be useful there can be difficulties both in the choices made by participants and subsequent data analysis. First, it is a well known phenomenon that people tend to *regress to the mean* when presented with a scale of choices; this means they tend not to use the ends of the scale with answers subsequently clustering in the middle. To avoid this some researchers might use a seven-point scale, again with a mid-point, as it provides a wider range of responses. You will notice in the example provided in Figure 11.4, however, that there is no mid-point to this scale as the researchers wanted to find out whether participants were positive or negative in their response (and to what extent). In terms of data analysis it is quite common to see researchers combining categories of agreement/disagreement when they report data (i.e. they may present their findings as 'XX per cent of participants either agreed or strongly agreed …'). My question to such researchers would be to ask why have different points on the scale if you are not going to use them? You should ask yourself the same question before setting up a scale.

Before leaving the issue of scales I want to point to the possibility of being inventive (especially with online survey instruments). In the example provided in Figure 11.5 a five-point scale has been used which caters for the non-user of digital technologies in the university setting being explored. In this example a combination of scales and forced choices could allow the researcher to find out, for example, more about participant knowledge, understanding and capability.

How frequently do you use the following features of presentation technologies in your teaching?					
	Frequency of use				
	Weekly or more often	**Occasionally**	**Rarely or never**	**I would like to do so but do not know how**	**I do not know what this means**
a. I use a presentation tool in my teaching (e.g. PowerPoint, Keynote or Prezi)	○	○	○	○	○
b. I embed audio/ video in my presentations	○	○	○	○	○
c. I use presentations in a non-linear way	○	○	○	○	○
d. I record a narrative in my presentations	○	○	○	○	○

Figure 11.5   Example of attitudinal scale with forced choice questions

Finally you may have noticed that in many of the questions there was an opportunity for the participant to provide an answer that was not offered to them in a forced choice question or was not listed in a multiple choice question. This is the use of an open text box in which the participant can offer alternative responses. In addition you could ask an open question (see Figure 11.6). A word of caution here: every time you invite comment you will have additional data to analyse, in this case in the form of words. The real benefit of using an open text box is that answers and ideas can be provided to you as a researcher that you may not have anticipated. If you are not careful, however, you could end up with huge amounts of data that needs coding and analysis before it can be presented as quantitative data. Imagine the survey of the use of digital devices in the university, for example, which could result in several hundred different responses. A better use of open text boxes might be to use them in the piloting stage of designing your research tool as this might reveal issues and ideas that have not emerged from your literature review or other research.

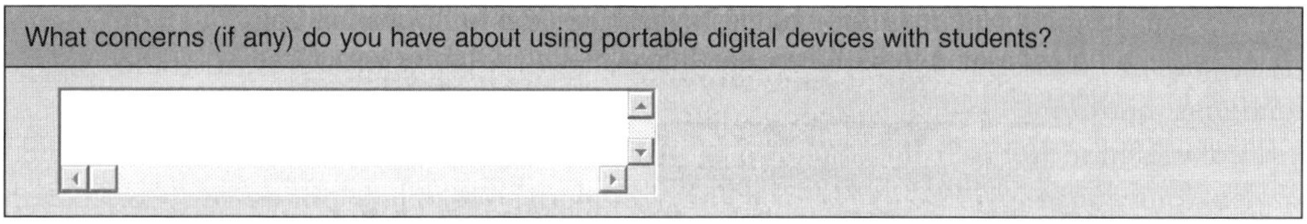

Figure 11.6 Open text box

By this point you should be ready to set out on your data collection, having determined questions that are valid and designed a research tool which is reliable and manageable. Consequently you now need to consider how you are going to manage the process of data collection.

Managing the Data Collection Process

The first element of good data collection is to ensure you treat the potential participants with respect. This is much harder to do when the process becomes impersonal, as much quantitative data collection inevitably does. It may be that you have decided to do a structured interview using a set of standard questions (much like those people who stop you in the street to ask you questions) or you have decided on a telephone survey. It is much more likely, however, that you will undertake a self-completion questionnaire as this is the most cost efficient method in terms of researcher time. In all instances you must remember that in asking them to answer your questions you are about to make an unwanted intervention into someone's life, so you have to find a way to make the process seem worthwhile for your prospective participants. One of the key features of outstanding quantitative research is a high response rate. This makes it important for you to gain and sustain the interest of those you wish to survey.

At this stage of your research you will have identified your population sample, chosen the range of questions you wish to ask, designed your research tool and are about to start the data collection process. The next step is critical to your success as you must try to anticipate what it will be like, as a prospective participant, to receive a request from you to answer your questions. Two things are vitally important at this point: make sure your research tool/process is high quality and that your invitation is attractive. It can be considered a little easier to interact positively with the prospective participants if you have verbal contact (assuming you have reasonable interpersonal skills), but it becomes harder when you are more remote, such as when using a self-completion questionnaire. Remember what was said earlier in this chapter by Robson (2011: 125) – people who respond to questionnaires do so out of an unknown mixture of 'politeness, boredom and their desire to be seen in a good light'. Your responsibility, therefore, is to make sure your research tool/process is of the highest quality. If it relies on personal contact then a high level of good interpersonal skills is required; if there is impersonal contact (e.g. email or a letter of introduction) then it needs to be carefully phrased and well presented. In order to try and find ways of doing this let's go back to the planned research into the use of portable digital devices in the university and think about how you might attract academic staff and students to engage with your questions.

First you have to catch the attention of prospective participants who, quite simply, will want to know what benefit there is for them through the research. In one survey I conducted, for example, I suggested the topic of my research was highly important in the development of policy and that participant contribution was vital if we were to address the challenges of the future. In conducting a survey into the use of portable digital devices in this university you could be supporting the future success of students by identifying where strengths and weaknesses lay in the current situation. The conclusion of such an argument is that it may be worth offering your research outcomes as being of benefit to all prospective participants. Alternatively you may seek to attract potential participants by offering a real or potential reward (not a good move if you don't have an attractive prize). A more novel approach might be to make use of technologies such as social networking, blogs, or creating an app, but the disadvantage of this is that you are more likely to only get those people who already use the technologies. The point is that you have to try and make participation seem attractive and worthwhile.

You then have to sustain such interest by being professional and efficient in the data collection process. Having made the decision to participate the next thing people want to know is 'how long is this going to take me?' Always be honest about this. I once got people to agree to spend about two hours on a self-completion questionnaire for me because I told them at the outset this is what they could expect. Of 50 people who accepted that invitation (many did not) I got full responses from 35 of them, a response rate of 70 per cent. To be fair, however, this was excessive and you should be looking at a maximum time of 15–20 minutes for a single piece of data collection and participants should be told as early as possible what their commitment will be. It also helps, especially with online self-completion questionnaires, for participants to know how much of the survey they have completed as they go through the questions. Most software packages for online surveys offer such a facility, which is surprisingly effective as a motivation to complete the questions.

The quality of your research tool then plays a major role in sustaining that interest from participants. Hopefully you will have sorted out (through your piloting stages) many of the difficulties that can damage participant interest and enjoyment (e.g. seemingly repeated questions, spelling errors, ambiguous questions, software glitches if using online services). What participants like to see if the data collection is through personal contact is high professionalism, and if it is through impersonal contact a quality document (for paper-based surveys) or a well laid out online questionnaire.

The implementation of the research tool should include the participants providing agreement to the conditions of informed consent that should be provided by you (see Chapter 3 on ethical practices in research). This should be a personal signature from them for data collection that is personal or paper-based and an agreement box to be completed within online surveys.

For impersonal data collection (i.e. self-completion questionnaires) you should aim to track responses so you know which participants have completed their return. It is quite legitimate for you to know the identity of the participant providing you have given appropriate assurances to the security of the data in the process of informed consent. Your data will be much more secure if you are able to confirm, for example, that responses you receive are from the people you asked to undertake your survey. This can be done quite simply by personally contacting a sample of your data population to confirm they were the participant. It is also advisable to be able to track who has replied so you can undertake follow-up to non-respondents. This is especially important if you are trying to get a high response rate. In one postal survey I conducted, for example, I received 736 replies from the first mailing, 435 more in a follow-up process a month later and a further 219 responses from a second reminder two months later. This pattern of returns corresponded to the 'typical pattern of responses' to postal questionnaires suggested by Cohen and Manion (1994: 99). The Office of Population Censuses and Surveys recommends the use of three reminders which, they say, can increase the original return by as much as 30 per cent in surveys of the general public (Cohen et al., 2011: 346). All of that is contingent, however, on you being able to track the questionnaire completion rate to individuals. In the paper-based survey I refer to above I did this by issuing each printed questionnaire with a serial number, thus allowing me to see who had submitted a completed return. Within online surveys there will be various routines of allowing you to track prospective participants, depending upon the software employed by different providers.

Finally, in this section, you need to determine a closing date for your survey. This is especially important with self-completion questionnaires which sometimes have a habit of turning up long after you have expected them. A factor to be aware of is that the answers from late returners of the survey can affect the quality of the data. The technical issue here is *response bias*, bringing with it the need to undertake both *respondent/non-respondent analysis* and *wave analysis* (Creswell, 2013). Both aspects of response bias relate to how non-respondents might have substantially changed the overall results of the survey (see Chapter 12 on how we analyse quantitative data). With wave analysis the procedure assumes that those who return surveys in the last stages are almost non-respondents. If their responses are not different from those received earlier, a strong case for absence of response bias can be established. Alternatively, a few non-respondents could be contacted to determine whether their responses differ substantially from those of respondents. The procedure constitutes a respondent/non-respondent check for response bias.

Informing the Population of the Results

This final section will be very short, but it is important that as a researcher you take the time and make the effort to inform the population of your results. This does not have to be a full report of the analysis, but an overview of what was said in the questions. In one postal survey I conducted, for example, I was able to produce a written report for each of the population strata, but with online survey instruments it is very easy to present an account of responses (see Figure 11.7).

How would you rate your own skill level in using these technologies?		
A computer (desktop or laptop) – Competency		
Expert:		50.0%
Some skills:		50.0%
Limited skills:		0.0%
This does not apply to me:		0.0%
iPodtouch or iPad – Competency		
Expert:		8.3%
Some skills:		37.5%
Limited skills:		12.5%
This does not apply to me:		41.7%
Presentation software – Competency		
Expert:		33.3%
Some skills:		54.2%
Limited skills:		12.5%
This does not apply to me:		0.0%
Internet for research – Competency		
Expert:		62.5%
Some skills:		37.5%
Limited skills:		0.0%
This does not apply to me:		0.0%

Figure 11.7 Example of report sent to participants

It is good practice to inform your participants about your research findings as it exemplifies the importance you place on their contribution. A short report showing the main findings can easily be mailed, sent electronically or posted to a website so that participants can see what other people have answered as well as knowing their own response.

Key Points to Remember

- Make sure you have enough participants to justify a quantitative investigation and subsequent analysis.
- Your sample should be representative of the population you are investigating.
- Recognise that potential participants are not always willing, so treat them nicely and with respect.
- Ensure there are good reasons to select the questions you use (validity).
- Be consistent in the ways you collect data (reliability).
- Try to limit the amount of time people have to spend on your questions to a reasonable length.
- Designing effective questionnaires takes much effort.
- Avoid using open text boxes as much as possible in questionnaires as these create further data analysis.
- Make sure participants have provided evidence of informed consent.
- Track your participant responses and be prepared to chase up those who have not responded.
- Finally, tell your participants the results of your investigation.

Further Reading

Bryman, A. (2012) *Social Research Methods* (4/E). Oxford: Oxford University Press.
Cohen, L., Manion, L. and Morrison, K. (2011) *Research Methods in Education* (7/E). Abingdon: Routledge.

Useful Websites

- Data Collection Methods
  http://people.uwec.edu/piercech/researchmethods/data%20collection%20methods/data%20collection%20methods.htm February, 2015.

- How to Collect Quantitative Data the Easy Way
  http://knowhownonprofit.org/how-to/how-to-collect-quantitative-data-the-easy-way Accessed February, 2015.

- Overview of Quantitative Research Methods
  www.sagepub.com/upm-data/36869_muijs.pdf Accessed February, 2015.

Online Questionnaires

- Survey Monkey: www.surveymonkey.com.
- SurveyExpression: www.surveyexpression.com/
- Bristol Online Survey (BOS): www.survey.bris.ac.uk

References

Bryman, A. (2012) *Social Research Methods* (4/E). Oxford: Oxford University Press.

Cohen, L. and Manion, L. (1994) *Research Methods in Education* (4/E). London: Routledge.

Cohen, L., Manion, L. and Morrison, K. (2011) *Research Methods in Education* (7/E). Abingdon: Routledge.

Creswell, J. (2013) *Research Design (International Student Edition): Qualitative, Quantitative and Mixed Methods Approaches.* Thousand Oaks, CA: SAGE.

Krznaric, R. (2013) *Have We All Been Duped by the Myers-Briggs Test?* Available at: http://management. fortune.cnn.com/2013/05/15/myers-briggs-problems/. Accessed June 2013.

Likert, R. (1932) 'A technique for the measurement of attitudes', *Archives of Psychology*, 140: 1–55.

Myers, I., McCaulley, M., Quenk, N. and Hammer, A. (1998) *MBTI Handbook: A Guide to the Development and Use of the Myers-Briggs Type Indicator* (3/E). Mountain View, CA: Consulting Psychologists Press.

Robson, C. (2011) *Real World Research* (3/E). Chichester: Wiley.

Scott, D. (1996) 'Methods and data in educational research', in D. Scott and R. Usher (eds), *Understanding Educational Research*. London: Routledge.

For additional online resources please visit the book's website:
https://study.sagepub.com/needhamandpalaiologou

12

ANALYSING QUANTITATIVE DATA

KEN SPENCER

Chapter Aims and Objectives

This chapter aims to help you to:

- overcome the 'fear' of statistical analysis;
- explain how you can analyse quantitative data;
- explore the different ways that you can use statistics in your research project;
- enable you to be confident to start using quantitative methods and statistical analysis.

Introduction

Have you ever wondered how long have we been measuring things, in other words, using quantitative methods? I have recently been working on my allotment, and realise that all the time I am using quantitative methods. I am measuring out paths and borders. I am calculating areas, estimating lengths of wood, working out how long it will take me to dig over the section devoted to potatoes. It strikes me that whatever I do seems to involve quantitative methods.

Recently Goldacre (2013), who has spent many years identifying and commenting on 'Bad Science', suggested that education and the social sciences could benefit from a more scientific approach to the collection and use of evidence, urging the careful collection of quantitative data.

> I think there is a huge prize waiting to be claimed by teachers. By collecting better evidence about what works best, and establishing a culture where this evidence is used as a matter of routine, we can improve outcomes for children, and increase professional independence.

This is not an unusual idea. Medicine has leapt forward with evidence based practice, because it's only by conducting 'randomised trials' – fair tests, comparing one treatment against another – that we've been able to find out what works best. (Goldacre, 2013: 7)

In evolutionary terms we know that our history is associated, over the past 500,000 years, with the development of tools, and we know that by 40–80,000 years ago we began to create art, leaving pictures inscribed on rocks and caves that have survived to this day. Language clearly drives this ascent of man, but because language is evanescent we do not have any records to see exactly how it evolved and was used. However, from the initial use of pictorial representations there is a very short step to a written form of quantification. One of the earliest examples of quantification comes from 8000–7500 BC in villages in the fertile crescent in modern-day in Iran, where tokens representing single animals were placed together on strings or enclosed in clay envelopes to indicate transactions (Schmandt-Besserat, 1989). There can be no doubt that quantification of items, such as flint arrow heads or cattle, was used before this time, but the new forms of tangible representation of quantities, their instantiation in Iran 10,000 years ago, occur at a nodal point for civilisation: they are the precursors of written language. When we developed written systems for recording speech and quantities, we greatly enhanced our capacities to control our environment, refine our methods of working with available resources, and began to predict the future. With such enhanced capacities, we began to build towns and the great cities of the ancient world.

Counting things is a necessary part of everyday life, and can often be summarised in tables and charts, such as bank accounts or invoices for bills. In research this way of dealing with quantities that we observe is usually the earliest stage, often referred to as descriptive statistics. I always think of the tedious astronomical observations made by Tycho Brahe that left an enormous amount of raw data for Kepler, his assistant, to inherit. After studying this data for 20 years, Kepler came to understand that the motion of the planets was clearly elliptical around the sun. Brahe provided the tables of data, the summaries of observations, but the more useful derivation of the laws of planetary motion was a later, inferential stage that allowed accurate predictions to be made about the location of the planets.

An Example of Descriptive Data Collection and Presentation

Recently I was asked to give a presentation on basic statistical ideas and processes, and I thought I should include reference to my own work. Usually I use inferential statistics – I want to make predictions or comparisons – but on occasions I simply wish to summarise my results. In the mid-1990s I was asked by a headteacher to think of ways in which I could help improve the school's profile for reading. The headteacher knew that I was working with very powerful portable computers that could 'talk', and suggested that we could devise a computer system that would read to the pupils who were from deprived backgrounds and this would compensate for a lack of parental reading. I was enthusiastic about paired-reading, which had been shown to produce beneficial results for children who had difficulty with reading, and thought that a computer program could be designed to simulate the interactions of a parent pointing to words and reading them aloud. After many months of preparation the program was presented to a number of children who were experiencing difficulties with reading. The computer had the text of their school reading scheme on the screen, and when the mouse was clicked the words were highlighted and read by the computer. Although we had a voice synthesiser that was similar to that used by Stephen Hawking, we decided to record the teacher's voice instead, to make it a more natural experience.

The children's reaction was amazing: they simply ignored the whole process of being read to; they didn't look at the screen as the words were highlighted, and hardly paid any attention to the words being read aloud. But, it wasn't a complete disaster. I had also spent some time investigating mastery learning, and thought that this could be used in the program. Thorndike had proposed in 1912 that it would be a good idea to prevent children from going on to page 2, unless they could show that they had understood what was on page 1 (Thorndike, 1912), and Pressey had devised a machine that did this in 1926 (Pressey, 1927). Mastery learning was simply an extension of this idea: students had to get 80 per cent on a test before going on to the next unit. They could take the test as often as was necessary, but they had to pass it to go to the next part of the course. It was rather like the UK driving test: you can fail and retake the test as often as is necessary to ensure that the high mastery standard is achieved before the learner driver can drive independently on the road. The children's reaction to this was quite unexpected: they loved the test, and kept working at it until they passed – we had built into the programme a remedial loop that indicated why they had failed and attempted to correct their errors. I re-programmed the computer to only give a series of tests, the simulation of reading to the child was completely dropped, and it was an immediate success with some of the children. The program recorded every response the pupils made, and presented new sets of words when they reached the established criterion level of performance for a group of 10 words, usually 80 per cent, but going as high as 90 per cent. There was so much data generated by recording every response that I was overwhelmed by it, and could not see how I could easily summarise it, how readers of my report would make sense of it. It is a similar problem that some of my students find when using qualitative methods, such as interviews: there is simply too much information, and it has to be reduced (usually into quantitative information). However, one measure that proved very useful was the length of time it took to learn how to correctly spell a group of words – the program presented the most common 100 words in groups of 10 – and that is how I displayed my results in the published article (Spencer, 1996), which are reproduced in Figure 12.1.

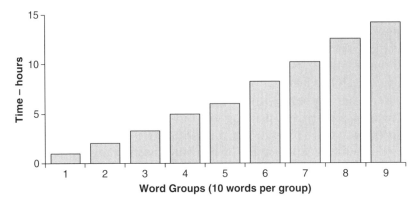

Figure 12.1   Cumulative time taken by Pupil A to master groups of 10 words (based on Spencer, 1996)

This chart shows the dramatic effect that the HyperRead programme had produced in Pupil A. He was 10 years old and, although he knew his alphabet, he could not read a single word, not even the most common word in English, 'the'. He had been in school for approximately 7,000 hours, but had failed to make any progress in reading. Within less than 15 hours (0.2% of his time in school) he had mastered the spelling and reading of 90 words. The programme had similar success rates with several other children. The research on the HyperRead programme was discontinued because similar approaches, called Integrated Learning Systems (ILS), based on cumulative research over 30 years, were being evaluated and were found to have similar effects to HyperRead in Primary schools (NCET, 1996). Figure 12.2 shows the results of one comparative experiment from Phase 2 of the ILS research conducted by the National Council for Educational Technology. The aim of this research was to establish the validity of claims made for such systems, and the initial results were certainly encouraging. The chart shows the average progress made for pupils using the ILS compared to a control group who did not have access to the new computer-based system, and continued with normal class activities.

The ILS group starts at a lower level of performance compared to the control group, and appears to make greater progress over the 16-month period. But this shows the limitation of simply using descriptive statistics: all we can say is that it looks as though the computer-based system does a better job of teaching the pupils than ordinary classroom practice. Inferential statistics takes us further and allows conclusions to be drawn about the statistical significance of sets of scores and the relative magnitude of any differences. For example, inferential statistics applied to the data in Figure 12.2 indicate that the ILS program has an Effect Size of 0.8, which means that 80 per cent of ILS pupils have a score equal to or greater than the average score of the control group. (Note: obviously, for the control group 50 per cent are above the average, so we can say that 30 per cent of the pupils who would have been below average under control conditions will become above average if they use the ILS programmes.)

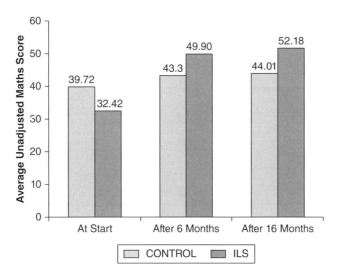

Figure 12.2 Average unadjusted maths score for integrated learning system group and control group (based on NCET, 1996)

Definition – Descriptive and inferential statistics

Descriptive statistics is the term given to the analysis of data that helps describe, show or summarise data in a meaningful way such that, for example, patterns might emerge from the data. Descriptive statistics do not, however, allow us to make conclusions beyond the data we have analysed or reach conclusions regarding any hypotheses we might have made. They are simply a way to describe our data.

With *inferential statistics*, you are trying to reach conclusions that extend beyond the immediate data alone. For instance, we use inferential statistics to try to infer from the sample data what the population might think. Or, we use inferential statistics to make judgements of the probability that an observed difference between groups is a dependable one or one that might have happened by chance in this study.

Thus, we use inferential statistics to make inferences from our data to more general conditions; we use descriptive statistics simply to describe what's going on in our data.

Table 12.1 presents descriptive data from an early experiment that I conducted to look at the relative benefits of increasingly costly audio-visual presentations (Spencer, 1977). Students studied three different science topics, and the topics were available in three different formats: a very low-cost audio recording of a lecture, with a paper booklet showing diagrams and equations; a low-cost video of an actual lecture, with the lecturer drawing diagrams and equations on a large board (as used in many of the Open University programmes in its infancy); a high-cost video presentation with expensive animated graphics and a full studio presentation (rather like a BBC science programme).

Table 12.1 Mean scores and Standard Deviations for audio-taped and video-taped self-study presentations (based on Spencer, 1977)

	Booklet + audio tape	Low-cost video tape	High-cost video tape
Four terminal networks			
Mean Score	8.5	8.1	8.4
Standard Deviation	1.2	1.0	1.3
Amplification properties of a junction transistor	7.9	8.4	8.4
Mean Score	1.9	1.0	1.3
Standard Deviation			
Load line			
Mean Score	7.7	8.1	8.8
Standard Deviation	1.3	0.9	0.7

As well as presenting the mean (average) score on the test given at the end of each study session, the table provides a measure of the variation (or spread) in the scores, a statistic termed the *Standard Deviation*. This statistic forms the basis for statistical tests that determine the statistical significance of differences in mean scores when groups are compared. It also forms the basis for calculating the *Effect Size* for comparisons of different methods. The reason for conducting this experiment was to consider the cost of an instructional programme in relation to the performance of students, in other words: as costs increased, was there a similar increase in student performance?

Figure 12.3 shows two different plots for the data. Plot 3(a) suggests that all test performances, irrespective of cost, are very similar, but by zooming in, as shown in 3(b), it looks as though there may be some differences. This is the point at which statistics become useful, taking into account not only the mean score, but also the distribution of scores. Applying statistics to the data in Table 12.1 showed that there was no statistically significant difference across the media with different costs: for increasing costs of production there was no statistically significant difference (*NSD*) in learning – the 'NSD effect' that was prevalent in much of the comparative media research in the last century.

Inferential Statistics

I view myself principally as a scientist – my background was in the physical sciences and biology. When I was studying at school much of what I had to deal with was based on well-established scientific principles, and I often felt that there was not the excitement within the physical sciences that I saw my peers enjoying in the arts and humanities. When I went to university I again found that there was little excitement in my studies because there was

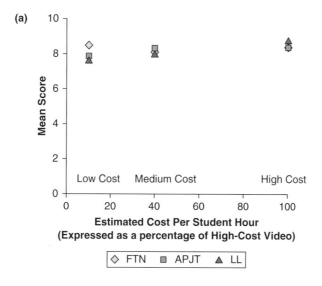

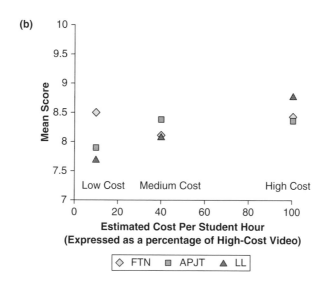

Figure 12.3 Mean scores for three science topics (FTN = Four Terminal Networks; APJT = Amplification properties of a junction transistor; LL = Load Line) and 3 teaching formats: (a) full range (b) restricted range (based on Spencer, 1977)

no opportunity, as a student, to engage in research. However, I was very lucky in my choice of a subsidiary subject when I chose the new science course in psychology. Traditionally psychology had been an arts-based subject associated with philosophy, but I was fortunate because for the first time a science of psychology was being established at my alma mater.

During the first year of this course we had to carry out a number of experiments, and an important aspect of those experiments was the experimental design, with students being asked to make contributions to the way in which data was gathered and analysed. I found this to be extraordinarily exciting, because we were being asked to engage in new research, not merely repeating age-old experiments that had very predictable results. Students were encouraged to think of new ways of recording behaviour, and analysing that behaviour, including the use of statistical techniques and various forms of graphical displays. For over 40 years I have enjoyed the benefits of this excitement as an academic pursuing a variety of research projects using quantitative methodologies. Although I can see the benefits of qualitative research methodologies, I am firmly of the opinion that much of what we do within these qualitative approaches can ultimately be turned into quantitative approaches. (This issue is discussed more fully in Chapter 10.)

Recently in a research meeting I ventured the idea that much of what was being discussed in qualitative terms could actually be incorporated into a quantitative approach, and the reason I gave for this was that I felt that the more quantitative data we obtained, with qualitative support, the closer we would move to pedagogy as an evidence-based process. One of the members of the group was so upset at the idea of working with a quantitative methodology that she explained that she had previously worked with a statistical pro-gramme (Statistical Package for the Social Sciences, aka SPSS) and still bore the scars of this distressing period of her career. I have noticed over many years that students, and also many members of staff, seem to have a fear of quantitative methodologies, and as a psy-chologist my desire is to reduce this quantitative phobia. In technical terms this is called the 'desensitisation of a phobia', and I hope that this chapter will be considered as a form of desensitisation of *quantiphobia*, to coin a new term.

Activity

My first recommendation is to watch the online video of Professor Hans Rosling, called 'The Joy of Stats' (www.gapminder.org/videos/the-joy-of-stats/), a brilliant and entertaining look at what we can do with quantitative data.

Let's look at some real data that is easy to understand and measure: a person's height, although this is an unusual approach to looking at quantitative methods. Usually there are long descriptions about what quantitative methods are, but ultimately it's simply about collecting and analysing data. Figure 12.4 represents height data on 25,000 18-year-olds from a South-East Asian city. In other words it's the data from the population of 18-year-olds in this particular city. So we are starting off with a population of 25,000 and we have measured their individual heights – the decision was taken to measure the heights of all the students who were 18 years old in this particular city, and also to measure their weight to assess body-mass index as a measure of health in this population – as you can see there is a huge amount of data with 25,000 individual data points, so many that you cannot even read the individual heights.

Figure 12.4 Heights of a population of 18-year-olds for a S.E. Asian city – 25,000 individual heights

Clearly it's quite a task to represent all of these data points in a chart, but we can make a start with Figure 12.5. It is an unusual chart for this type of data, but it is one you are probably familiar with – it is a bar chart (although each bar is rather narrow) with the bars representing the height of each individual: just imagine the entire population of 18-year-olds standing next to each other from the smallest (just under 1600 millimetres, or 1.6 metres) to the tallest (just over 1.9 metres); if they were all very thin Figure 12.5 is what they would look like.

There are some interesting observations to be made from such a chart: 28 per cent of the population are between 1.6 and 1.7 metres tall, and 8 per cent of the population are taller than 1.8 metres; the remainder, 64 per cent are between 1.7 and 1.8 metres tall. The average or mean height (1.727 metres tall) is halfway along the horizontal axis (usually called the x-axis), with 50 per cent of the population being taller than this, and 50 per cent being smaller. The average height, of course, is calculated by adding up all the heights and dividing by the number of individuals. In this case that is 43,175,711 divided by 25,000. This type of information is part of statistics, and, as we have seen, is referred to as descriptive statistics, because, obviously, all we are doing is describing the data that has been collected.

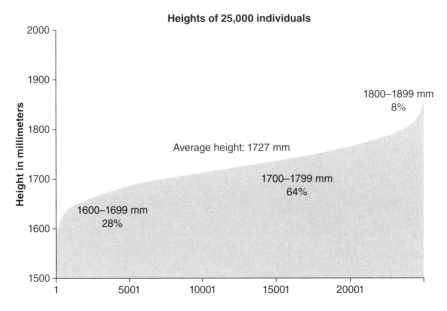

Figure 12.5 Bar chart of heights of a population of 25,000 18-year-olds for a S.E. Asian city

The descriptive statistic that is often provided with the average (mean), as shown in Table 12.1, is the standard deviation, which describes the spread of the data about the mean. A colleague recently lamented the fact that many students and lecturers do not know what a standard deviation is, although it is a basic concept in quantitative methods, and suggested that it was this lack of knowledge that led to a fear of statistics and quantitative methodologies. To explain this concept, the data in Figure 12.4 are plotted in a different manner, a way that you may be familiar with, called a histogram (see Figure 12.6). A histogram is a special form of the bar chart, and plots quantitative data with ranges of the data grouped into bins or intervals – this is often misunderstood. Let me explain: Another way to represent the heights of our population of 18-year-olds is to COUNT UP THE NUMBER OF PEOPLE OF EACH HEIGHT (in millimetres) and then PLOT THE NUMBER OF PEOPLE FOR EACH HEIGHT.

Table 12.2 Number of individuals of each height (in millimetres) about the mean (1727mm) within the range 1720mm to 1734mm

Height	Number of Individuals
1720	187
1721	198
1722	184
1723	214
1724	197
1725	197
1726	246

Height	Number of Individuals
1727	**224**
1728	227
1729	194
1730	207
1731	183
1732	212
1733	189
1734	192

The intervals (or bins) in Table 12.2 are each 1 millimetre, which shows the numbers of individuals of heights starting at 1720 mm, and increasing by 1 mm to 1734 mm. There are 187 individuals of height 1720 mm, and 198 individuals just one millimetre taller. The histogram in Figure 12.6 shows the data when the numbers in Table 12.2 are plotted, with the length of each bar representing the number of individuals at that height.

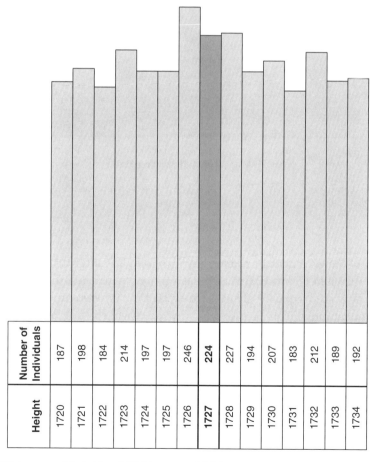

Number of Individuals	187	198	184	214	197	197	246	224	227	194	207	183	212	189	192
Height	1720	1721	1722	1723	1724	1725	1726	1727	1728	1729	1730	1731	1732	1733	1734

Figure 12.6 Histogram of heights of 1720 mm to 1734 mm

I must point out again that this is real data, it is actually based on a population of 25,000 individuals, and as such the data can be rather spiky when represented in graphical form. Figure 12.6 is just a small part of the full data set. Figure 12.7 shows the histogram for the full data set of 25,000 heights, but with much thinner bars, each of which represents a particular height in millimetres, and although it is rather spiky the general shape is one that is very familiar: the normal distribution, or bell-shaped curve.

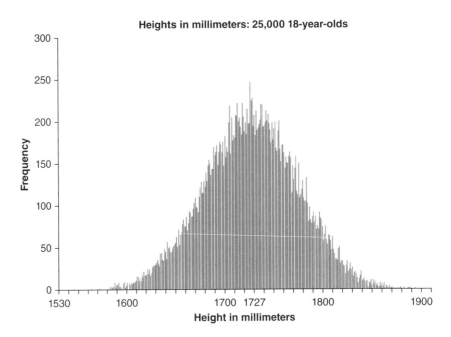

Figure 12.7 Histogram of heights of 1531 mm to 1909 mm (full data set of 25,000), intervals of 1 mm (mean = 1727)

The spikiness of the graph can be reduced by increasing the intervals (or bins) from 1 mm to 10 mm, as shown in Figure 12.8, which has a more obvious bell-shape.

But notice how the frequency changes for each of the intervals in Figure 12.7: there are ten times as many individuals in the 'bins' that are each 10 mm in size, as there are in interval bins that are 1 mm in size.

The reason I have chosen this set of data is because it conforms to the ideal bell-shaped, normal distribution, and consequently it has certain properties that can be explained and tested, using real individuals as our data source. One of the properties of this type of distribution is that the spread of data about the average can be described in standard deviation units. Figure 12.9 shows the height data described in standard deviations.

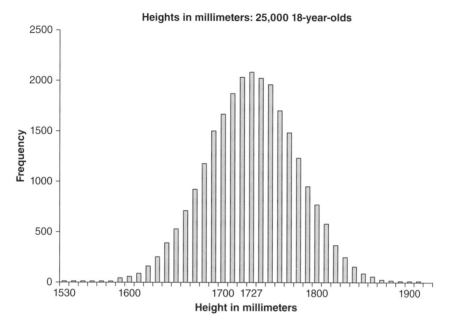

Figure 12.8 Histogram of heights of 1531 mm to 1909 mm (full data set of 25,000), intervals (bins) of 10 mm (mean = 1727)

Definition – Standard Deviation

The calculation of the standard deviation for a given set of data is quite straightforward, and I will demonstrate the calculation after describing what a standard deviation means. For the height data the standard deviation is 48 mm – this has been calculated by my computer. This means that 34 per cent of the population will be between 1727 mm (the mean height) and one standard deviation (48 mm) above the mean: that is 34 per cent of the population will be between 1727 mm and 1775 mm tall.

It is important to realise just what this means. Beneath the curve of our bell-shaped distribution lie all of the individuals in the population: the curve effectively encloses everyone who has had their height measured, and the area below the curve, and between the mean and one standard deviation, is 34 per cent of the total area (and hence 34 per cent of the total population). Similarly, 34 per cent of the population are one standard deviation below the mean, that is between 1669 mm (i.e. 1727 – 48) and 1727 mm. Between one and two standard deviations above or below the mean there are fewer individuals (the area below the curve is smaller). In fact, only 14 per cent of the population are between one and two standard deviations above (and below) the mean. In other words, 14 per cent of the population are between 1775 mm and 1823 mm tall, and 14 per cent are between 1631 mm and 1679 mm. The proportion of the population between two and three standard deviations above and below the mean is much smaller, representing just 2 per cent of the population in each direction. Looking at Figure 12.9 we can see that when we add up the percentages (14 + 34 + 34 + 14) 96 per cent of the population are between 2 standard deviations above and below the mean, i.e. between 1631 mm and 1823 mm. We can make some predictions based on this information: if we randomly select an individual from the population we will find that 96 per cent of the time they will be between our limits of 2 standard deviations above and below the mean. Another way of looking at this is in terms of unusual occurrences. For example, how likely is it that when I choose an 18-year-old at random their height will be greater than 1823 mm? They will be in the top 2 per cent of the population heights, and so for every 100 selections at random I will find 2 individuals taller than 1823 mm, and this is usually written in reports as having a probability of 0.02 (or 2%). The probability of randomly selecting individuals greater than 1823 mm or less than 1631 mm is 0.04; in other words for every 100 selections, 4 individuals will be outside the limits established by 2 SDs above and below the mean height.

> Note: I am using 2 SDs because it is easy to demonstrate and calculate, but traditionally statistical significance has started at the 5 per cent level, and 1.96 SDs above and below the mean accounts for 95 per cent of the population, leaving 5 per cent beyond these limits (2.5 per cent above and 2.5 per cent below). So, if a result is statistically significant with a probability less than 5 per cent ($p < 0.05$) it is outside the limits of 1.96 SDs above and below the mean.

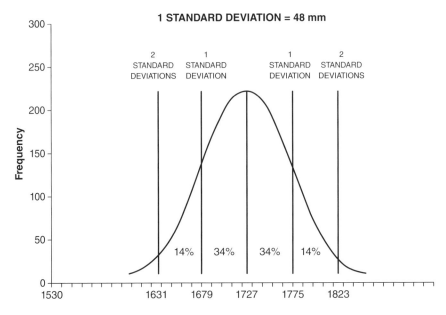

Figure 12.9   The bell-shaped normal distribution, showing percentage of measurements (heights) associated with Standard Deviations

It should be noted at this point that although the shape of the distribution may change, and the standard deviation may change in value, the proportion of the population described by one standard deviation above (or below) the mean remains the same: 34 per cent. Figure 12.10 illustrates this with two distributions, each with the same mean value of 50. The lower distribution has a much wider spread of data, with a standard deviation that is twice that of the top distribution, 20 units as compared with 10 for the upper distribution. Nonetheless, the same proportion of the data (individual scores on a test, perhaps) is represented by one standard deviation in both distributions.

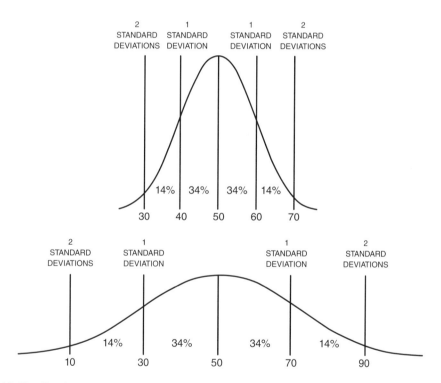

Figure 12.10 Two bell-shaped normal distributions, each with the same mean value, but different Standard Deviations (Top: 10 units; Bottom: 20 units), showing percentage of measurements associated with each Standard Deviation

Calculating the standard deviation for a normally distributed set of data is quite simple, but the formula seems to be quite intimidating for many non-mathematicians (and some mathematicians use it to intimidate quantiphobes). The formula is shown overleaf.

$$\sigma = \sqrt{\frac{\Sigma\left(x - \bar{x}\right)^2}{n}}$$

σ = standard deviation

Σ = sum of

x = each value in the data set

$\bar{x}$ = mean of all values in the data set

n = number of values in the data set

This simply means that the standard deviation is the average of the difference of all the heights from the mean height. You take the mean (average) for your population away from each measurement (height), and square the result. The squaring of the result is necessary because half the values (by definition, in our normally distributed data) will be negative and half will be positive, so they will cancel each other out if they are added up to find the average. Having added up all the squared differences, divide by the total population (25,000) to find the average squared difference, and then take the square root to find the Standard deviation.

Example: A standard deviation calculation

Here is a quick example, assuming a population of 8 rather than 25,000:

Population values: 2, 4, 4, 4, 5, 5, 7, 9.

Average of the eight data points: 2 + 4 + 4 + 4 + 5 + 5 + 7 + 9 divided by 8 = 40/8 = **5**

Take the average away from each value and square the result:

$(2 - 5)^2 = (-3)^2 = 9$	$(5 - 5)^2 = (0)^2 = 0$
$(4 - 5)^2 = (-1)^2 = 1$	$(5 - 5)^2 = (0)^2 = 0$
$(4 - 5)^2 = (-1)^2 = 1$	$(7 - 5)^2 = (2)^2 = 4$
$(4 - 5)^2 = (-1)^2 = 1$	$(9 - 5)^2 = (4)^2 = 16$

Then add the squared differences up: 9 + 1 + 1 + 1 + 0 + 0 + 4 + 16 = **32**

And find the average (squared difference), this is termed the variance: 32/8 = **4**

Then find the square root, which results in the standard deviation: $\sqrt{4}$ = **2**

So, the STANDARD DEVIATION (a.k.a. the square root of the average squared difference) = **2**.

But you may be wondering why the Standard deviation is important in Education and Social Sciences. It is because, when assessing different approaches in education or the social sciences, researchers are tending to use the EFFECT SIZE to judge the effectiveness of one approach over another.

Definition – Effect size

An Effect size is:

[Mean of new method – Mean of old method]/Standard Deviation (of old method)

This expresses differences between mean scores for a new method and a control group as a proportion of the standard deviation for the control group (although it may involve averaging the standard deviation of both groups). An effect size of 1.0 shows that the mean score for the new method is an improvement of one standard deviation above the mean of the control. In performance terms this means that 34 per cent of the group that previously performed below the average, are now above the average.

Generally, for educational outcomes, an effect size of 0.2 is small with only 8 per cent of students performing better with the new method; an effect size of 0.4 is medium (16 per cent of students perform better); and an effect size of 0.6 is large (20 per cent of students perform better). Hattie (2009) has used the effect size (d) to judge the effectiveness of many research interventions in thousands of research studies in education, demonstrating both the complexities of quantitative research outcomes, and the disparities between assumptions about effectiveness and actual outcomes from research (Table 12.3).

Table 12.3 The largest effect sizes for educational variables (based on Hattie, 2009: 297)

Rank	Domain	Influence	d
1	Student	Self-report grades	1.44
2	Student	Piagetian programs	1.28
3	Teaching	Providing formative evaluation	0.90
4	Teacher	Micro teaching	0.88
5	School	Acceleration	0.88
6	School	Classroom behavioral	0.80
7	Teaching	Comprehensive interventions for learning disabled students	0.77
8	Teacher	Teacher clarity	0.75
9	Teaching	Reciprocal teaching	0.74
10	Teaching	Feedback	0.73
11	Teacher	Teacher-student relationships	0.72
12	Teaching	Spaced vs. mass practice	0.71

(Continued)

Table 12.3   (Continued)

Rank	Domain	Influence	d
13	Teaching	Meta-cognitive strategies	0.69
14	Student	Prior achievement	0.67
15	Curricula	Vocabulary programs	0.67
16	Curricula	Repeated reading programs	0.67
17	Curricula	Creativity programs	0.65
18	Teaching	Self-verbalization/self-questioning	0.64
19	Teacher	Professional development	0.62
20	Teaching	Problem-solving teaching	0.61
21	Teacher	Not labeling students	0.61
22	Curricula	Phonics instruction	0.60
23	Teaching	Teaching strategies	0.60
24	Teaching	Cooperative vs. individualistic learning	0.59
25	Teaching	Study skills	0.59

The Population, Sample Size, and Sample Errors

The basis for most quantitative data research is the sample. Although many textbooks discuss the sample in terms of how it is selected and how large it should be, they fail to relate the sample to the population in any meaningful way. This tends to be because data used to explain quantitative concepts are drawn from samples rather than whole populations. Which is why I have chosen to illustrate the following concepts based on the entire population of 25,000 18-year-olds whose height was measured in 1993 (see Figure 12.8). Of course, we will not always be able to measure an entire population, so we select a smaller group, the sample, and make our measurements (height, IQ or other test scores) on this sub-group. But, how large should the sample size be, and how should it be selected? I am sure you will agree that a sample size of 50 per cent of the population, with each member of the sample selected at random, would probably fairly represent the whole population, but how confident would you be with a sample of just 16 individuals drawn at random? Not very confident, I hope, although such small samples are not uncommon in student projects (for further information on sample size see Chapter 11).

Statistics can help define the limits of our certainty for normally distributed data derived from randomly selected samples. The standard deviation of a randomly selected sample reflects the error in the sample in a quite simple way, and enables the calculation of an estimate of the actual population mean, or at least the range of values it will have and their associated probabilities. Here is the equation:

$$\text{standard error of the mean} = \frac{\text{sample standard deviation}}{\sqrt{\text{sample size}}}$$

The equation gives the standard deviation of the error (called the standard error of the mean, or SEM). For example, for a sample of 100 students with a mean test score of 50, and a standard deviation of 10, the standard error of the mean would be:

$$\text{SEM} = \frac{10}{\sqrt{100}} = \frac{10}{10} = 1$$

Because the standard error is actually the standard deviation of sample errors (i.e. the difference between the actual population mean and a large number of sample means), we can be sure that in 96 out of 100 random samples, the population mean will be between 2 SEMs above and below the sample mean, which in the above hypothetical case will be between 48 (which is 50 – 2 SEMs) and 52 (50 + 2 SEMs). Scores outside these values will be unusual, occurring in only 4 per cent of random samples. Most of the time we simply have to accept that the maths works. Most of the time we do not know the population mean (because we cannot collect all the population data), so we cannot check the validity of the statistics. Because I am naturally sceptical, I do not like to find myself in such a position, and will usually want to see the evidence, preferably with an experiment. Fortunately, for this exercise, we have the population data for height, and can run an experiment. We know that the actual mean value for height in the population of 18-year-olds is 1727 mm, so I can randomly select 100 individuals for my sample and see if the theory matches the experiment. This will take a few minutes to run on my computer!

Example: The results

From my random sample of 100 individuals, the mean value is 1721, and the Standard Deviation is 49.28, giving a Standard Error of the Mean of 4.9 (49.28/$\sqrt{100}$). So, we can be 96 per cent sure that the actual population mean is between two Standard Errors (let's round it to 5 rather than 4.9) either side of our sample mean, that is between 1711 and 1731. And we know that this is true because our actual population mean is 1727. In fact, the mean of the sample is 6mm shorter than the actual mean – not a bad approximation, although it is from a good sample size. Another experiment, this time with just 16 in the random sample.

Here are the results: from the random sample of 16 individuals, the sample mean is 1720, and although the Standard Deviation is similar to the larger sample at 54.83, the Standard Error at 13.70 (i.e. 54.83/$\sqrt{16}$) is almost 4 times that of the larger sample. So, in this case we can be 96 per cent certain that the population mean will lie between the sample mean and 2 SEMs or between 1693 and 1748.

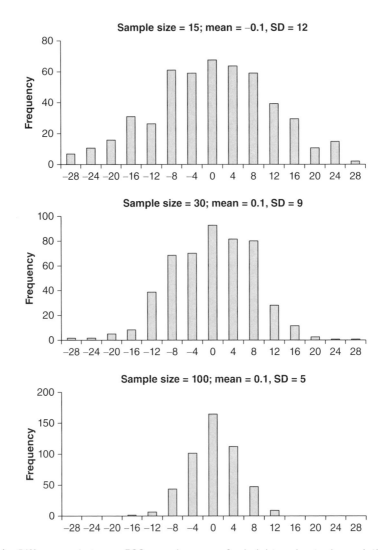

Figure 12.11   Differences between 500 sample means for height and actual population mean height in millimetres, for 3 sample sizes (15, 30 & 100)

To get a more accurate picture of the distribution of errors we have to collect lots of samples of various sizes and compare their means with the actual population mean. I have done this for Figure 12.11, which shows the actual difference between the population mean 1727 and each of 500 random samples of sizes 15, 30 and 100 individuals. As you can see from Figure 12.11 the range of actual errors is much wider for the small sample, reduced for the medium sample, and narrow for the large sample. Don't forget, these are actual samples taken from real population data, and the standard deviation of errors for the large sample (5) is identical to the hypothesised SEM value from our sample of 100 – so, I am convinced by the data, not just the maths. Remember: small samples produce large errors.

These two measures (SD and SEM), which are relatively easy to calculate, provide the basis for a range of statistical tests, and for most of these, although the calculations are no more difficult than for the SD, computer statistical programmes are used in research studies. However, on occasions even schools are being encouraged to calculate performance statistics using formulae shown in Table 12.4 (OFSTED, 2011).

Table 12.4 Comparing school and national average point scores (based on OFSTED, 2011)

$$\frac{X_s - X_n}{\left(\frac{\sigma_s}{\sqrt{n_s}}\right)} > +2 \text{ then Significance is positive}$$

$$\frac{X_s - X_n}{\left(\frac{S_s}{\sqrt{n_s}}\right)} > -2 \text{ then Significance is positive}$$

Where: x_s is the school's average point score for English, Maths and Science
x_n is the National average point score for English, Maths and Science
σ_s is the school's standard deviation
n_s is the school's number of entries (pupil scores)

The top part of the formula is the difference between the mean score for the school and the mean for the entire population. If it is positive the school is significantly better than the national mean; if negative, it is worse than the national mean. The bottom part of the formula, you may recognise, is the SEM for the school. So, this test is simply measuring the number of school SEMs that are between the school and population means. If this difference is greater than two SEMs it is classed as statistically significant because it is likely to be found by chance only 4 per cent of the time.

Note: Actually the value used by the English schools data information system RAISE online to test significance is 1.96, rather than 2, because traditionally a result is statistically significant if it occurs in less than 5 per cent of cases, and 1.96 SDs covers 95 per cent of cases (whereas 2 SDs, you will remember, covers 96 per cent).

Comparing Groups

The z-statistic shown in Table 12.4 is a useful way of comparing a sample, in this case a school's performance, with the population mean. However, for many research projects comparisons are often between two or more groups, and there are a number of tests for statistical significance that can be applied to such comparisons. For research data that is normally distributed the tests are referred to as *parametric tests*, if the data is not normally distributed *non-parametric tests* are used. Microsoft Excel offers a number of parametric tests (see Table 12.5) but at the time of writing does not provide non-parametric tests.

Table 12.5 Microsoft Excel Statistical Tests

ANOVA: Single Factor

ANOVA: Two Factor With Replication

ANOVA: Two Factor Without Replication

Correlation

Regression

t-Test: Paired Two Sample for Means

t-Test: Paired Two Sample Assuming Unequal Variances

t-Test: Paired Two Sample Assuming Equal Variances

z-Test: Two Sample for Means

The commonly used statistical programme, Statistical Package for the Social Sciences (SPSS), includes both types of test. The parametric tests are basically variations on the theme of means, standard deviations and standard errors. A frequently used test for comparisons of two groups is the *t-Test*. Here is the basic equation for the t-Test:

$$\frac{X_1 - X_2}{\sqrt{\left(\frac{SD_1}{\sqrt{N_1}}\right)^2} + \sqrt{\left(\frac{SD_2}{\sqrt{N_2}}\right)^2}}$$

Although it looks complicated, there is nothing here that hasn't already been dealt with in this chapter. The top part is the difference in the mean scores for the two groups (X_1 and X_2); the bottom part shows the Standard Error of group 1 ($SD_1/\sqrt{N_1}$) and the Standard Error of group 2 ($SD_2/\sqrt{N_2}$) – these are squared (giving the variance), added together and then the square root is taken of the sum, giving what is known as the 'SE of the sampling distribution of differences'.

   This is in effect the standard deviation of differences, and as would be expected, differences larger than two of these measures will occur by chance 4 per cent of the time. (*Note: generally statistical significance is set at 5 per cent, so a value of more than 1.96 SDs, rather than 2, is expected.*) For very large samples, the critical value for the t-Test is indeed 1.96; but, for smaller samples with equal numbers in each group the range is from 2.05 for 15 subjects per group, to 1.98 for 50 subjects in each group. Of course, just because it is statistically significant does not mean it is educationally significant – the Effect Size will provide a basis for such a judgement. Table 12.6 shows the results for an independent t-Test from an experiment I created, based on the height database. Group 2 is a simple random sample from the 25,000 database; whereas Group 1 has been manipulated (they have been given a drug that may have an effect on growth – I've actually just added in a mathematical equivalent of such a drug). Now, because I didn't know exactly how the drug would affect the height of the sample, I cannot predict the direction of any difference, so I use what is known as a *two-tailed test* (if I had made a prediction that the height would be increased, I would have used a one-tailed test, which has a lower threshold). The output in Table 12.6 shows that the mean height of the sample receiving the drug is higher than Group 2, which is the straightforward random sample: the difference is 16mm. The t-Test statistic, calculated by Excel (using the equation shown above), is 2.40 and the critical value for the t-Test is 1.97 (for a probability of occurring by chance 5 times in 100 or 5 per cent of the time, which is expressed as: $p < 0.05$, with p representing *probability*). So, we may conclude that the drug has produced a statistically significant effect. In fact, Excel, and most other computer-based statistical packages will compute the exact probability associated with a particular t-value, in this case it is a probability of 2 per cent, or $p = 0.02$, for $t = 2.40$. When writing up this information in a report, there is no need to put all the details from the table. It is sufficient to write that the difference between the groups is statistically significant, with $t = 2.40$; df = 198; $p < 0.05$ (or to be more precise, $p = 0.02$). The table provides values from which the Effect Size can be calculated, using the pooled variance or the variance for the control group (Group 2); this comes to 0.3 $[(1747-1731)/\sqrt{2135}]$, a relatively small effect, although statistically significant.

Table 12.6 t-Test output from Microsoft Excel

	Group 1	Group 2
Mean	1747.03	1731.32
Variance	2190.31	2081.19
Observations	100	100
Pooled Variance	2135.75	
df	198	
t Stat	2.40	
P(T<=t) two-tail	0.02	
t Critical two-tail	1.97	

A similar test for differences between more than two groups is the *Analysis of Variance* test or *ANOVA*. In a recent research project I collected reading data on groups of 6-year-olds over four years (Spencer, 2010). Although the teaching methods and teacher remained constant over these years, I was concerned that there might be some cohort variation in their reading scores. If there was no cohort variation I could combine all the data and analyse it as a group of 105 pupils; but if there was a statistically significant variation in the year groups, the data would have to be analysed separately by year group. The *One-Way Analysis of Variance* was applied to the data and the output from Microsoft Excel is shown in Table 12.7. The F-Statistic for the four groups is 0.36 and this does not exceed the critical value of 2.69, so there was no statistically significant difference between the groups, and I could therefore legitimately combine them. Again, there is no need to put the entire table in a report, and in my paper the table is expressed as: 'ANOVA results revealed no statistically significant differences between the 4 year groups for the standardized reading scores

$(F(3, 101) = 0.36$, MSE $= 221.26$, p $= .78).$' If there had been a statistically significant result from this ANOVA I would only know that there were differences between the groups, and I would need to perform multiple t-Tests to compare the groups in order to determine the nature of those differences.

> Note: A key feature in the analysis is the degrees of freedom (df) for each measure (between groups, within groups and total): there were four groups, and the associated degrees of freedom are $4 - 1 = 3$; for the within groups calculation, with 105 subjects and 4 groups, the degrees of freedom are $105 - 4 = 101$.

Table 12.7   ANOVA Single Factor output from Microsoft Excel

Source of Variation	SS	df	MS	F	P-value	F crit
Between Groups	237.99	3	79.33	0.36	0.36	2.69
Within Groups	22347.40	101	221.26			
Total	22585.39	104				

Note: SS = Sum of Squares; df = degrees of freedom; MS = Mean Square, (SS/df); F = MS Between Groups/MS Within Groups

The t-Test and ANOVA are parametric tests, which means that the data should be interval or ratio quantitative data (height, weight, scores on a test, income, years teaching etc.) and should approximate to a normal distribution. Other data types such as ordinal data (preferences in a questionnaire) or nominal data (gender, type of school or subject taught) should be analysed using non-parametric tests, which are not based on the same assumptions as parametric tests, and are referred to as assumption-free tests. A non-parametric equivalent to the independent t-Test is the *Mann-Whitney test*. It is not available in Excel, at the time of writing, and so a more advanced statistical programme, such as SPSS, must be used. Table 12.8 shows the results of our height-inducing drug experiment when the data is analysed with the SPSS Mann-Whitney test. Notice that it gives the same statistical significance (0.02) as the output from the parametric t-Test in Table 12.3, as we should expect.

Table 12.8   Mann-Whitney test output from SPSS

Hypothesis Test Summary

	Null Hypothesis	Test	Sig.	Decision
1	The distribution of Height is the same across categories of Groups.	Independent-Samples Mann-Whitney U Test	.019	Reject the null hypothesis.

Asymptotic significances are displayed. The significance level is .05.

When the non-parametric version of the one-way ANOVA, the *Kruskal-Wallis test*, is applied to my reading tests data, the results in Table 12.9 clearly show that there is no statistically significant difference between the four groups, although the actual significance (0.84) is slightly different to the parametric test (0.78).

Table 12.9   Kruskal-Wallis test output from SPSS

Hypothesis Test Summary

	Null Hypothesis	Test	Sig.	Decision
1	The distribution of NFER Standardised Reading score is the same across categories of yeargroup.	Independent-Samples Kruskal-Wallis Test	.842	Retain the null hypothesis.

Asymptotic significances are displayed. The significance level is .05.

For more details of these statistical tests, and how to run them in SPSS, I strongly recommend Field (2009), as do most of my colleagues.

Questionnaires

A student recently informed me that their project was a qualitative study using a questionnaire, and I had to point out that questionnaires actually are mainly quantitative instruments. Even open-ended questions that have free-form responses will have to be coded and counted. The general format of questionnaires for student projects is to have two sections: a 'demographics' section that asks questions about age, experience, etc.; and an 'issues' section that poses the questions dealing with the research interest. The issues section is often in the form of statements that require the respondent to agree or disagree with them. Usually these are presented as *LIKERT* items, with five options: strongly disagree, disagree, uncertain (don't know), agree, strongly agree. Although writing a questionnaire seems to be an easy task, unless the questions are carefully constructed, analysis and interpretation will be very difficult – a lot of data can be collected, but figuring out what they mean can become impossible. A simple solution is to use questions that have been asked in published articles, or are available from dissertations and theses: the originals can then be compared with the new data. (For more about designing questionnaires see Chapter 11.)

   Data analysis from a questionnaire can take the form of a simple description of the number of respondents who have selected each of the alternatives, for example, the number of children in a class who agree/disagree with the statement: 'I like reading'. However, a more interesting analysis of this question would be to compare the responses of, for example, boys and girls. This type of analysis, making use of the demographic data in a questionnaire, can still be reported in a descriptive manner, but it can also be analysed using a variety of tests to determine the statistical significance of any differences. This approach can be applied in Excel, but is time-consuming, whereas a statistical program, such as SPSS, produces tables, as shown in Table 12.10, within seconds.

Table 12.10 Frequencies output from SPSS

Teachers at the school use advanced technology in their teaching

		Frequency	Percent	Valid Percent	Cumulative Percent
Valid	Strongly Disagree	38	9.8	9.8	9.8
	Disagree	75	19.4	19.4	29.3
	Do not know	62	16.1	16.1	45.3
	Agree	156	40.4	40.4	85.8
	Strongly Agree	55	14.2	14.2	14.2
	Total	386	100.0	100.0	100.0

Table 12.10 shows the frequencies and percentages for responses to the statement 'Teachers at the school use advanced technology in their teaching'. This shows that just over half the parents who were asked this question agree or strongly agree. However, the project was set up to determine whether there were differences in perceptions between parents whose children were in private schools and those who were in public schools.

Table 12.11 Crosstabs output from SPSS

Type of school * Teachers at the school use advanced technology in their teaching Crosstabulation

			Teachers at the school use advanced technology in their teaching					Total
			Strongly Disagree	Disagree	Do not know	Agree	Strongly Agree	
Type of school	Private School	Count	13	26	23	90	40	192
		% within Type of school	6.8%	13.5%	12.0%	46.9%	20.8%	100.0%
	Public School	Count	25	49	39	66	15	194
		% within Type of school	12.9%	25.3%	20.1%	34.0%	7.7%	100.0%
Total		Count	38	75	62	156	55	386
		% within Type of school	9.8%	19.4%	16.1%	40.4%	14.2%	100.0%

Table 12.11 shows the Crosstabs output from SPSS, with responses split between the two types of parents. With this split it looks as though parents of children in private schools are more confident that teachers are using the latest technologies in their teaching, compared with parents whose children are in publicly funded schools, with 68 per cent of the private school parents agreeing or strongly agreeing compared with 42 per cent of publicly funded school parents. Statistical tests can be applied to this data to determine whether the differences are statistically significant, and because this data is often classed as non-parametric data, being ordinal data rather than ratio (i.e. we do not know if a response of 'strongly agree' is the same distance from 'agree' as 'agree' is from 'do not know'), the *Chi-Square test* is applied. Table 12.12 shows the output from SPSS, with 3 different Chi-Square test results.

Pearson Chi-Square is the most common form of the test, and here the significance is shown as 0.000. If the result is likely to occur less than 5 per cent of the time (for example, beyond 1.96 SDs in the t-Test) it is written as having a probability of 0.05, which is written as p < .05 in reports. When a probability of 0.000 is shown in SPSS it means that it is more likely to appear by chance 1 in 1000 times. So, 0.000 is highly significant.

Note: don't worry about the degrees of freedom or the term asymptotic, SPSS takes care of these issues, although following them up in a manual such as Field (2009) will give you confidence to conduct this analysis.

The conclusion here is that there is a statistically significant difference (p < 0.001) in the views of parents who send their children to either private or public schools.

Table 12.12 Crosstabs statistical output from SPSS

Chi-Square Tests

	Value	df	Asymp. Sig. (2-sided)
Pearson Chi-Square	30.018[a]	4	.000
Likelihood Ratio	30.688	4	.000
Linear-by-Linear Association	25.930	1	.000
N of Valid Cases	386		

a. 0 cells (.0%) have expected count less than 5. The minimum expected count is 18.90.

I have said that questionnaire data are non-parametric and suggested Chi-Square as the appropriate statistic, and this certainly is supported by one of the most downloaded articles on the subject (Jamieson, 2004):

The response categories have a rank order but the intervals between values cannot be presumed equal... the appropriate descriptive and inferential statistics differ for ordinal and interval variables and if the wrong statistical technique is used, the researcher increases the chance of coming to the wrong conclusion. (Jamieson, 2004: 1217)

However, not everyone agrees, and Norman (2010) suggests that it is perfectly acceptable to analyse Likert items by parametric methods, claiming that 'as it turns out, parametric methods are incredibly versatile, powerful and comprehensive' (2010: 627) and demonstrates how the same results tend to be found for both types of analysis. Accepting the parametric analysis of this data type opens up many opportunities that are denied if only parametric methods are available. When the data from the questionnaire in Table 12.12 are re-analysed by t-Test, the mean difference in score is found to be 0.63, and this is significant with p < 0.001 – the same result as with the non-parametric test.

Statistical Association

I have so far considered a major element of quantitative methodologies, the description of measures for groups and the comparison of measures between groups. Another way of measuring and looking at data is to consider how they are associated or correlated. A good example of how measures are correlated comes from our population height data. The study was conducted to look at both height and weight, with a view to looking at the association between the two measures. Figure 12.12 shows the histogram for the population weights in 100 gm bands – it has the same spiky appearance as Figure 12.7 for the heights.

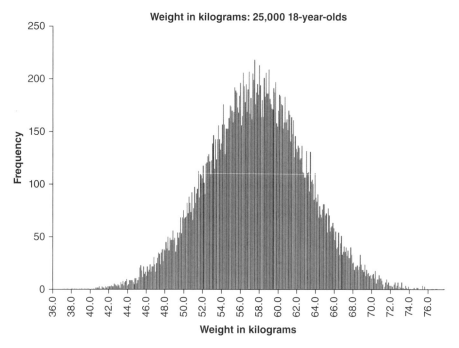

Figure 12.12 Histogram of weights of 35.4 kg to 77.5 kg (full data set of 25,000), intervals of 100 gm (mean = 57.6 kg)

A method of showing the relationship between height and weight is to produce a *scatter plot*. Figure 12.13 shows the mean values for the normally distributed weight data on the vertical axis (termed the Y axis) and the mean for the normally distributed height data on the X or horizontal axis. Figure 12.14 fills in the scatter plot with samples of varying size and provides the corresponding correlation coefficient. Each dot represents the weight and height of a single individual selected at random from the population of 25,000. The figure shows that the sample of 100 has a correlation coefficient of 0.56, which is a good estimate of the overall correlation for the 25,000 individuals of 0.50, as shown in Figure 12.15. As the sample size increases the overall shape of the plot (called the 'swarm' of data points) becomes fixed and there is a high degree of correspondence between the actual population correlation and the sample. The correlation for these data is positive, which means that as one measure increases (or decreases) so does the other. If one measure increases when the other decreases the correlation will be negative. The diagonal line in Figure 12.15 is the 'line of best fit' for the data, and is known as the regression line, and clearly shows that the relationship is positive: as height increases, so does weight. It represents the line with the shortest distance between each data point out of all possible lines, and is centred on the point at which both means cross in the graph. This line is associated with an equation that allows predictions to be made. For Figure 12.15 we can use the equation to predict a weight of an individual from any height. The equation for the regression line for the data is:

$$\text{weight} = (\text{height} \times 0.0551) - 37.5$$

If the mean height of our population is entered into the equation the result is 57.6 kg, which is, of course, the average weight of our population.

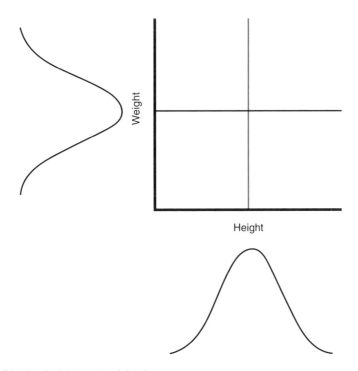

Figure 12.13 Plotting height and weight data

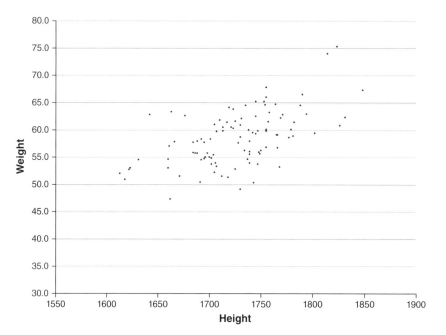

(a) Sample size: 100; correlation coefficient = 0.56

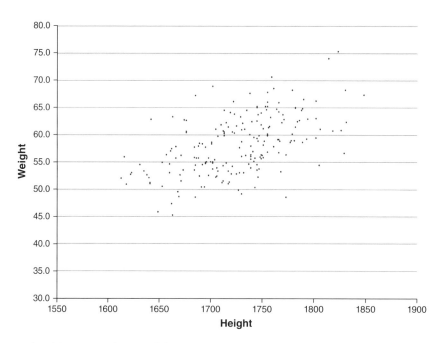

(b) Sample size: 200; correlation coefficient = 0.53

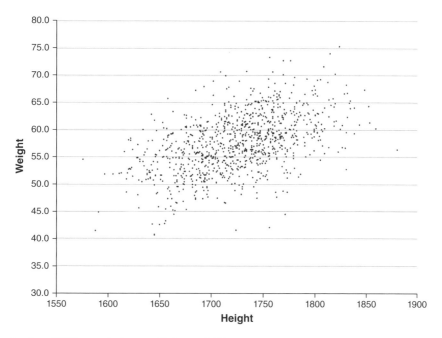

(c) Sample size: 1000; correlation coefficient = 0.50

Figure 12.14 Scatter plots of height (X axis) and weight (Y axis) data from 3 sample sizes (100, 200 & 1000)

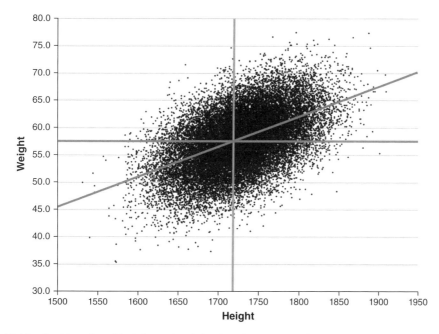

Figure 12.15 Scatter plot of height and weight data from population (25,000), with regression line; correlation coefficient between height and weight = 0.50

The correlation coefficient that is produced from parametric data is the *Pearson Product-Moment Correlation coefficient*. Both Microsoft Excel and SPSS provide Pearson coefficients, and although the calculation is tedious (which is why computer programs are so useful) the mathematics are quite simple!

Figure 12.16 shows two data points, each of which is a given distance from the mean value (for weight and height). The covariance is calculated first, and is simply the distances of each data point from the respective means multiplied together. The results for all data points are added together and divided by the number of data points (actually, divided by n – 1). So, in Figure 12.16 the covariance is: $(-1 \times -2) + (+2 \times +1)..../n - 1$. The result is standardised by dividing by the standard deviations of both measures. The standardised correlation coefficient = covariance/ SDmeasure 1 x SDmeasure 2. As with effect sizes, correlation coefficients are classed as small (0.10), medium (0.30) and large (0.50).

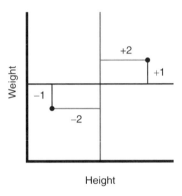

Figure 12.16   Calculating the product-moment correlation coefficient

I have been using correlations recently to look at the performance of university students. There is great interest in adding value to students of all ages, but the adding of value is obviously related to an initial measure of a student's performance, and for university students we tend to use the entry tariff scores, which are based on examination performance before entry into university. I was intrigued by the data that is now generally available linking entry tariff and good honours degree (2:1 and 1st classifications). I was aware of research that showed only a weak association between entry scores and degree classification in the 1970s (Sear, 1983), and decided to plot the more recent data on individual universities that has been made available to, and published in, UK newspapers. The results are presented in Figure 12.17, and show a very high correlation between the entry standard and the percentage of good honours degrees awarded to students. This is not at the individual level, of course, but it does show that generally the higher the entry tariff for a university the larger the percentage of good honours. The equation for the regression line even suggests the proportion of good honours a university should be giving if its entry tariff is known, and this has led to some under-performing universities calling on staff to boost their graduate outcomes!

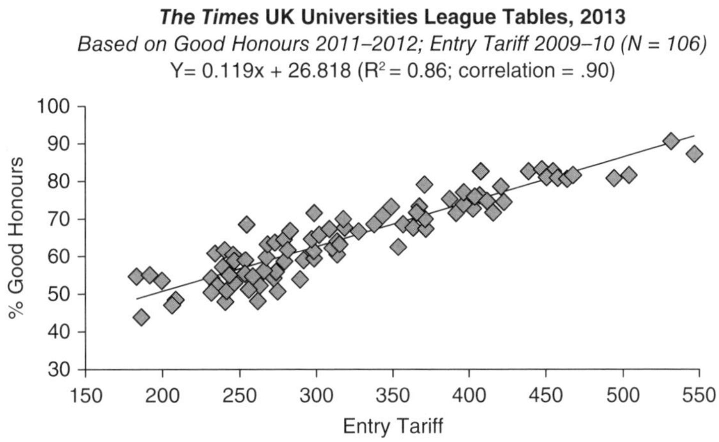
The Times UK Universities League Tables, 2013
Based on Good Honours 2011–2012; Entry Tariff 2009–10 (N = 106)
Y= 0.119x + 26.818 (R² = 0.86; correlation = .90)
% Good Honours
100
90
80
70
60
50
40
30
150
200
250
300
350
400
450
500
550
Entry Tariff

Figure 12.17 Scatter plot of % good honours and entry tariff (on admission); correlation = 0.90

In my latest research on the damaging effects of the English writing system (Spencer, 2010) I was interested in correlations between the number of students who could read a word and a variety of word metrics, such as its frequency in the language, the number of unnecessary letters, and even how often the letters for the vowels are used in the language. The word metrics were calculated from a variety of different studies. Table 12.13 shows the correlations between the readability of a word (which is basically how many children in a class can actually read the word: Y1R, in the table) and transparency metrics (the frequency of certain combinations of letters and sounds). The results demonstrate a most unexpected effect: it had been assumed that reading measures of transparency would be highly correlated with measures of word readability, but the results show that these reading measures (*14. GP* to *19. GP*) are not correlated with readability, whereas spelling measures (*8. PG* to *13. PG*) all have large correlations.

It is possible to use more than one measure (*independent variables*) to predict another (*the dependent variable*), using a *multiple regression analysis*. The underlying mathematical processes are extensions of the covariance calculation described above, and the tedious calculating of the results is now performed in seconds by statistics programmes. I put the transparency measures shown in Table 12.13, together with word frequency and a measure of word complexity (the number of letters minus the number of sounds or phonemes in a word) as independent variables in a regression analysis, and found that combined they accurately predicted how many children in a class could read a variety of different words. The diagram in Figure 12.18 shows the complex interactions between the independent variables: they are all inter-correlated, but also make individual contributions to the model's predictive power. The model allows me to accurately predict how many children can read any given word, if I know the frequency, complexity and transparency of the word, which in turn allows me to conclude that English is a dyslexic language (Spencer, 2000).

Table 12.13 Correlation matrix of reading transparency metrics

	Source	1	2	3	4	5	6	7	8	9	10	11	12	13	14	15	16	17	18	19
I. YIR		—	.48**	.46**	.49**	.59**	.57**	.48**	.45**	.45**	.51**	.58**	.5I**	.44**	-.03	-.09	.16	.08	.02	.18*
2. SG Ty	SC		—	.89**	.79**	.78**	.75**	.80**	.65**	.58**	.54**	.59**	.55**	.51**	.23**	.21**	.34**	.17	.15	.24*
3. SG Ty	SA			—	.91**	.75**	.76**	.81**	.53**	.52**	.51**	.51**	.49**	.45**	.23**	.24**	.33**	.18*	.15	.19
4. SG Ty	H				—	.72**	.74**	.75**	.52**	.54**	.59**	.55**	.55**	.49**	.08	.09	.30**	.06	.02	.23
5. SG To	SC					—	.98**	.90**	.73**	.71**	.70**	.80**	.76**	.67**	.11	.06	.22**	.15	.10	.27**
6. SG To	SA						—	.92**	.69**	.69**	.67**	.75**	.74**	.66**	.09	.06	.19*	.12	.09	.24
7. SG To	G							—	.65**	.63**	.61**	.66**	.65**	.68**	.14	.10	.19*	.13	.11	.28**
8. PG Ty	SC								—	.94**	.84**	.85**	.84**	.81**	.20*	.10	.27**	.15	.07	.10
9. PG Ty	SA									—	.90**	.85**	.89**	.84**	.11	.02	.17*	.08	-.01	.07
I0. PGTy	H										—	.85**	.88**	.78**	-.05	-.11	.12	-.04	-.12	.03
11. PGTo	SC											—	.94**	.80**	.06	-.05	.16*	.13	.01	.17
12. PGTo	SA												—	.83**	.02	-.06	.07	.07	.00	.11
13. PGTo	G													—	.03	-.07	.09	.03	-.03	.21
14. GP Ty	SC														—	91**	.56**	.87**	.83**	.15
15. GP Ty	SA															—	.60**	.78**	.83**	.18
16. GP Ty	H																—	.46**	.46**	.31**
17. GPTo	SC																	—	.95**	.26**
18. GPTo	SA																		—	.31**
19. GPTo	G																			—

Note: Y1R = word readability; SG = sonograph metric; PG = spelling metric; GP = reading metric; ** = 0.01 significance; * = 0.05 significance

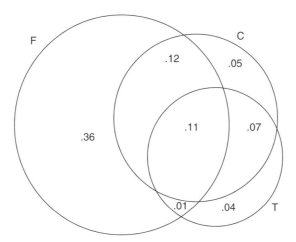

Figure 12.18   Proportional Venn diagram of three variable models for word readability

Note: T = transparency; C = complexity; F = frequency

Key Points to Remember

- Quantitative methodologies in education and the social sciences are inescapable in the modern world, and although tutors in these subjects may feel inadequate when it comes to analysing quantitative data, and prefer to recommend qualitative methodologies, students should be given the opportunity to make decisions about appropriate methodologies in their research, and that means having a basic understanding of both approaches.
- Having such a grounding in a range of methodologies and particular methods, enables students to choose between alternatives and to combine suitable elements together in a mixed methods approach. Understanding the basis for all approaches is empowering for students, and their tutors.

Further Reading

Salkind, N. (2014) *Statistics for People Who (they think) Hate Statistics* (5/E). London: SAGE.

This is an excellent book with interactive statistics to get you started in statistical analysis.

References

Field, A. (2009) *Discovering Statistics Using SPSS* (3/E). London: SAGE.

Goldacre, B. (2013) Building Evidence into Education. Available at: http://media.education.gov.uk/assets/files/pdf/b/ben%20goldacre%20paper.pdf. Accessed May 2013.

Hattie, J. (2009) *Visible Learning: A Synthesis of over 800 Meta-analyses relating to Achievement*. Abingdon: Routledge.

Jamieson, S. (2004) 'Likert Scales: How to (ab)use them', *Medical Education*, 38: 1217–1218.

NCET (1996) *Integrated Learning Systems: A Report on Phase II of the Pilot Evaluation of ILS in the UK*. Coventry: National Council for Educational Technology.

Norman, G. (2010) *Advances in Health Science Education*, 15: 625–632.

OFSTED (2011) 'A guide to calculations of RAISEonline reports: Methodology Library v5.1'. Available at: www.raiseonline.org/documentlibrary/ViewDocumentLibrary.aspx, Accessed May 2013.

Pressey, S.L. (1927) 'A machine for automatic teaching of drill material', *School & Society*, 25: 549–552.

Sear, K. (1983) The correlation between A level grades and Degree results in England and Wales. *Higher Education*, 12(5), 609–619.

Schmandt-Besserat, D. (1989) 'Precursors of writing: Plain and complex tokens', in W.M. Senner (ed.), *The Origins of Writing*. Lincoln, NE: University of Nebraska Press. pp. 27–41.

Spencer, K.A. (1977) 'An Evaluation of the cost-effectiveness of audiotaped and videotaped self-study media presentations', *British Journal of Educational Technology*, 8(1): 71–77.

Spencer, K.A. (1996) 'Recovering reading using computer mastery programmes', *British Journal of Educational Technology*, 27(3): 191–203.

Spencer, K.A. (2000) 'Is English a dyslexic language? Orthographic transparency and multilingual teaching', *Dyslexia*, 6: 152–162.

Spencer, K.A. (2010) 'Predicting children's word-reading difficulty for common english words: The effect of complexity and transparency', *British Journal of Psychology*, 101: 519–543.

Thorndike, E.L. (1912) *Education: A First Book*. New York: Macmillan.

For additional online resources please visit the book's website:
https://study.sagepub.com/needhamandpalaiologou

13

RESEARCH ANALYSIS AND DISCUSSION

GLYNN KIRKHAM

Chapter Aims and Objectives

This chapter aims to help you:

- understand the difference between presenting results and analysis;
- understand what analysis/discussion is;
- understand how you write and present your conclusions.

Introduction

If you have read the other chapters of this book you should be able to understand the dominant approaches to research methods in education and how we analyse them. From your reading (see the following Activity), you will have gained an understanding of the nature of research and why it is important. You will also have seen the elements necessary to be included in your personal research which can assist you in your developmental journey as a researcher. You have now reached an important part of the book with regard to providing your personal signal to the reader of your work that you are rigorous and systematic (Clapp and Myers, 1999; de Almeida Biolchini, 2007; Walls, 2012).

Activity

What have I read so far?

Tick the areas that you have read so far:

The purpose of research: Why do we do it?	
Making sense of research methodology	
Ethical issues associated with educational research	
Constructing the hypotheses/Creating the research question(s)	
Managing the project	
Writing the proposal	
Constructing the literature section	
Selecting appropriate research methods for an educational context	
Collecting qualitative data	
Analysing qualitative data	
Collecting quantitative data	
Analysing quantitative data	
Research analysis and discussion	
Writing and reporting the research	

If, however, you are in the middle of writing up your research and you have decided you do not know what to do at this stage, read on, since the key to this chapter is how you can show the reader or examiner of your own research that you are not only rigorous and systematic, but also are able to draw together strands from the relevant literature that you have read with the findings from your own small- or larger-scale research. It is only in this part that you can bring the hypothesis/research question and the findings together with your reflections on the process and the outcomes.

Analysis/Discussion

This chapter contains an introduction to the purpose of the analysis/discussion, and highlights the relationship of the analysis to the original hypothesis, findings and tentative conclusions. Areas for further research which have emerged as significant from the research and which are related to the original focus are also outlined within the discussion section.

The discussion section of your project report also contains commentary on ways in which the research might have been improved. Through taking a critical stance on the pros and cons of your research (the findings and how they relate to the findings of others), there is demonstration of revision of an epistemic standpoint (new knowledge has been acquired), reflection and subsequent learning and understanding from that learning.

This chapter or section of your work provides the basis for a successful dissertation, thesis or small-scale research activity. As in any writing, it is important to keep the storyline clear to the reader/marker. Thus, a very brief summary at the beginning of the chapter representing the emergent principles from the results, their relationship with what is already known and that which has been shown in the earlier part of your research report in the literature section, and the generalised trend demonstrated by the results will assist. In the 'Discussion' section, however, the purpose is to discuss, not to reiterate (except in synthesis) the results, which will enable the reader (who may have taken a break while reading your work) to be able to pick up the story from your words.

Practical Tip

It is a good idea to indicate to the reader how you intend to present the analysis and discussion. You can do this in a number of ways: purely textual, textually and with graphics, graphics alone, other visual forms including, if you are really confident in your ability to carry this off, by means of what the French call 'bandes dessinées' or cartoon strips. Such an approach would certainly gain a response from the reader/marker. On a good day and with the right examiner, if you have done it well you would gain marks for individuality and creativity. On a bad day and with the wrong examiner you could lose a lot of marks for failing to comply with orthodoxy.

With the technological capabilities that are today available, it would be possible to present digitally the whole of the research, be it a research project, your dissertation or your thesis. (Some universities already have an expectation that dissertations and theses are presented for repositories in digital form. Check to see what the requirements for your university are.) Claims would have to be made for parity with those presenting such research embodiments for examination where the product is the outcome of the research, as in some Fine Arts' courses. A digital presentation (in the form of a videoed mini-viva or in-depth TV/Radio-style interview or interrogation), for example, between you and an interviewee about your research would be one opportunity for you to include such things as a presentation of your analysis and consequent discussion of the key points and cross-reference to the prevailing relevant literature. Be careful, however, as it is generally still the expectation that your report will be presented in the traditional way.

In some papers published in peer-reviewed journals, you will find that the discussion of the analysis sometimes includes the conclusion; in others there is a separate conclusion. Two examples of these differing, but acceptable approaches, are Benwell and Stokoe (2002) (where the conclusions are included in the discussion section) and Wall et al. (2013) (where the conclusions are presented in a separate section). In a paper by Cheuk (2007), having highlighted the findings as 'key learning points', he follows with perceived benefits and limitations and, finally, conclusions. The messages about approaches to the discussion section of your work are:

1. that there must be such a section, however conceived and presented;
2. that the style fits the nature of the task, the nature of the inquiry and is consonant with the style of the rest of the work.

If you are on a degree course, you must verify with your supervisor (who will also know the likely response of the external examiner if your work happens to be part of the sample s/he might see) which is the preferred university or faculty style. Alternatively, if you choose another format you should state at the beginning of your text which way you intend to present and why this is your preferred method with appropriate reference to models from the literature.

Sources of Support

There are numerous advice sites available online (and sound counsel may be found on some). An example here is *thesiswhisperer.com*, which is a generic site relating to theses and focused on the needs of doctoral students; there Mewburn (2012) declares that, 'Essentially the discussion chapter tells your reader what your findings might mean, how valuable they are and why.'

Note Mewburn's emphasis here on you giving evidence of your ability to interpret the findings emerging from your research, putting them into the context of the existing body of knowledge and evaluating them accordingly. It is important in your writing to know and to declare what might be tentative and what is more certain to claim on the basis of your evidence from the literature and your own research.

Whereas Hinshaw (in Azar, 2006), suggests that 'The point of a discussion, in my view, is to transcend "just the facts," and engage in productive speculation.' Here, he is correct that the purpose of the discussion chapter is not to re-state the findings ('the facts'), but to go beyond description and analysis to inject real-world meaning(s). (Please note the plural of 'meaning' is used here to indicate that the discussion section is where it may be possible to interpret findings in more than one way. Based on analysis, synthesis and thesis of the evidence, the discussion would then identify, which was to be the strongest outcome.) Note also that Hinshaw (op. cit.) uses the adjective, 'productive' in relation to 'speculation' to emphasise the need to avoid mere conjecture and to show the practical (or indeed theoretical) value in the outcomes from your research.

In the box below you will find – in the form of questions to which to respond – a possible format for the 'Discussion' section of your research report.

1. What will the reader find within this chapter and why?
2. What were the key findings?
3. What were my initial reference points and conclusions from the literature review, the elements from which any epistemic standpoint or hypothesis was built?
4. How does what I have found cohere with what already exists in the literature that I have consulted?
5. Was the methodology appropriate to test my hypothesis and to answer the questions and sub-questions posed?
6. Was my form of analysis the best way to undertake the task? What if I had adopted a different approach, might the outcomes have been different and why? (Be careful here, however, not to conjecture too much. You did what you did. What you learned from it is the important factor.)
7. What are the claims emerging from the research and how might they be described in relation to the sample size and generalisability? Are the claims strong and, if so, how strong are they?
8. What might be the implications for theory and practice and potential impact of the research?
9. What conclusions might be drawn? What areas emerge as potentials for further investigation and future research?

Following the introduction, then, move to the findings and their relationship to what is already known. One way of building your own framework for this chapter is the use of a table (or spreadsheet) on which you link a list of the products of analysis with the key anchor-points from the literature and reach a 'so what?' factor or emerging consequence as a point for further discussion. You can imagine research examining different factors in leadership. Below is an example of such a structured analysis for discussion.

Table 13.1 A possible framework for the relationship between research findings and known literature

	Findings from analysis	Related literature	Emerging discussion point
1.	Leaders' height above average	Bonuso, 1983; Giessner & Schubert, 2007	Concurrence, but what of 'smaller than average' leaders?
2.	Leaders' own education	Ribbins, 1997; Pascal & Ribbins, 1999; Bennis & O'Toole, 2005	Contradiction, business leaders differ from school leaders
3.	Leaders' background	Medina, 2001; Li, 2003; Persson & Zhuravskaya, 2011	Stereotypes and non-stereotypes, political orthodoxies, eastern and western cultures

Kretchmer (2006) supports the notion of a visualised representation of the evidence to develop your argument and suggests that 'Before beginning you should try to develop an outline to organize your thoughts in a logical form. You can use a cluster map, an issue tree, numbering, or some other organizational structure.'

Making Claims

Although it is quite certain that he was not thinking of writing a discussion chapter for a dissertation, Mercer's (1944) lyrics for the song 'Accentuate the Positive' give wise advice for the researcher seeking so to do.

> "You got to ac (yes, yes) –cent-tchu-ate the positive
>
> Eliminate (yes, yes) the negative
>
> And latch (yes, yes) on to the affirmative
>
> Don't mess with Mister In-Between
>
> No, don't mess with Mister In-Between"
>
> *Source:* www.lyricsdepot.com/Johnny-mercer/accentuate-the-positive.html

Ask yourself what are the positive aspects that have emerged from the research that may be claimed as potential new knowledge. There is a sense whereby every piece of social science research produces new knowledge since no research can be carried out and then replicated with the same population using the same methodology and procedures without there having been changes in the population. For example, the participants have grown older and/or have learned more; the weather has changed and with it the demeanour of the researched. In the discussion chapter, such variables, including changes in the researcher him/herself, must be seen to be recognised and their potential impact on the results evaluated by the researcher.

To eliminate the negative is not always possible since honesty and integrity are expected of researchers. What it is possible to do is to recognise what might have been done better and how improvement might have been effected and how it might have an impact on the overall results. Speculation on what might have been when taken beyond a certain narrow degree of freedom is, however, unacceptable.

Latching on to the affirmative is again a positive approach to a critical appraisal of both method and findings. What went well and how findings verify (or nullify) the original hypothesis or research question demonstrates consonance within the research. It is imperative to note where links are made with the literature and the results support or even contradict one another. Just because there is a published article on a particular phenomenon does not mean that it is the truth for all times. Remember that people once believed the Earth was flat or that the Earth was the centre of the universe. It was not until

Copernicus in 1563 and Galileo in 1610 that the heliocentric theory was brought to mainstream thinking in Europe (and even then it was opposed).

Advice From Universities to Students on Degree Courses

Your university's library or learning centre will no doubt have a hand-out, other literature or e-accessible resource giving clear advice and generic guidance on the structure and layout of your work at different levels, undergraduate, postgraduate and doctoral. Read this advice carefully and give evidence that you have read it by following the guidelines. (You might also include it in your references if you have made reference to it and if you have followed the advice.)

As examples, below you will find advice from two universities about writing your discussion section followed by an analysis of what the examiners are expecting to see in this section. That advice is worded differently and emphasises different aspects demonstrates well the need for you to read what your university expects.

Plymouth University's advice to students about what to write in the discussion section is brief and concise – see box below.

> One of the most interesting and important parts of your dissertation is the analysis/ discussion of results. This is where you will try and draw some useful conclusions from the research you have carried out. What you are trying to do in this section is to put your findings into the context of previous research (most usefully this would be the research you identified in the lit review). Questions you might want to consider when writing this section are: have you confirmed your expectations and those of other researchers in the field or have you found something different/new/contradictory/ anomalous? Can you make sense of your findings? Can you offer some sort of explanation, however tentative? What are the professional/practical/political implications of your findings (Hannan, 2008)?

Leicester University's (2013) Study Guide on 'Writing a Dissertation' gives the following counsel about the discussion section:

> This is where you review your own research in relation to the wider context in which it is located. You can refer back to the rationale that you gave for your research in the literature review, and discuss what your own research has added in this context. It is important to show that you appreciate the limitations of your research, and how these may affect the validity or usefulness of your findings. Given the acknowledged limitations, you can report on the implications of your findings for theory, research, and practice.
>
> University of Leicester Student Learning Development

What can be gathered from examining the expectations from these two universities are the commonalities and also the minor differences in guidance. Both advise critical reflection on your findings from your research in relation to the existing available literature (or at least to that which you have referred). Further, they agree about the opportunity to raise questions in the discussion section or chapter. These questions will be both methodological and consequential.

It is, therefore, good to know what are the expectations of students at the universities of any external examiners who may be scrutinising your work and how, if at all, they differ. This should not change your own stance in relation to the research you are submitting because your work will be examined against the criteria in your university. Nonetheless, especially in the quality of discussion, knowing that your work is equivalent to or better than elsewhere is a psychological boost. As you will see from the box below UK universities usually make use of External Examiners who provide that comparative view for all their degree courses.

> One aspect of higher education that must be remembered by those studying in the United Kingdom is that part of the quality assurance process is the system of external examiners. Such agents of quality assurance bring with them their experience of the systems and expectations of their own institutions as well as an understanding of the examination and marking across a number of universities. Among other aspects of their role, they advise university departments and faculties about parity.

In conclusion what needs to be discussed in reports, dissertations and theses can be seen in the box below.

> (1) Findings: how do they compare with what already exists in the literature reviewed in the literature chapter? What could be the reasons for differences? What are the similarities?
> (2) A rigorous examination of the impact of your chosen methodological approach on findings, using comparisons with similar research in the field.
> (3) What of the variables you identified? How did they impact on the results, as expected or otherwise?
> (4) Were there differences in the results between gender groups, age groups, experience? How do you interpret these differences or why do you think there were similarities?
> (5) Have you avoided bias in interpretation and included only clearly evidenced assertions?
> (6) Is there sufficient evidence to make strong claims from your findings? Are any claims possible at all?

Making Strong Claims

An example of a strong claim from a rigorous review of the literature and research on a particular form of professional development for teachers can be seen in the following extract from a research report where (under the subheading of 'discussion') in their opening paragraph the authors have written:

> As the field of virtual professional development is still in its infancy [...], an important finding from this study is that it is imperative not to settle for the *status quo* of virtual professional development even if it appears on the surface to be better than what teachers traditionally have experienced in their past traditional face-to-face contexts. This study indicated that while virtual school professional development experiences may be in greater alignment with what is known about teacher professional development, a programme of school action research can push the envelope on the ways teachers engage as learners and collaborators with one another to better understand and enact the online teaching phenomenon. (Dana et al., 2013: 254)

This technique of opening an analysis/discussion section with a strong assertion or claim is a way of engaging the reader, drawing the attention of the reader and leading the reader to think positively about the research. Note the use of words like 'important' and 'imperative', which shout, 'Listen to what we have to say!' or, more accurately, 'Read what is here!' Note also the use of 'traditionally' and 'traditional' in the same sentence which reinforces the negativity of old-fashionedness suggested by the term. The use of the term 'push the envelope', meaning 'extend' or 'make greater use of' further promotes their claim. Later in the paper, again in support of their research, they reflect on the link between their findings and selective existing literature and have to follow separate sub-headings of 'Implications', 'Further research' and 'Conclusions', which parts are sometimes seen within the discussion section. Their very strong claim is made following a study of only 30 'virtual' teachers (real teachers in a virtual environment) engaged in action research! Note, too the use of reference to relevant and reviewed literature in an opening paragraph.

  When using a quantitative methodology, strong claims can also be demonstrated as in the article by Kearney et al. (2013: 331). Again, they catch the reader's attention in the first sentence and leave reference to related literature to a later stage but still within the first paragraph and conclude it with a second reference to other studies:

> The authors now turn to a brief discussion of the results from each of these variables in turn. While mindfulness is not the only aspect of effective leadership, we posit that it is one important dimension exhibited by many successful school leaders. In designing this study, the authors acknowledged it would be important to include control variables that have also been demonstrated to impact student achievement. For example, SES (socio-economic status) has consistently demonstrated its impact on school level achievement. As a result, any school success study that did not include socio-economic status would be falsely skewed. Accordingly, this research included the following demographic control (independent) variables: attendance rates; socio-economic status; and school size. These variables were selected based on their previously demonstrated impact on school success [....] It is no surprise that relative wealth (SES) of the schools in this study were highly correlated with student success ($r = 0.6668$, $p < 0.01$). Historically, SES has consistently been one of the best predictors of student success [...]. It is also not surprising to find that the largest schools underperformed compared to the smaller schools in this study ($\beta = -0.139$, $p < 0.05$) as this is also consistent with prior studies [...].

The thoughts of the nineteenth-century Danish philosopher, Kierkegaard, remind the researcher that it is impossible to predict outcomes in every case in life if one seeks to understand.

> It is quite true what philosophy says: that life must be understood backwards. But then one forgets the other principle: that it must be lived forwards. Which principle, the more one thinks it through, ends exactly with the thought that temporal life can never properly be understood precisely because I can at no instant find complete rest in which to adopt a position: backwards. (Kierkegaard, 1967)

Thus, precision in reporting is essential if understanding of phenomena is to be achieved. Christopher Columbus set out to find a new route to the Spice Islands of the East and the riches to be found there; instead he came to a different land and a different set of riches. His original hypothesis of the potential for circumnavigation (that since the Earth was round it would be possible to reach [the Orient] the East by going West) was correct. He actually found somewhere which was not known to him (nor to many others in Europe), but even on reflection he believed that it was the Indies. Since he came back with riches and told his story well (though some hearing his tale had doubts), he was believed. Argue your case and tell your story well! It may be that you may have to recognise that someone will later prove that you too were mistaken.

What can be learned from the outcomes of the research relates both to the epistemic bases and the focus of the research (which is and is to be in the public domain) and to your own competence (knowledge, skills and attitudes) as a researcher. Depending upon the advice and guidance you receive from your supervisor or critical friend, you may include within the section your reflections about your own learning as a researcher, which may or may not be part of the intended outcomes from your project. Nonetheless, this is an important aspect of your personal development as an individual 'academic'. Many in the early stages of research believe that the task is easy. 'Anyone can write a questionnaire!' some declare. Similarly since almost all UK students will have seen Jeremy Kyle, the popular daytime television presenter, they may also believe it is easy to interview people to elicit 'truth'. After reflection on their experiences, however, there is often a greater appreciation and understanding of the breadth of paradigms, methodologies and methods, forms of analysis and interpretation, the ability to analyse and synthesise, and the actuality of needing to find exactly the right words, *les mots justes*, to extract the data to derive the information sought both in their research and the writing up. Not everyone analyses their own learning following the research activity, but to do so can give you new insights into your strengths and your areas for development.

It's all Ps

In summary, it seems that it is possible to remember the Discussion section as a series of words beginning with the letter 'P' (see box below).

Panache: This is the style with which you write and it should be attractive to the reader. Ask a friend whether s/he finds your work readable.

Perils: Ignoring (or failing to identify) any weak elements of the work is not good practice, but nor is focusing the whole of the discussion on highlighting these. For example, if there were a number of people involved in carrying out the research, it is possible that the manner in which they carried out their roles will have had an impact on the findings. Not having recognised this as a possibility is one potential weakness, but to labour the point as more significant than it might have been is not helpful to the reader; nor is repeating it time and again in the text. Any research should be balanced in reporting and the commentary around findings.

Personality: Is the discussion based on personal reflection? How much of you emerges from the perspectives given? Will the reader follow you and your line of thinking? Are you purely an external observer (if that is at all possible?)? This P can also recognise that all human beings are individuals and that individuality can impact on the area of research and the researcher.

Perspectives: These are the ways in which your findings might be interpreted. This P also relates to the ontological stance you have taken; how your views of reality impact on your writing.

Perspicacity: This P is your ability to discern – to perceive differences –and then make relevant and evidence-based judgements as to their value in relation to your research question(s).

Perversity: This is recognising that things do go wrong (and how you dealt with what went wrong).

Potential(s): Relating to the functional or practical outcomes for your research which includes recommendations for specific action and further research, this P also includes the power of your claim.

Practicalities: These are the challenges and issues that your research brought to you and how you managed them. They are also the things that you have to do to complete the section.

Presentation: of the material relating to the research, but it also represents you as a researcher: your ability to be rigorous and systematic, but also your ability to develop arguments that support your findings. Your ability to write up the research in a way that engages the readers and encourages them to read more (or at least) the complete paper, dissertation or thesis is also being examined.

Problem: The starting point for your research when you asked yourself the question, Why … ? or How …. ? or What if … ? is how this P might be considered. It should always be an overt consideration when you discuss the findings and their analysis since they both relate to the initial questions.

Process: This is the way in which you carried out the research and this section of it. How are you going to approach your writing of the 'Discussion' section?

(Continued)

(Continued)

Product: This is what you have accomplished through the process: your final submission. It is also your contribution to what is known.

Proof: This is the evidence emerging from your findings from which you are able to make your claims. When you have enough proof, you can decide what phenomenon can then be charged with being responsible.

Try to think of more Ps or differing definitions, or maybe you can find a different alliterative approach to describing the discussion section?

Writing the Conclusion

Azar (2006: 2) presents a helpful insight from one of his postgraduate students, Michael David, who declares that the discussion section is where you should 'find a balance where you set a tone that indeed celebrates interesting findings without too many leaps, while at the same time reporting limitations *without being unnecessarily negative*,' (my emphasis). The brevity of his comment also sets the tone for a concluding section. The conclusion of your discussion section should not bring in new facts but should draw the section to a close in a precise and concise manner. Your words should leave the readers able to tell your research story in their own words, but knowing your beginning, middle and end. From the discussion section they should be able to recount the key points from your research.

In Kim's (2012: 446–447) article using cultural-historical activity theory (CHAT) from which I have selected key sentences, she includes the conclusion at the end of the discussion and analysis section, writing:

In conclusion, a CHAT perspective revealed that the use of ICT-mediated metaphors led to increasing contradictions between beliefs on how children learn as expressed by theorists (e.g. Piaget, Vygotsky, Bruner, Dewey) and as expressed by pre-service teachers. [...] The main finding was that pre-service teachers did not have relevant pedagogical knowledge, resulting in contradictions and tensions which can lead to change. [...] The most important implication of these results is that teacher education needs to focus more on helping pre-service teachers develop culturally-appropriate psychological tools such as ICT-based metaphor. They need metaphors that would enable them to become story makers engaging in reflective narrative inquiry for knowledge construction with their students, as well as redefining their own theories of teaching and learning.

Notice how in her synthesis, she has carefully included things for the reader to remember: the focus of the research, the main finding and suggestions for possible changes in practice, all imbued with a theoretical underpinning.

In the next extract look at how the writers, two university teachers, Timoštšuk and Ugaste (2012: 431), who researched student teachers' professional identity and emotions, capture the essence of their work. They open with a paragraph reminding the reader of the specific focus of the work.

> Our study sought to understand more thoroughly the emotions that help form professional identity, what factors relate to these emotions and, through an understanding of students' teaching-related emotions, decide what factors should be addressed in the university and what kind of support students need from their own teachers. Our results, however, do not describe objective characteristics of teaching – they reveal subjective meanings of teaching experiences.

Note how they guide the reader and the expectations from the work. They have also indicated the learning and functional outcomes expected from the research.

Practical Tip

At the beginning and end of each chapter, it is good practice to 'top and tail' your work to enable the reader to pick up your writing about your research, your dissertation or your thesis and proceed from chapter to chapter. 'Topping and tailing' requires that, at the beginning of the chapter, you tell the reader what to expect to find in the chapter and, at the end of the chapter, you tell the reader (briefly) what you want the reader to remember (the key points) from the content of the chapter while leading the reader into the next chapter.

An example of ending a chapter with a summary is provided in the box below. The whole of the dissertation discussion and findings example can be found in the 'New Essays' website, the link for which can be found at the end of this chapter.

> In summary of this chapter it is evident that Facebook is an effective means of advertising products and brands by means of product pages. It is also clear that although it is primarily the younger generations who are attracted by Facebook as a marketing tool, there is also scope for other generations. Finally, this research has revealed a number of relationships between variables which add particular insight to this topic. Thus, the following chapter provides final conclusions to the study and poses a series of recommendations for practitioners and academics for areas of further research. (Source: New Essays website: http://www.newessays.co.uk)

Such practice helps you provide evidence of your ability to summarise (if not synthesise) the content of your chapters. One test of the effectiveness of this practice is to just read the first and final chapters of your work. Better still ask a friend to read them! If your friend understands what you have done in your research then you can be confident that you have summarised the story of your research well.

In the next three short paragraphs from Timoštšuk and Ugaste (2012) findings that are paraphrased are that there is insufficient emotional support for student teachers, there is a need for further research, the phenomenon of unpredictability arises from the act of teaching and more context and domain-specific approaches are needed to understand emotions. In their final paragraph, they write:

> Our research clearly showed the strong and inevitable influence of emotions in the early stages of teacher education. We recommend, therefore, that teacher educators should, from an early stage, encourage students to express their emotions and read the emotions of others as a key component of self-regulation; that researchers should apply measures beyond self-reportage such as observation and psychological measures in order to gain a more complete picture of the complex issue of teachers' emotions, and, finally, that further research should be undertaken into the use of positive experiences in initial teacher education in order to develop an accepting attitude towards changes and insecurity in the teaching profession. (Timoštšuk and Ugaste, 2012: 433)

In this final paragraph, they have made their claim about the strength of their findings and the significance of their research. They establish what needs to be done, thus fulfilling the need to have a functional outcome and indicate the need to increase the knowledge base in the area, again with a desire for a practical outcome. With their claim about their research they have brought their own work to a conclusion, but they recognise there is more to be done and, with an eye to the future, they make recommendations for further action.

Final Words

It would probably have been easier to write what you should not do in the discussion chapter:

- Do not waste your time writing meaningless verbiage. At all times be coherent and relate what you write to the issues that have arisen.
- Do not go off at a tangent. Keep the discussion focused and directed around the research outcomes that might be inferred from the results and, where appropriate, implications for practice or, in very exciting cases, implications for modification of existing theory or the creation of a new theory.

For those who need such a checklist and then for the sake of balance, please look at the boxes belowwhich have been adapted from international sources for brief, but sound advice on *what not to do* and then *what to include*. You will find that there is consistency with what you may already have read above.

Errors to avoid

10 most common dissertation discussion mistakes

1. *Starting with limitations instead of implications.*
2. *Going overboard on limitations, leading readers to wonder why they should read on.*

3. *Failing to acknowledge limitations or dismissing them out of hand.*
4. *Making strong claims about weak results.*
5. *Failing to differentiate between strong and weak results as you make conclusions about them.*
6. *Lapsing into causal language when your data were correlational.*
7. *Repeating the introduction.*
8. *Restating the results without interpretation or links to other research.*
9. *Presenting new results; such data belong in the results section.*
10. *Offering no concluding statements or ending with the limitations.*

Source: Nolen-Hoeksema (2006)

Elements to include

1. Organise the discussion from the specific to the general: your findings to the literature, to theory, to practice.
2. Use the same key terms, the same verb tense (present tense), and the same point of view that you used when posing the questions in the introduction.
3. Begin by re-stating the hypothesis you were testing and answering the questions posed in the introduction.
4. Support the answers with the results. Explain how your results relate to expectations and to the literature, clearly stating why they are acceptable and how they are consistent or fit in with previously published knowledge on the topic.
5. Address all the results relating to the questions, regardless of whether or not the findings were statistically significant.
6. Describe the patterns, principles, and relationships shown by each major finding/result and put them in perspective. The sequencing of providing this information is important; first state the answer, then the relevant results, then cite the work of others. If necessary, point the reader to a figure or table to enhance the 'story'.
7. Defend your answers, if necessary, by explaining both why your answer is satisfactory and why others are not. Only by giving both sides to the argument can you make your explanation convincing.
8. Discuss and evaluate conflicting explanations of the results. This is the sign of a good discussion.
9. Discuss any unexpected findings. When discussing an unexpected finding, begin the paragraph with the finding and then describe it.
10. Identify potential limitations and weaknesses and comment on the relative importance of these to your interpretation of the results and how they may affect the validity of the findings. When identifying limitations and weaknesses, avoid using an apologetic tone.
11. Summarise concisely the principal implications of the findings, regardless of statistical significance.

(Continued)

(Continued)

12. Provide recommendations (no more than two) for further research. Do not offer suggestions which could have been easily addressed within the study, as this shows there has been inadequate examination and interpretation of the data.
13. Explain how the results and conclusions of this study are important and how they influence our knowledge or understanding of the problem being examined.
14. In your writing of the discussion, discuss everything, but be concise, brief, and specific.

Source: Scientific, Medical and General Proofreading and Editing (n.d.)

Above all be honest, self-critical and critical of others' research. Make your claims without apology. Make your recommendations as practical outcomes which can be seen (and ensure that you have made that transition potentially possible for the reader). Draw the work together through a cogent argument to a clear conclusion.

Key Points to Remember

- This chapter explored what should be found in the analysis and discussion section of your research report.
- It has offered a number of examples of good practice in writing elements of the section and shown how the writers used the evidence to develop and support their interpretation of the results and their line of argument to reach conclusions and make recommendations.
- It is important to remember that there is a distinction between results and analysis/discussion. Results should be focusing on answering the question: 'What have I found?'
- During the discussion analysis you do need to refer back to the key influential studies of your literature review as you have raised these as important to your research. A key question throughout the discussion/analysis is 'What you have found; does it add anything to the current body of knowledge?'

Further Reading

Robson, C. (2013) *How to do a Research Project.* Oxford: Blackwell.

Useful Websites

(All URLs verified April 2013 unless otherwise stated)

For guidance from universities on dissertations:

- Leicester University (2013)
  www2.le.ac.uk/offices/ld/resources/writing/writing-resources/writing-dissertation

- Plymouth University

  www.learningdevelopment.plymouth.ac.uk/LDstudyguides%5Cpdf/Writingadissertation.pdf

Example of a discussion chapter:

- "Dissertation Findings & Discussion Chapter: Sample"
  www.newessays.co.uk/wp-content/uploads/2011/12/10Findingschapter.sample.pdf

References

(All URLs verified April 2013 unless otherwise stated)

Azar, B. (2006) *Discussing your Findings*. gradPSYCH. Available at: www.apa.org/gradpsych/2006/01/findings.aspx

Bennis, W. and O'Toole, J. (2005) 'How business schools lost their way', *Harvard Business Review*, 83(5): 96–104, 154.

Benwell, B. and Stokoe, E. (2002) 'Constructing discussion tasks in university tutorials: Shifting dynamics and identities', *Discourse Studies*, 4: 429–453.

Bonuso, C. (1983) 'Body type: A factor in the hiring of school leaders', *The Phi Delta Kappan*, 64: 374.

Cheuk, B. (2007) 'Social networking analysis: Its application to facilitate knowledge transfer', *Business Information Review*, 24(3): 170–176.

Clapp, J. and Myers, D. (1999) *Graaskamp and the Definition of Rigorous Research*. Available at: www.greercorp.com/Research_files/USC_-_Graaskamp_and_Definition_of_Rigorous_Research.pdf

Dana, N., Dawson, K., Wolkenhauer, R. and Krell, D. (2013) 'Pushing the envelope on what is known about professional development', *Professional Development in Education*, 39(2): 240–259.

de Almeida Biolchini, J. (2007) 'Scientific research ontology to support systematic review in software engineering', *Advanced Engineering Informatics*, 21(2): 133–151.

Giessner, S. and Schubert, T. (2007). 'High in the hierarchy: How vertical location and judgments of leaders' power are interrelated', *Organizational Behavior and Human Decision Processes*, 104(1): 30–44.

Hannan, A. (2008) *Writing Up Research*. Faculty of Education: University of Plymouth. Available from: www.edu.plymouth.ac.uk/resined/resedhme.htm Accessed 31 May 2012.

Kearney, W., Kelsey, C. and Herrington, D. (2013) 'Mindful leaders in highly effective schools: A mixed-method application of Hoy's M-scale', *Educational Management Administration & Leadership*, 41(3): 316–335.

Kierkegaard, S. (1967) In Hong, H. and Hong, E. (eds, translators) *Soren Kierkegaard's Journals and Papers*. Bloomington: Indiana University Press.

Kim, M. (2012) 'Cultural-historical activity theory perspectives on constructing ICT-mediated meta-phors of teaching and learning', *European Journal of Teacher Education*, 35(4): 435–448.

Kretchmer (2006) *Fourteen Steps to Writing an Effective Discussion Section*. Available at: www.sfedit.net/discussion.pdf

Li, C. (2003) 'Educational and Professional Backgrounds of Current Provincial Leaders', *China Leadership Monitor*, 8: 1–19.

Medina, J. (2001). 'Types of positions, job responsibilities, and training backgrounds of outdoor/adventure leaders', *Journal of Experiential Education*, 24(3): 150–162.

Mewburn, I. (2012) 'How Do I Start My Discussion Chapter?' *The Thesis Whisperer*. Available at: http://thesiswhisperer.com/2012/01/23/how-do-i-start-my-discussion-chapter/

Nolen-Hoeksema, S. (2006) *10 Most Common Dissertation Discussion Mistakes*. Available at: www.apa.org/gradpsych/2006/01/findings.aspx

Pascal, C. and Ribbins, P. (1999) *Understanding Primary Headteachers: Conversations on Character, Careers and Characteristics.* London: Cassell.

Persson, P. and Zhuravskaya, E. (2011) *Elite Capture in the Absence of Democracy: Evidence from Backgrounds of Chinese Provincial Leader*s. Paris: Paris School of Economics Working Paper, 1–53.

Ribbins, P. (1997) *Leaders and Leadership in the School, College and University*. London: Continuum.

Scientific, Medical and General Proofreading and Editing (n.d.). *14 Elements for the Discussion Section*. Available at: www.sfedit.net/discussion.pdf

Timoštšuk, I. and Ugaste, A. (2012) 'The role of emotions in initial teachers' professional identity', *European Journal of Teacher Education*, 35(4): 421–433.

Wall, K., Higgins, S., Remedios, R., Rafferty, V. and Tiplady, L. (2013) 'Comparing analysis frames for visual data sets: Using pupil views templates to explore perspectives of learning', *Journal of Mixed Methods Research*, 7: 22–42.

Walls, G. (2012) 'Is systematic quantitative research scientifically rigorous? Methodological and statistical considerations', *Journal of American Psychoanalytic Association*, 60(1): 145–152.

For additional online resources please visit the book's website:
https://study.sagepub.com/needhamandpalaiologou

14

WRITING AND REPORTING THE RESEARCH

GARY BEAUCHAMP

Chapter Aims and Objectives

This chapter aims to provide advice upon how to write academically and appropriately within each part of the process of research and how to report findings to others in order to:

- find a voice;
- write up the voices of others; and
- express lucidly what you have learnt in writing.

Introduction

If you have followed the advice in the rest of this book you will have gathered a large amount of information in a methodical and rigorous manner, using appropriate methods which (hopefully!) all make perfect sense to you. During this process, but especially near the end, you are faced with the challenge of making this accessible and understandable to a wide range of readers – potentially including an international online audience. Not only that, but you are normally faced with a deadline to have the finished product ready for the editor, your supervisor or examiner. The same challenges face writers at all stages of their academic career and it is suggested that 'many beginning academic writers struggle and not just with technical writing skills, but with the emotions that writing stirs up and with the challenging process of developing a sense of self as an academic writer' (Cameron et al., 2009: 269).

You should not underestimate the emotional demands you will face during the writing process, but remember that your peers will be facing the same issues and will often be grateful to realise they are not the only one feeling stressed or not up to the task. It is always useful to have a network of peer reviewers, or indeed proof-readers, whose opinions you value and are able to listen to. You should also not discount others, including friends and family. I have spoken, for example, to many students whose parents or wider family have read their work and have not understood it, but having to explain it to them has made the students realise they could have said things in a much more simple and straightforward way.

In this chapter, it is only possible to consider key ideas and approaches, but many higher education providers offer a range of detailed real-time (synchronous) face-to-face and in your own time (asynchronous) virtual/web-based support in developing academic writing – often tailored to particular courses. It is important that you are aware of these and make use of them wherever possible – after reading the rest of this chapter first of course! It is also important to note that such study skills support is not just aimed at those who find such writing difficult. Although some universities operate a 'deficit' model in offering support primarily to those they perceive who need it (Wingate, 2010), such advice is normally available to *all* students.

In the remainder of this chapter we will work through the process of writing and reporting your research. It will be impossible to cover all writing contexts, but we will endeavour to look at a range of generic issues which will contribute towards success in as many as possible.

Writing Research

Depending on the context of your writing, the framework or structure may be predetermined (such as the structure of a dissertation) or more open-ended (such as a journal article) – although few are completely open. It is crucial that you understand all these essential requirements before you begin. This can include such basic features as required word count, setting up a word processing file with the required font and line spacing, or more complex ideas such as the correct form of referencing required. It is much easier to get all of this right at the start, rather than to have to go over the whole of your writing again when it is complete.

Practical Tip

This can also apply to the tense that you write in. For instance, you may currently be writing about the methods you are going to use to conduct your research in the future. Although the temptation is to write this in the future tense, it is much easier to write in the past tense as it will appear in the finished piece of work.

What is the Academic 'Voice'?

The factors we have begun to consider above are some of the many challenges you will face when finding your voice, or writing style. One of the first things you will realise is that trying to copy the voice, or style, of someone else adds another unnecessary challenge, so it is easiest to keep things consistent by using and improving your own 'voice'. Neville (2009: 123–124) defines this as taking ownership of your work by:

- deciding yourself which position or direction to take;
- selecting evidence that allows you to present a strong set of arguments or descriptions;
- summarising or paraphrasing in your own words what you have read;
- writing in a style that comes from within.

Practical Tip

A report which features a range of different voices, or writing styles, which are not acknowledged by speech marks and supporting references is an early indicator to readers that it is the work of more than one person – such as work which has been cut and pasted or copied without acknowledgement, which would constitute plagiarism.

In finding your academic voice, it is important to remember that *you* are the person doing the writing, about *your* ideas. An added complexity to this, however, is that you will also need to read, interpret and present the voices of other writers. Sometimes you can do this by using direct quotations, but more often you will need to summarise the key ideas and write them in your own words and in your own style. In my experience, many students and early career researchers faced with writing in an academic style for the first time feel they need to adopt an 'academic' tone and, as a result, often reject the style that has got them through the course or their education to date. Often they might save time and effort by refining their existing style rather than trying to reinvent themselves. A common example of this is incorrectly using unfamiliar ('academic') vocabulary they have read in the work of others, when a word they know would be just as good.

Academic writing does not need to be wordy or complicated. As Thomas (2009: 238) correctly points out, 'writing is about communicating; it is not about trying to sound clever'. Although a series of long words and complicated sentences may sound impressive, a much worthier achievement is making your meaning clear in short and straightforward sentences. An added bonus in adopting this approach is that this makes punctuation much easier to use and to understand. Having said all this, throughout your writing you will be faced with many choices of terminology and developing your vocabulary is important as sometimes a more 'complicated' word *is* the best choice. For instance, in describing certain concepts it is very difficult to use words other than the 'labels' given by the person(s) who developed the idea. An example may be the use of the word 'Piagetian' when describing a view of child development. This gives the (informed) reader a clear idea of what you mean without having to go into a lengthy explanation (although in this instance you need to make sure you understand Piaget's work before you do this, as this is often misused and simplified).

Before we progress further, it is worth considering what constitutes an academic tone in writing. Rosen (2009) suggests academic writers:

1. Review and constructively criticise the work of others;
2. Build support for their conclusions by using logic and evidence from information in the research of others;
3. Acknowledge all sources that they use, both in the text and at the end of their writing;
4. Maintain a serious, formal tone.

The end result should be writing which is 'informed, logical, clear, well structured, and based on evidence' (Rosen, 2009: 1), both in discussing your own work and how it relates to that of others. In making judgements about the work of others, we move from describing to analysing. The ability to constructively criticise (in other words, to be critical) is an important feature and, although there are many definitions of being critical, this summary from Manchester University Academic Phrasebook is helpful:

> As an academic writer, you are expected to be critical of the sources that you use. This essentially means questioning what you read and not necessarily agreeing with it just because the information has been published. Being critical can also mean looking for reasons why we should not just accept something as being correct or true. This can require you to identify problems with a writer's arguments or methods, or perhaps to refer to other people's criticisms of these.

To this could be added the suggestion that being critical can also mean looking for reasons why we *should* accept something, perhaps because it makes a particularly strong case based on the arguments, methods used and what other people have said about its strengths. This may be particularly the case with longitudinal, large-scale international studies undertaken by established academics. Even in this case, however, it is important to note when the study took place and any major changes in education (such as a revision to the National Curriculum or the introduction of the Foundation Stage in England or the Foundation Phase in Wales) since that time which may affect the validity or currency of the findings. It is also worth noting where the study took place and any implications of this – such as following a different curriculum or having different educational resources or funding.

Not all writing is analytical as there are times when something needs to be described in order to help make judgements. Cottrell (2008: 286) provides a useful summary of the distinction between descriptive and critical writing in the table below.

Table 14.1

Descriptive writing	Critical analytical writing
states what happened	identifies the significance
states what something is like	evaluates strengths and weaknesses
gives the story so far	weighs one piece of information against another
states the order in which things happened	makes reasoned judgements
says how to do something	argues a case according to the evidence
explains what a theory says	shows why something is relevant or suitable
explains how something works	indicates why something will work (best)
notes the method used	identifies whether something is appropriate or suitable
says when something occurred	identifies why the timing is of importance
states the different components	weighs up the importance of component parts
states options	gives reasons for selecting each option
lists details	evaluates the relative significance of details
lists in any order	structures information in order of importance
states links between items	shows the relevance of links between pieces of information
gives information	draws conclusions

To give an idea of how this can be reflected in your writing let us look at a sample sentence and how a more critical tone can be introduced. First we start with:

Beauchamp (2011) suggests that interactive whiteboards are a good idea in the primary school.

One simple first step is to insert a judgement word when reporting the work of others, for instance:

Beauchamp (2011) *makes the valid suggestion* that interactive whiteboards are a good idea in the primary school.

This can then be developed to include factors such as sample size, methods used, when the study took place or the year of the study to show criticality:

Beauchamp (2011) makes a strong [*judgement word*] case for the use of interactive whiteboards in the primary classroom based on a large-scale recent [*sample size and year of study*] study across seven European countries [*context*], although the different educational systems in each of the countries mean the results need to be treated with caution when applied to UK classrooms. [*academic caution*]

Neville (2009: 38) proposes six other ways of approaching critical analysis which may be useful in your writing:

1. Agreeing with a particular point of view, but presenting reliable evidence to support the position taken.
2. Rejecting a particular point of view, but again using reliable evidence to do this.
3. Conceding that an existing point of view has merits, but that it needs to be qualified in certain respects, and stating what these are.
4. Proposing a new point of view, or re-formulating an existing one, backed with supportive evidence.
5. Reconciling two positions, which may seem at variance, by bringing a new perspective to bear on the topic.
6. Connecting or synthesising different ideas, so that new approaches and points of view can be advanced.

Audience

An important, or perhaps *the* most important, consideration in developing your voice is the audience for your writing. You need to be totally clear about who is going to read your work and how they will judge it. Often the judgements in student work can be found in formal assignment criteria, so make sure you read them, understand them and refer back to them often as you write (not just at the end). In other contexts, such as academic articles, a less formal judgement may be made about your academic credibility, which can in turn affect your career.

You also need to be very clear about what you can assume your readers already know, what you will need to explain and in what order. In my experience this has become much more of an issue in recent times with the wider availability of work to an international readership with very different educational systems and relevance to an international audience being common criteria for journal reviewers.

Activity

Is your work accessible to a wide audience?

Consider the piece of writing below and discuss if, and how, you may need to change it. Consider what assumptions it makes of the reader and what they might be considered to know, as well as any national contexts. The intended readership is students on Education Studies degree courses within the United Kingdom, but may also be read by international readers.

> *This study explores the implications of the new standards and their impact on the education of teacher training students. The study follows a group of students as they teach Key stage I classes following the programmes of study for science in the national curriculum. The study used a qualitative methodology where semi-structured interviews were conducted with the students both before and after the lessons. Analysis of the results showed that their epistemological beliefs were affected by contradictions between their professional knowledge gained in the classroom and their theoretical grounding from their university studies.*

Note: the answers for this activity can be found at the end of the chapter, after you have read the whole chapter.

Time Management

Having considered your audience and how you will be judged, it is important to consider how you can manage your time to ensure that not only do you complete your work, but also allow time for it to be proof-read, corrected and, if necessary, bound. There are many ways that you can plan your time but one of the most frequently used is a Gantt chart (see Figure 14.1, below). In this chart you can break down tasks against units of time from hours, to days, months or even, in the case of a PhD, years. The example below shows how you *may* manage a one-year dissertation project. It is important to note that some activities (such as writing) take place throughout the whole time period, whereas others (such as data collection) may be constrained by practical considerations such as getting access to schools within their term time.

The Gantt chart is useful because it also makes you think about the sequence of activities and ensures that you allow time to undertake necessary piloting or revisions. Although many of the activities in the example below have already been covered in this book, the most important feature here is to note how writing is a continuous process, with some particularly busy periods at key parts of the research process. The importance of reading will be returned to below, but this will also continue beyond the initial period allocated to the literature review as new work becomes available and needs to be incorporated into your study.

Timetable	Sept	Oct	Nov	Dec	Jan	Feb	Mar	Apr	May
Problem Identification and choice of Methodology	■								
Reading and literature review	■	■	■						
Development of research instruments and piloting			■	■					
Gathering of Data					■	■			
Data analysis						■	■		
Writing	■	■	■	■	■	■	■	■	■
Editing									
Final document								■	
Proof reading		■	■	■				■	
Binding of document – submission									■

Figure 14.1 Example of a Gantt Chart

Activity

Discuss and develop a Gantt chart for your current writing project. It may be easiest to use a spreadsheet program or a table in a word processing package as a starting point. An important decision will be whether to represent the columns as months, weeks or perhaps even days depending on the length of your project.

Practical Tip

For students on degree courses remember that everyone on your course (and possibly others) will probably be trying to get their work bound at the same time, so ensure you leave plenty of time or that you know where else you can get it bound in the locality.

Planning/Structuring Your Written Work

A key feature of writing management is having a clear plan or structure to your work. Often this is provided by the assignment brief which may stipulate how many chapters or sections the written work must contain. When the writing is not for an academic assignment, however, this is less clear-cut but it is often possible to use models from previous versions of the work (such as an academic article or report) published by the same journal or commissioning body. In general terms, most academic writing requires you to:

- Outline the issue, its context and the research questions;
- Review relevant literature in the area;
- Give details of the research methods used – in sufficient detail to allow the reader to make a critical judgement of their appropriateness;
- Provide details of the results or findings presented in a suitable format (see more below) – again in sufficient detail to allow the reader to make a critical judgement, this time of the rigour of the analysis and any statistical analysis undertaken;
- Discuss the implications of this – and sometimes outline further areas of study or changes in current practice – and any limitations to the study.

The precise word allocation and level of detail for each of these are normally provided. It is essential in all cases to read this extremely carefully, as it would be foolish to lose marks or have your article rejected because you failed to abide by basic requirements which have been clearly outlined.

Practical Tip

Most academic journals, and indeed professional journals or publications, include such guidance either on the inside or back cover of the publication or within a few pages of this. They may be called different things but common titles are 'notes for contributors' or 'instructions for authors'. In this section you will also normally find guidance on writing style, the use of tables or figures, referencing style and how the manuscript can be submitted – this is increasingly done in an online format and you may need to register for the website before you can submit.

Use of Headings and Subheadings

Even if some subheadings are removed in the final writing, the use of headings and subheadings helps you decide on the relative importance of themes and ideas which you are going to explore. At an early stage of your writing, or even before you start writing (particularly for dissertation), it may be worth developing an initial table of contents with different levels of headings. This can help you decide both the overall structure (to make sure you have covered everything), and also the relative importance of each section. For example, in the chapter headings below we can see not only the sequence of ideas but how important each one is:

2   Main chapter heading

   2.1 Second level

      2.1.1 Third level
      2.1.2 Third level

   2.2 second level

      2.2.1 Third level
      2.2.2 Third level
      2.2.3 Third level

An example of this (but by no means perfect) for an early years ICT research project looking at ICT in outdoor learning may be:

2   Literature review

   2.1 Early years education

      2.1.1 History of early years education in the UK
      2.1.2 Theoretical perspectives
      2.1.3 Outdoor learning

   2.2 ICT in education

      2.2.1 ICT and pedagogy
      2.2.2 ICT and interactive teaching
      2.2.3 Features of ICT
      2.2.4 Affordances
      2.2.5 Mobile technology

   2.3 ICT in primary education

      2.3.1 Dialogic teaching with ICT
      2.3.2 Interactivity
      2.3.3 Computer use at home and school
      2.3.4 ICT and inclusion
      2.3.5 Home use of technology

   2.4 ICT in early years education

      2.4.1 'Playful' use of ICT
      2.4.2 Creativity and ICT
      2.4.3 The 'curriculum' context

   2.5 Inspection evidence and official reports

┌─ **Practical Tip** ───

The structure of the table of contents can be developed from a mind mapping of your overall ideas on your own or with others.

───

Writing – Finding Your Academic 'Voice'

All of the preparation we have discussed above contributes to developing an 'authorial identity', defined as 'the sense a writer has of themselves as an author' (Pittam et al., 2009: 154). Although it may sound obvious you do need to believe that you are capable of being an author. This may not come easily or quickly. Having planned the structure of your writing, and allocated specific time periods to it, the hard work begins. Writing is not an easy process and you will have many false starts, changes of emphasis and even setbacks as your research develops and you read more widely. All writers have to work extremely hard and it is essential to realise this from the outset. This applies at all levels of writing from a new undergraduate to an established academic. While it may get easier with more experience, there are still challenges to be faced as you set your own expectations higher and those of others around you increase. At all stages of your writing career, however, one of the most important ways of developing your writing is to read the work of others writing to the same format or for the same audience as yourself.

Perhaps the most fundamental challenge of all is writing the first sentence. For example, many students I have worked with spend a great number of hours reading and making notes about what they have read and end up writing twice as many words as they need to before they begin actually writing their assignment or dissertation.

As soon as you do begin writing, a major challenge for all writers is keeping track of different versions of the work. It is essential to keep your files well organised and clearly labelled. It is a matter of personal choice whether you maintain many different word processing files (perhaps the different chapters, perhaps on different themes and so on) or you keep one file with all your writing in it. Even if you just keep one file, it is often worth keeping a separate file ('cuts from dissertation' or similar) for all of the words that you cut or delete from your master copy. It is always hard to say goodbye to words you have worked so hard on, but it may be useful to have them to return to or even to use in other work in the future.

It is well worth considering using a 'Cloud'-based storage system which allows you to synchronise (back-up) copies (see Practical Tip below), but even renaming your file ending in the current date can prevent you mixing up files (e.g dissertation 06.05.16). This approach may also be useful when working with a tutor, supervisor or a co-writer as they can rename the file (using 'save as' instead of 'save') with their initials and the date (e.g. dissertation GB 07.05.16). Finally, you can also email a copy of your writing to yourself at one or more addresses to keep back-up versions. While all this may seem slightly paranoid, it does prevent much heartache and stress as sometimes even with the best planning things may go wrong through no fault of your own – such as when a student house was broken into and all the laptops, containing final drafts of their dissertations, were stolen.

---| **Practical Tip** |--

Back up your work often and in different places from day one

Whatever approach you take, it is absolutely vital that you keep back-up copies of all your work from day one of your writing. With the increase of secure virtual, or Cloud, services (current examples include Dropbox or OneDrive) many writers now use this method of storage either in place of or in addition to portable storage devices. The advantage of such services is that not only do they synchronise work between different devices (such as work you do on your laptop at University being synchronised with your desktop PC at home when you turn it on), but they also allow you to access your work anywhere with an Internet connection. This in turn, is the disadvantage of such an approach as it relies on having an Internet or wireless connection. Nevertheless, most universities provide a wireless connection and it is increasingly available at home as well. An additional advantage is that these files can be accessed on mobile devices, such as an iPad, or even your smartphone if you need to check or amend anything.

If you are using a word processing package, it is normally possible to change the auto save feature to make sure your work is saved automatically more often (such as every minute). You can normally find this in the preferences or options feature of the software and it is worth checking the default setting and amending it, depending on your level of concern about losing your work.

Reading to Support and Develop Your Writing

In preparing to start your writing you will have undertaken a lot of reading, particularly of academic sources. As well as providing information to support and develop your argument, this reading should also help to develop your own writing, both in style and vocabulary, as we have discussed above. In particular disciplines, including education, there are specific words, phrases and acronyms that you need to understand, as well as those that apply to research in general. We have already discussed the importance of the audience for your writing, but it is also necessary to decide which of these need some form of explanation when they are first used. However, more importantly, when you read you also need to develop your ability as an 'active' reader. Epstein et al. (2005: 13) provide valuable advice when they suggest that:

> When you read academic work, you need to engage actively with the material by interrogating it. Ask yourself questions as you go along. Do I really agree with this? How convincing is this argument? What holes can I pick in that one? What would I say to the author if they were explaining their ideas to me in person? How can I make use of these ideas or data to inform my own? What key concepts is the author working with and why?

By adopting this method you are adopting a critical approach to reading, which you can then reflect in your writing. All this will take time and you need to allow for this when you are planning your work – see 'Time management' above.

--- Practical Tip ---

References: Most scholars and all universities have access to a range of electronic databases, thus making it increasingly common to download PDF copies of articles you are using. When you choose to save these from the database the default option is normally a string of numbers or similarly unhelpful text. It is an easy step to insert author, surname, year and keywords from the title as the file name and save them in a folder (preferably on a Cloud-based storage system so that you can access them anywhere) so that they will appear in alphabetical order making them easier to find. It is also worth exploring whether the database you are using allows you to email a copy of the article to yourself as a backup. Some also allow you to include the citation in the email in a variety of formats which you can then just cut-and-paste into your written work.

As you read from the very beginning you should also write from the very start of the project. The common use of the phrase 'writing up' implies that writing will only commence once data has been collected, but this approach is questioned by many (for example, Badley, 2009) – although it does have its uses if you are writing as part of a team 'where ideas develop as the team interacts during the process of the research' (Thody, 2006: 19).

Another reason it is important to write from early in your research is to develop the habit of writing. Even if you go back and edit out many of your words, it is much better to write little bits often rather than try to work your way through large chunks of text later. This also enables you to read back through what you have written the next time you write and quickly get back into the flow of what you are trying to say.

As you write it is also a good idea to collect a bank of suitable words or verbs to demonstrate both judgements and criticality. For instance, when reviewing literature you often have to report the words of others but using more than one verb to describe this throughout makes it much more interesting for the reader. You could use any of the following verbs depending on the context:

- suggests
- contends
- asserts
- stresses
- emphasises
- proposes
- highlights
- recommends

--- Practical Tip ---

Synonyms

Many word processing packages have a synonym feature which can be useful in developing your vocabulary. In Microsoft Word, for example, if you highlight a word and right click it you can scroll down to a menu suggesting various alternatives.

We have already discussed above how to structure work into different sections, but it is worth briefly considering how to write different components within it. Perhaps a good starting point is to consider how to structure a paragraph, which can be planned (like a mini-essay) as follows:

1. sentence introducing the point;
2. sentence making the point with necessary detail;
3. illustration of point using reference: research example, case study, figures, etc.;
4. critical analysis of point;
5. sentence summing up the point and showing how it addresses the question or contributes to your argument. (University of Reading, n.d.)

Such an approach, used consistently, should help to make a more coherent final piece of writing.

Use of Tables and Figures

There will be occasions, particularly in quantitative research, where you need to report numerical data. If so, you need to consider whether tables or figures are more appropriate than using numbers in the text. In addition, having used a table you do not need to describe everything it says in the table as your reader will hopefully have made sense of the information you provide there. You do, however, have to make sure that you refer to the table in the text (for instance, 'see Table 14.1'). When using tables Priebe (2008: 22) suggests that they 'have strong visual impact, are informative and easy to comprehend, and can stand alone' and that you should 'use the fewest tables and illustrations needed to tell the story'.

Editing and Redrafting

Once you have written drafts of individual sections, chapters or even the whole piece of writing it is necessary to edit and redraft. Editing can be a difficult process if you have spent a long time developing a piece of writing. It is, however, an essential task to ensure you stay within any word count, make the most of every word, and also ensure that your writing has the necessary formality and clarity of expression. Before sharing with any other readers, you need to undertake this process yourself, during which time you can make great use of the provisionality feature of ICT-based writing, where you can use the undo and redo features to check how something will look; if you don't like it you can go back to the original (Kennewell and Beauchamp, 2007). For instance, look at a paragraph you have written and use the strikethrough feature (normally near the bold, italic and underline) to draw a line through words or phrases you think may not be needed. If you read through the paragraph and the words you have crossed out are not needed then delete them permanently (although you can always 'undo' it if you change your mind). You can then read the text to see if you can replace phrases with single words which mean the same thing, hence saving words. For example, later in the chapter I was going to write:

I have mentioned the use of others in many parts of the writing process

But changed it to lose four words:

I have mentioned the use of others throughout the writing process.

In another instance I was going to write:

One of the key things you need to consider …

Which became:

One of the key considerations …

This can even apply to expressions, so 'very large', could change to 'substantial'. Rosen (2009) suggests that you should also revise sentences that begin with *it is, there are* and *there were* to make sentences more direct. He gives the example:

Wordy: *There were several reasons why* Josephine Baker fared better in Europe than in America.

Direct: Josephine Baker fared better in Europe than in America for several reasons.

Rosen (ibid.: 426) also suggests that 'long-winded expressions' should be avoided and gives the examples:

Long-Winded	*Direct*
at this moment (point) in time	now, today
at the present time	now, today
due to the fact that	because
in order to utilise	to use
in view of the fact that	because

If you have saved words within an individual sentence or paragraph, you can begin to imagine how many words you will save over an extended piece of writing. Another task which you can undertake is to ensure that you have not made claims which the data cannot support, and that you have used what might be described as 'academic caution' to qualify your statements. For example:

Beauchamp (2004) *proves* that there is a transition process for learning to use the interactive whiteboard.

Beauchamp (2004) *suggests* that there is a transition process for learning to use the interactive whiteboard.

This is not to advocate that you be too cautious in your assertions, but merely to suggest that you exercise a degree of criticality when making claims for the research of others and yourself.

Another easy activity to undertake is to check that you have supported all claims with evidence. For instance, I have read many assignments recently where students have written phrases such as:

'There is much research to suggest that ....' *or* 'Many studies have shown that ...'

There is nothing inherently wrong with such phrases if *supported by evidence*. For instance:

'There is much research (Jones, 2011; Smith, 2013; White, 2010) to suggest that ...'
or 'Many studies (for example, Jones, 2011 and Smith, 2013) have shown that...'

This approach does not, however, mean that you go through your work using a 'reference pepperpot' (Epstein et al., 2005: 24) to add multiple citations; just take care to support your statements with evidence. Once you have undertaken these tasks yourself, and made a thorough check of grammar, spelling and punctuation, you can then consider whether you wish to share your writing with others to gain another perspective.

Role of Tutor/Supervisor and Critical Friends

Throughout this chapter I have mentioned the use of others during the writing process and nearly everybody will discuss their ideas with somebody else at some stage. This is particularly important when writing with others, but it also applies to someone writing on their own. Indeed, some writing processes such as the 'patchwork' type of assignment rely on a critical interaction with others (Ovens, 2003).

As the whole point of writing is for somebody to read it, you should not be afraid to share your work with others. You do not necessarily need to listen to everything they say, but they may raise questions which cause you to consider whether you have expressed yourself clearly or whether you have taken something for granted which needs further explanation. If we return to where we started, writing can be an emotionally challenging task and you should take advantage of all the support that is available to you. It is not the preserve of a special elite, it is something that everybody can do if they work on it.

We have considered above some generic features of the writing process, but the most important aim of this chapter is to encourage you to have confidence in your ability to describe your work to others. You need to work hard on your writing, so that others do not have to.

Rejection or Failure

Despite your best efforts there are occasions where your work may fail to reach the required standard or be rejected by a publisher. If it is an academic assignment, there is normally another chance to submit your work and in the case of the academic journal this may be true as well, or there are other journals available to which you can submit your work. In nearly all instances you will receive some form of feedback from the marker or review. There are occasions where you may not agree with these judgements, and other occasions where you may receive contradictory feedback (such as reviewers from journals), but in all cases it is best to try and take as much as possible from the feedback and move on.

Case Study

Journal publication

A PhD student was nearing the end of his thesis and had some findings to share on the initial period of data collection. He felt ready to submit a paper to an academic journal. He discussed this with his supervisors, as he wanted their support in writing, and agreed that they would also be named on the paper, but that his name would be first as he would be doing most of the work. [Although it may seem a small thing, it is always worth discussing the order of names at an early stage.]

The first step was to research suitable journals to submit the paper to. This involved looking at past issues of the journal to see if they had published anything similar in this area. If they had, these articles were read and the references checked and read if appropriate. If necessary these were used later on in the writing process. An essential next step was to check the guidance to authors provided by the journal to find out key information such as how many words were allowed (do not exceed this), what format the document had to be submitted in and what kind of referencing format should be used. This last was very important as the journal stipulated a different referencing format than he was using at that time and the required format could be used in the drafting of the article to save time later on and avoid possible rejection.

Note: As a reviewer it is very frustrating to have to comment on avoidable issues such as an incorrect referencing format. If you already have doubts about a paper, such things added together can influence your overall recommendation or the amount of revisions that are required. Reviewers give up time to provide constructive feedback and they need to feel that you have spent your time checking the specific requirements of the journal and ensuring that you are submitting your best work, specifically targeted at that journal.

The student wrote an initial draft of the paper and then revised it many times over a period of weeks before he sent it to his supervisors in turn, who returned it with comments. After several iterations of this over a period of weeks, a final draft was agreed. The next step was to check how the article was submitted to the journal. In this case it was an electronic submission and a student needed to register on the journal website before he was able to submit. The submission process was relatively straightforward, except that it asked for keywords which had not been added to the article. This was relatively easy to do, but it was also useful in pinpointing what was important in the article.

The next step was waiting! The student knew from reading the author guidance that the article would be sent to two reviewers and also reviewed by the editor. What he did not know was how long this would take. In the event, this was about two months which is a quicker turnaround than some journals.

Tip: It can be very tempting to contact the editor to check on the progress of a review, but in reality the editors and reviewers are normally very busy people who try to fit reviews in and on top of their existing workload. You should normally be prepared to wait months rather than weeks for feedback.

Unfortunately, the feedback from the journal was negative and they would not publish the article. The editor provided feedback from the reviewers, which was discussed by the student and his supervisors. Two of the supervisors were very experienced reviewers themselves and there was considerable discussion about the quality of the feedback, but the overall decision of the writing team was that there was still something of worth in the article so the student would work on it again and try and respond to some of the feedback provided before submitting to a different journal.

Although you may not have the benefit of a supervisory team to discuss amendments, it is worth discussing these with your peers or colleagues. As rejection can be a difficult experience, and some comments of reviewers can appear overly critical, it is worth waiting a short period until this is less raw before you discuss with others. You may not want to share some of the reviewers' comments with others but is important that they get the full picture of the feedback in order to help you fully.

As the changes agreed were relatively minor this only took a few weeks to complete. During this period, the student also researched other journals to which he could submit the article. He was aware that he could not submit his article to more than one journal at a time, but now that it had been rejected by one he could submit it to another. When the revised draft of the article was agreed by all concerned, it was submitted electronically to the new journal – again after registering on the site. The same period of waiting began again, although the feedback from the editor was slightly quicker this time. In this case, the editor informed the student that the paper would be suitable for publication if he was prepared to undertake 'minor amendments' suggested by the reviewers.

Given this positive outcome, the student undertook the revisions and sent the article back to the editor with a table showing in the first column the required amendments and in the second column what he had done to address them. This made it easier for the editor to see what had been done as it had been some time since he had seen the last draft.

The editor accepted the changes and informed the student that the article would be published in three months' time in the next edition of the journal.

Summary

In this chapter we considered how to develop your writing style. It has not been possible to cover all aspects of this, but there are many textbooks devoted solely to it so look at a variety of these as well. A very useful summing up of the whole process of academic writing for coursework assignments is provided below (courtesy of University of Wolverhampton):

---| **Practical Tip** |--

Ten tips for better academic writing

1. Analyse the question – make sure you are answering the question set, not the one you think has been set.
2. Plan your essay – Planning your workload will help you get your work done on time. Make a plan, be realistic, stick to it.
3. Keep sentences short and straightforward – By keeping your sentences simple you will lessen the chances of errors of grammar and punctuation.
4. Take care with spelling, particularly subject specific words – if you are not sure how to spell a word, check a dictionary.
5. Only include one argument or point of information per paragraph – this will make your work easier to read and understand.
6. Do not include any new information in your conclusions – the conclusions of your work should draw only upon what has already been written. If there is new information to be presented, it should be included in the main body of your assignment.
7. Ensure all information is correctly referenced – any ideas you have taken from others, whether quoted directly, paraphrased or summarised, must be referenced.
8. Proof-read your work – check our guide to proof-reading to see what an important step this is.
9. Check your assignment brief for any specific format requirements – if specific format requirements have been set, i.e. for line-spacing or font, then you must adhere to them.
10. Proof-read your work – this is included twice but it is important!

(University of Wolverhampton, n.d.)

Key Points to Remember

This chapter aimed to discuss how we develop your research project either for academic journals or to be submitted as a dissertation or thesis. It offered a number of examples and the key message is that a good report is the one that:

- from the start outlines the issue and the context of the research project and clearly states the research questions;
- discusses the relevant research and addresses how this research project makes a contribution to the body of knowledge;
- explains the methodology and the research design – how data was collected – to allow the reader to make a critical judgement of their appropriateness;
- finally, provides details of the results or findings and discusses the implications of this in relation to the issues that were investigated.

Activity discussion

Is your work accessible to a wide audience?

Earlier in the chapter you were asked to consider a piece of writing relating to teacher training. At that stage I asked you to consider that this project report could also be read by a variety of educationalists, including those from other countries and systems. Here is the same section with some annotations:

This study explores the implications of the new standards [1] and their impact on the education of teacher training students. The study follows a group of students [2] as they teach Key stage I [3] classes following the programmes of study [4] for science in the national curriculum. [5] The study used a qualitative methodology where Semi-structured interviews were conducted with the students both before and after the lessons. Analysis of the results showed that their epistemological [6] beliefs were affected by the contradiction between their professional knowledge gained in the classroom and their theoretical grounding from their university.

1. What standards are these? You could assume it was teacher training standards, but even these can be called different things (in Northern Ireland they are called competences).
2. We could assume these are in higher education, but even then it would be good to know whether they were initial teacher training students, undergraduates or postgraduates.
3. Although totally understood in England, there is no KS1 in Wales or indeed in other countries in Europe so giving the age range of pupils in brackets afterwards would be useful.
4. Does everybody on Education Studies courses know what this means?
5. Some international readers may not understand the concept of a national curriculum. Also, which country did this take place in?
6. Is this the best word for my audience? Is there a better word?

Further Reading

Badley, G. (2009) 'Academic writing as shaping and reshaping', *Teaching in Higher Education*, 14(2): 209–219.

Epstein, D., Kenway, J. and Boden, R. (2005) *Writing for Publication*. London: SAGE.

Rosen, L.J. (2009) *The Academic Writers Handbook* (2/E). London: Pearson.

Useful Websites

Many universities offer online support for academic writing and some examples are given below. Some of these are aimed at those learning English as a second language but they still provide very valuable advice.

- Manchester University Academic Phrasebank
  www.phrasebank.manchester.ac.uk

- Queen's University Academic skills
  www.qub.ac.uk/directorates/sgc/learning/AcademicSkills/WritingSkills/

- University of Reading
  www.reading.ac.uk/internal/studyadvice/StudyResources/Writing/sta-style.aspx

References

Badley, G. (2009) 'Academic writing as shaping and reshaping', *Teaching in Higher Education*, 14(2): 209–219.

Cameron, J., Nairn, K. and Higgins, J. (2009) 'Demystifying academic writing: Reflections on emotions, know-how and academic identity', *Journal of Geography in Higher Education*, 33(2): 269–284.

Cottrell, S. (2008) *The Study Skills Handbook* (3/E). Basingstoke: Palgrave Macmillan.

Epstein, D., Kenway, J. and Boden, R. (2005) *Writing for Publication*. London: SAGE.

Kennewell, S. and Beauchamp, G. (2007) 'The features of interactive whiteboards and their influence on learning', *Learning, Media and Technology*, 32(3): 227–241.

Neville, C. (2009) *How To Improve Your Assignment Results*. Maidenhead: Open University.

Ovens, P. (2003) 'A patchwork text approach to assessment in teacher education', *Teaching in Higher Education*, 8(4): 545–562

Pittam, G., Elander, J., Lusher, J., Fox, P. and Payne, N. (2009) 'Student beliefs and attitudes about authorial identity in academic writing', *Studies in Higher Education*, 34(2): 153–170.

Priebe H-J. (2008) 'Results' in G.M. Hall (ed.), *How To Write A Paper* (4/E). Oxford: Blackwell, pp. 19–30.

Rosen, L.J. (2009) *The Academic Writers Handbook* (2/E). London: Pearson.

Thody, A. (2006) *Writing and Presenting Research*. London: SAGE.

Thomas, G. (2009). *How To Do Your Research Project*. London: SAGE.

University of Reading (n.d.). *Study Skills: Writing Style*. Available at: www.reading.ac.uk/internal/studyadvice/StudyResources/Writing/sta-style.aspx. Accessed November 2014.

University of Wolverhampton (n.d.) *Academic Writing Skills*. Available at: www.wlv.ac.uk/lib/skills_for_learning/academic_writing.aspx Accessed: November 2014.

Wingate, U. (2010) 'The impact of formative feedback on the development of academic writing', *Assessment & Evaluation in Higher Education*, 35(5): 519–533.

For additional online resources please visit the book's website:
https://study.sagepub.com/needhamandpalaiologou

INDEX

Figures and Tables are indicated by page numbers in bold print.